Irrational Triumph

Wilbur S. Shepperson Series in History and Humanities

GEOFFREY JENSEN

Irrational Triumph

Cultural Despair, Military Nationalism, and the Ideological Origins of Franco's Spain

University of Nevada Press Reno & Las Vegas

Wilbur S. Shepperson Series
in History and Humanities
Series Editor: Jerome E. Edwards
Publication of this book was made possible in part by the support of the Program for Cultural Cooperation between Spain's Ministry of Education, Culture and Sports and the United States Universities.

University of Nevada Press
Reno, Nevada 89557 USA

Manufactured in the
United States of America
The paper used in this book meets the requirements of American National Standard for Information Sciences—Permanence of Paper for Printed Library Materials, ANSI Z39.48-1984. Binding materials were selected for strength and durability.

Frontispiece: The mural, *Alegoría de la Guerra Civil* by Arturo Reque Meruvia, is in the Archivo Histórico Militar, Madrid. Courtesy Oronoz.

FIRST PRINTING
11 10 09 08 07 06 05 04 03 02
5 4 3 2 1

Library of Congress
Cataloging-in-Publication Data

Jensen, Geoffrey, 1965–
Irrational triumph: cultural despair, military nationalism, and the ideological origins of Franco's Spain / Geoffrey Jensen.
p. cm.—(Wilbur S. Shepperson series in history and humanities)
ISBN 0-87417-481-3 (hardcover)
1. Sociology, Military—Spain—History—20th century. 2. Spain—Armed Forces—Officers—History—20th century. 3. Ideology—Spain—History—20th century. 4. Nationalism—Spain—History—20th century. 5. Spain—Intellectual life—20th century. I. Title. II. Series.
UA780.J46 2001
306.2'7'094609034—dc21 2001001403

For my parents

Contents

Acknowledgments

This book comes at the end of a long journey of research, reflection, and writing, and I owe my gratitude to more people than I can possibly name here for offering assistance along the way. An outgrowth of my 1995 Ph.D. dissertation, it is above all the product of many years of encouragement, criticism, and advice from James M. Boyden, without whom I could never have pursued the project in the first place. My other advisors at Yale, Michael Howard and Geoffrey Parker, made important contributions to my endeavors as well. Carolyn P. Boyd not only carefully read and commented on drafts of each chapter, but she, likewise, provided me with an invaluable critique of the finished dissertation. Stanley G. Payne also shared his erudition and counsel during my days as a graduate student, and his comments on the dissertation played a similar role in shaping the present book. Sandie Holguín offered astute observations and advice during the early stages of the project, steering me toward apt and profitable avenues of investigation. In Spain, I benefited greatly from Jorge Aspizua Turrión's suggestions and immense knowledge of contemporary Spanish history and military affairs. Manuel Burguete Herrero and José Enrique Ruiz-Fornells Bonet generously granted me access to private family papers.

I owe special thanks to Duncan Anderson, Sean McKnight, Niall Barr, and everyone else who aided me at the Royal Military Academy Sandhurst, where I was granted the opportunity to spend an academic year teaching classes in war studies to officer-cadets and the course of the Junior Command Staff College to captains. Military education in Britain today may differ markedly from its Spanish equivalent a century ago, but my time at Sandhurst nevertheless helped me to gain a fuller understanding of military pedagogy and culture in general. I would also like to thank the staff of the Sandhurst Library, especially Andrew Orgill, Diane Hillier, and Sarah Oliver, for their help.

In addition, I have received substantial support of various kinds at the University of Southern Mississippi, and I am especially grateful to Orazio Ciccarelli, Doug Mackaman, Michael Mays, Brian O'Neil, Shelia Smith, Marjorie Spruill, and Andrew Wiest for all they have done for me since I began teaching there.

Many others assisted my research and writing as a graduate student or thereafter, though I alone accept full responsibility for the contents of this book. Those who provided assistance of one kind or another include Miguel Alonso

Baquer, James Amelang, Jorge Cachinero, Mary Coffey, David Cohen, Inman Fox, Joshua Goode, Ellen Healy, Greg Kendrick, Juan Linz, John Merriman, Philip Minehan, Pamela Radcliff, Ellen Sackelman, Patricia Zahniser, and Carl Ziegler. José E. Álvarez of the University of Houston graciously allowed me to read a preliminary version of his military history of the Spanish Foreign Legion. I would also like to thank the following institutions for providing me with financial support: Yale University's Center for International and Area Studies and its Council on West European Studies, the MacArthur Foundation, the Andrew W. Mellon Foundation, the Fulbright Commission of Spain and the United States of America, and the University of Southern Mississippi and its College of Liberal Arts. For all their essential help in bringing this project to its conclusion, I also wish to thank the editors and staff at the University of Nevada Press, especially Margaret F. Dalrymple and Sara Vélez Mallea. Laura Morgan and her family also deserve my thanks for their love and support during my final efforts to complete the project.

Finally, I must express the most profound gratitude of all to my family. My parents' love and belief in me made everything possible, and they, along with my sisters, Jennifer and Tracy, have always meant more to me than they can possibly realize.

Introduction

The massive mural in the Spanish army's center for historical research, the Servicio Histórico Militar, always makes a strong impression on visitors. In the center of the mural stands an oversized and very idealized likeness of the late dictator Francisco Franco, armor clad and clutching a massive sword. Behind him kneel representatives of the groups that provided him with vital support in the civil war, or "crusade," he successfully waged against the Spanish Second Republic between 1936 and 1939. Several soldiers, including a blue-shirted militiaman from the Spanish fascist party, the Falange, and a fez-wearing Moroccan, gaze in awe at the figure of the Caudillo towering before them, and Italian and German infantrymen stand in the background. A friar, his hands extended in supplication, joins the soldiers in adulating this new incarnation of the Cid. Above them all, Saint James, carrying a sword in one hand and a banner in the other, rides across the heavens on a white horse.

An apparent anachronism in today's democratic Spain, the mural stands as a stark reminder of the nationalist vision that served, albeit with dwindling success, as an ideological tool of the Franco regime until its demise in 1975. Above all, militarist and religious imagery, supported but by no means overshadowed by imagery representative of fascism, stands out as an unsettling reflection of the regime's ideological program. Although the armed forces and the church had played decisive roles in Spanish history long before Franco took power, under his rule ideas and values from military culture and traditionalist Catholicism were forced upon civil society to an unprecedented degree.

Yet regardless of how accurately the mural may reflect the official values of the Franco government, in some ways it leaves viewers with a false impression of history. For not only does it perpetuate the specious, Francoist vision of the armed forces as Spain's traditional, homogenous bulwark of conservative religious and medieval warrior values, but it also paints Spanish nationalism itself as an exclusively rightist phenomenon. In fact, even at the height of his regime's propaganda onslaughts Franco encountered noteworthy resistance from many of his fellow men in arms, including monarchists, Falangists, and more liberal-minded officers. And during the first three decades of the twentieth century Spanish military institutions had been anything but the exclusive domain of the kind of reactionary, antimodern, and intensely religious officers whose views seemed to predominate after the Civil War. Although military culture served as an undeniable source of early-twentieth-century Spanish nationalism, within the officer corps liberals, progressives, and advocates of modernization in general promoted a vigorous nationalist program just as forcefully as did their conservative Catholic counterparts. Hence military nationalism—a barely studied but crucial component of modern Spanish nationalism—was not a purely right-wing affair.

Indeed, during the late nineteenth and early twentieth centuries the officer corps was home to some of the most forward-looking, progressive elements in Spanish society, and officers had easier access than most civilians to institutions and programs fostering education, the advancement of scientific knowledge, and intellectual debate in general. In part because of the Franco regime's success in projecting an image of Spain's supposedly unique and uniform ideological makeup, scholars have largely ignored the different, often conflicting, ideas held by military officers, especially those of strongly "modernist" and "European" outlooks.[1] The tendency to overlook the intellectual diversity that thrived in Spanish military culture may be understandable given murals like the one at the Servicio Histórico Militar and even some official publications of the armed forces that continue to see print.[2] But it has led historians to neglect an important element in the development of modern Spain.

* * *

In the pages that follow I attempt to show how the intellectual conflicts and syntheses resulting from such wide ideological diversity helped shape both Spanish military culture and subsequent Spanish history in general. In particular, through their ideas of national identity and nationalism officers eventually provided—although in many cases unwittingly—significant support for the antidemocratic, authoritarian political forces in Spain that would prove so effective for much of the twentieth century. *Spanish* nationalism—unlike its Catalan and Basque counterparts—has only recently begun to receive much scholarly attention, and scholars have identified various reasons for the relative weakness of modern Spanish nationalism, such as the lack of any long-term foreign threat to the national territory.[3] But Spanish nationalism was far from absent altogether, and the role of military culture in its development and rise still remains almost entirely ignored. By analyzing the case of Spanish military nationalism I aim not only to compensate for some of this neglect, but also to shed light on modern European nationalism in general. Above all, I argue that military culture—surprisingly ignored by E. J. Hobsbawm, John Breuilly, and many other leading scholars in the field—can have a decisive function in the development of modern European nationalism.[4]

How can one seek to identify and comprehend the origins, character, and consequences of military nationalism in modern Europe? How can the production of a nationalist culture within the military community affect society as a whole? For Spain, the answers to such questions can be found to no small degree in the period bounded roughly by the 1898 war with the United States, which brought an end to the centuries-old Spanish empire, and the establishment of Primo de Rivera's dictatorship in 1923. These years not only saw a rise among officers of antidemocratic opposition to parliamentary politics and government, but also set the stage for the subsequent rejection of liberalism by many more officers as the twentieth century progressed. Ultimately this general philosophical shift helps explain the subsequent dictatorship of Primo de Rivera, the failed democracy of the 1930s, and the long-lasting and seemingly anachronistic authoritarian regime of Franco.

Of course, the perceived crisis of the late nineteenth century and the first two decades of the twentieth extended well beyond the world of the armed forces, even if it was military defeat that heightened the general sense of urgency that pervaded much of the country. During these years leading intellectual figures, responding in part to the "Disaster" (the 1898 military loss to the United States), struggled to comprehend how a former world power like Spain could have become a poor land of scant international significance, and they argued passionately over possible means to "regenerate" their country. As members of the so-called Generation of '98—an artificial title often imposed on a very disparate group of Spanish writers—these intellectuals have received considerable attention from literary scholars.[5] The ideas of Spanish military officers during this period, however, have attracted little notice, despite the formidable influence the military has exerted on Spanish society as a whole.

In fact, although most of the works by military writers lacked the literary merit of works by their civilian counterparts, they were probably at least as important as those in influencing the course of Spanish history. Since they shaped as well as reflected the various schools of thought thriving in the officer corps, they also help us to understand the period that followed. For during the dictatorships of Primo de Rivera (1923–30) and Franco (1936–75) many of the country's most powerful government administrators were, like the dictators themselves, products of the military culture I examine. Hence my analysis will, when appropriate, draw attention to continuities—some of which linger to this day.

Yet Restoration Spain, the period of constitutional monarchy that lasted until 1923, remains the primary focus of my work. After all, the intellectual developments within the Restoration officer corps merit attention in their own right, regardless of their interest to scholars of the period that followed. Besides the role they played in the making of modern Spanish nationalism, they also reveal a surprisingly significant participation by Spaniards in the new intellectual movements that attracted so much attention elsewhere in fin-de-siècle

Europe. The ideas of modern thinkers such as Nietzsche and D'Annunzio, for example, found powerful supporters within the Spanish officer corps, as did some of the mystical notions of the occult and theosophy that had a far greater impact on many Europeans at the time than is generally recognized today.

Some officers, however, were also receptive to the tenets of Spanish traditionalism, a movement characterized by antiliberal, counterrevolutionary, and strongly conservative Catholic ideals.[6] And Franco eventually turned to traditionalist thought as the most important source of ideological support for his regime, as exemplified so dramatically in the mural described earlier. Yet even this use of a conservative, mystical vision of history as a model for the future was by no means unique to Spaniards, regardless of traditionalist arguments for the supposedly unique qualities of the "Spanish essence." Moreover, within the officer corps—as elsewhere in Spanish and European society—traditionalist doctrine resembled its modernist counterpart in a very important way: it stemmed from a rejection of the liberal, rationalist legacy of the Enlightenment. In Spain this reaction against liberalism and reason was particularly significant in the military world, where, as I will show, liberal and rationalist principles had previously found an especially receptive audience. Taken together, then, Spanish traditionalism and modernist, Nietzschean thought worked from opposite directions to undermine the liberal tradition of the officer corps—a development of crucial importance for modern Spanish history.

Although historians have analyzed the political, professional, and social transformations within the military that occurred during this period, the more fundamental philosophical shift that underlay the decline of liberalism within the Restoration officer corps remains largely unexamined.[7] In fact, the struggle within the officer corps between competing ideologies—a term I use in its broadest sense[8]—lay the groundwork for a Spanish form of the same "reactionary modernism" that gained significant support elsewhere in Europe during the first part of the twentieth century. Although the concept of reactionary modernism was developed by Jeffrey Herf to describe the enthusiasm for modern technology of German thinkers who rejected Enlightenment reason, it can also serve as a useful term to describe a more general European intellectual trend.[9] Important segments of the radical right in France, for example, simultaneously embraced royalist tradition and Nietzschean precepts, and Italian fascism embodied traditionalist as well as futurist values. In Spain, of course, conservative and traditionalist ideas eventually played a far greater role in shaping the official Francoist worldview than did their modernist counterparts. But the influence of the latter in the weakening and defeat of liberalism and democracy was at least as significant as elsewhere, and even the most important shaper of the Francoist propaganda offensive from the military world—José Millan-Astray—made ample use of modernist fin-de-siècle imagery and rhetoric.

Hence Spain was not always as "different" from the rest of Western Europe as the Franco regime's tourist slogan would later proclaim, despite the enduring tendency to think so that is found in the work of scholars within and outside the country. Although the persistence of the Franco dictatorship after World War II was certainly outside the norm of the democratic West, we should not let this undeniable contrast blind us to the many ways historical developments in Spain before Franco resembled those of other liberal European states. As the social historian Adrian Shubert argues, the same questions posed by Geoff Eley and David Blackbourn regarding the supposed "peculiarities" of German history can be raised about an alleged Spanish *Sonderweg* as well.[10] Historians such as Stanley G. Payne have pointed out, moreover, that the various political forms assumed by the modern Spanish state—like the social developments Shubert studies—largely mirrored their counterparts elsewhere.[11] And, as this work makes clear, the new intellectual movements that attracted attention in other fin-de-siècle European countries found a more significant reception in Spain than has previously been thought. In particular, the military clubs, press, academies, and intellectual societies provided forums for the exchange of ideas to the Spanish officer corps at a level not available to most Spaniards while at the same time fostering the production of nationalist culture. These forums were especially important given Spain's lack of a significant modern, radical right-wing political movement along the lines of Action Française or Italian Fascism, because they served as important centers in Spain for the development of similar ideological programs.

* * *

This book begins with a chapter on the historical background to the rise of such nationalist ideas, examining the world of the armed forces in nineteenth-century Spain. It then turns its attention to the lives and ideas of four particularly noteworthy officers of the Restoration army. Although each of these men had considerably different interests and outlooks, together they form a representative picture of the intellectual world of the officer corps in general. The first, Ricardo Burguete, was a decorated combat veteran who rose to become one of the most important Spanish generals of the twentieth century. A fervent admirer of Nietzsche, he was a powerful advocate of the philosophical movement of vitalism, which was enjoying a revival during this period thanks in part to the influential French thinker Henri Bergson. Vitalism was, in the eyes of Bergson and his many followers, a movement representing both an affirmation of the primacy of nature's "vital forces" and a rejection of nineteenth-century science and positivism, a view Burguete also espoused. And just as Bergson developed his vitalistic evolutionary theory, which presupposed that the universe had begun with a "vital impulse [élan vital]," as an alternative to

Darwinian mechanism, Burguete betrayed a similar vitalist reverence for the irrational, spontaneous forces he believed to fuel biological, social, political, military, and cultural evolution.[12]

Because Burguete's extraordinary ideas and actions warrant a discussion of considerable length, my analysis of his life and writings extends through three chapters. His activities in the political arena were, after all, well known during the first part of the twentieth century both within and outside of the military community. And in the eyes of some contemporaries from Spain's literary world, he actually transcended the civil-military division to earn a place among the more famous writers associated with the "Generation of '98." Although he was hardly the first army officer to play an active role in Spain's mostly civilian intellectual milieu, he attracted attention from renowned Spanish writers that was exceptional for an army officer. He was no more prolific than some of the other military figures discussed in this book, but he alone displayed a noteworthy, if somewhat flawed, understanding of the major ideas of the fin-de-siècle European intellectual vanguard. And by helping to popularize the antirationalist, antimaterialist militarism later associated with radical right-wing movements elsewhere in Europe he contributed to the eventual demise of parliamentary liberalism in Spain. That he himself became an ardent republican who strongly opposed Primo de Rivera and Franco makes little difference. For, just as extreme rightist movements in France, Italy, and other European states often made use of ideas from earlier works by leading thinkers often classified as "leftist," in Spain Burguete unwittingly helped supply his later enemies with much of the linguistic and ideological material they would use in their struggle against liberalism and democracy.[13]

In stark contrast to Burguete, fellow officer Antonio García Pérez, the second figure I examine, publicly acknowledged no interest whatsoever in the new philosophical movements surfacing in Spain and elsewhere in Europe. In fact, García Pérez not only eschewed virtually every aspect of modern social, political, military, and philosophical thought in his writings, but even when working within the ideological world he so loved—that of Spanish traditionalism—he failed to reveal literary or critical skills in any way comparable to those of Burguete. Nevertheless, he probably played at least as important a role as Burguete in shaping military culture in Restoration Spain. A longtime instructor at the Infantry Academy in Toledo and the author of more than seventy-five books and pamphlets and countless periodical articles, he helped fuel the growth of the more conservative outlook that contributed so decisively to the demise of the Spanish officer corps' liberal tradition. And it was above all the traditionalist ideology he so fervently promoted that eventually became a staple of the Franco regime's cultural politics.

A leading liberal, scientifically inclined military writer and educator, Enrique

Ruiz-Fornells, serves as the next subject of this book. A firm believer in what he perceived as Enlightenment values, Ruiz-Fornells most clearly and forcefully represented the school of thought within the army that struggled to maintain the intellectual legacy of nineteenth-century military liberalism. Although he was a severe critic of many facets of the development of the armed forces in Restoration Spain, he staunchly rejected calls to shift the focus of the military's educational institutions and general staff away from what he perceived as their customary scientific focus. He eventually made his most noticeable mark in history during the early 1930s, when he assisted Republican War Minister Manuel Azaña in his attempt to reform and rationalize the military, a controversial undertaking that provoked much resentment in significant sectors of the armed forces. But his activities during the preceding four decades merit at least as much attention as those during the 1930s, even if they have since been largely ignored. During this period Ruiz-Fornells played a prominent role in Spanish military pedagogy, writing the textbook on "military morals" assigned to all infantry cadets. And his unpublished memoirs, made available to me by his grandson, provide fascinating insight into the world of the Restoration military.

The fourth officer studied in this book, José Millán-Astray, remains a notorious figure in Spain even today. As the founder of the Spanish Foreign Legion and Franco's first propaganda chief during the Civil War, the one-eyed, one-armed war hero is probably best remembered for assaulting the great Spanish writer Miguel de Unamuno with cries of "Long live death!" and "Death to intellectuals!" at a 1936 celebration in Salamanca. In spite of his ostensibly anti-intellectual outlook, however, he in fact had a strong interest in ideas and their role in history. Indeed, in many ways his views represented the ideological culmination of the antirationalist tendencies fostered from radically different perspectives by Burguete and García Pérez. Embracing Catholic traditionalist doctrine as well as the vitalist rhetoric and fascination with foreign ideas characteristic of Burguete, Millán-Astray was a principal figure in the rise and triumph of the unnatural union of irrationalist and conservative elements from military culture that the Franco regime would try to impose on Spanish society as a whole. Indeed, Zeev Sternhell's description of the synthesis that fostered the rise of Italian and French fascism applies as well to the national-Catholic, "crusade" ideology promoted by Millán-Astray: "on the one hand, a rejection of democracy, Marxism, liberalism, the so-called bourgeois values, the eighteenth-century heritage, internationalism, and pacifism; on the other hand a cult of heroism, vitalism, and violence."[14]

The chapter on Millán-Astray also explores possible links between the antirationalist, violent imagery and historical myths that came to characterize extreme right-wing Spanish nationalism and the actual conduct of battle. Grounded in a very conservative idea of the *patria,* mystical notions of death, sacrifice, and the righteousness of the "Spanish" cause were essential ingredients of the nationalist vision shared by many of the hardened officers of the brutal campaigns in North Africa. This vision, in turn, corresponded well to tactical, operational, and strategic ideas that favored frontal attack over the defensive, the need for "total pacification" of conquered areas, and a general faith in the predominance of "moral" forces in war over such material factors as defensive fortifications and weaponry. Military thinking of this sort did not, moreover, remain confined to the Moroccan campaigns of Millán-Astray's Foreign Legion, but it was also learned by the Legion's second in command, future dictator Francisco Franco. Indeed, the *africanista* mind-set he acquired as a young officer clearly informed his outlook and actions when he subsequently led troops in the suppression of civilian unrest and later in the Spanish Civil War.

In the epilogue I attempt to trace this influence of Millán-Astray as well as that of Burguete, García Pérez, and Ruiz-Fornells on Spanish history after 1923, shedding light on certain continuities extending beyond the demise of the Restoration system of government and into the periods of the Primo de Rivera dictatorship, the Second Republic, and the Civil War and Francoist triumph. Although I do not claim that the intellectual movements I study in the main body of my work led directly or inevitably to the major historical events they preceded, I do maintain that they helped lay the groundwork for certain key developments. By examining how the subjects of my work influenced and responded to important events after 1923, moreover, I explore the long-term effects of nationalist cultural production as well as the relationships between ideas, professional concerns, and actions.

These effects and relationships also inform the organization and emphasis of this book. I begin by stressing how the opposing ideologies of liberalism and traditionalism both left their marks on the nascent nationalism of the nineteenth-century Spanish military. I then turn to Burguete, the "vanguardist" of the group who most forcefully contributed modern, vitalist notions of national identity and regeneration to military culture after 1898. By immediately following the introductory chapter with an analysis of Burguete and the modernist component of early-twentieth-century military thought, I hope to combat the common impression that an overwhelmingly and peculiarly traditionalist character has always separated Spain from the rest of modern Europe.

This is not to argue, however, that the more reactionary current in the Spanish officer corps or the liberal, rationalist school failed to outlive the nineteenth century. Indeed, the chapters on García Pérez and Ruiz-Fornells demonstrate how those legacies from the previous century responded to modernist attacks and how they continued to evolve during the remainder of the Restoration and thereafter. Burguete's modernism may have represented the most spectacular and dynamic strain of military thought to arise in the immediate aftermath of the 1898 military loss to Cuban rebels and the United States, but it by no means achieved hegemony in military culture. It did, however, help shape the twentieth-century versions of the older schools of military traditionalism and liberalism, especially their notions of Spanish identity. Even otherwise liberal and scientifically inclined officers would now propagate a very romantic, historicist vision of nationalism and war, sometimes even citing the likes of an antirationalist such as Ernst Jünger. And at roughly the same time Burguete's vitalist strains would also merge with traditionalism to form the unnatural ideological union later associated with the nationalist program of Millán-Astray.

* * *

Several other themes run through all the chapters in this work. Although each chapter assumes a largely biographical form, my primary aim is to impart an understanding of the broader world in which the military writers lived. By examining their perceptions and actions as individuals one can learn a great deal about the broader structures defining the officer corps as well as Spanish society as a whole. In particular, the institutions of military education and publishing—which have received relatively little attention from historians—functioned as powerful, surprisingly autonomous forces within, and to a certain degree outside of, Spanish military culture. Of course, the realization that military education has played an important role in Spanish history is nothing new, and Paul Preston's recent biography of Franco includes a brief discussion of the importance of his subject's days as a cadet.[15] But few scholars have conducted detailed studies of Spanish military academies themselves, especially during the Restoration.[16] Since all four of the officers I study devoted notable efforts to analyzing the state of military education in Spain, and two—García Pérez and Ruiz-Fornells—labored for much of their careers in the army's pedagogical wing, this book adds to our knowledge of this little-explored aspect of Spanish history.

Another common theme that surfaces repeatedly from the writings of these officers is a strong interest in history, which profoundly shaped their political, social, and philosophical outlooks. It is difficult, if not impossible, to overemphasize the importance of historical perceptions in modern Spain. As Richard Herr has written, "One cannot conceive of a Spaniard who does not know in a vague way that Spain once belonged to the Roman Empire, that it was conquered by the Moors in the *Reconquista,* that under Ferdinand and Isabel Columbus discovered America where Spain founded a vast empire, that Spanish arms fought the heresy of Luther, or that Spanish guerrillas foiled Napoleon's conquest of their country. These are collective memories that make Spain a nation."[17] Even if Herr exaggerates to some degree, he rightly emphasizes the vital role played by historical consciousness in shaping the outlook of many Spaniards. As scholars have pointed out, the widespread interest in history during the nineteenth and early twentieth centuries stemmed in large part from the debates that raged in intellectual circles over national identity and the legitimacy of political authority.[18] Equally important, popular visions of Spain's supposed historical destiny as an imperial power, embraced by many military officers and civilians alike, fueled movements in favor of military expansion in northern Africa. My discussion of the historical perceptions of army officers therefore stresses their observations on Spain's past and future activities in Africa. After all, Morocco has played an important part in many Spaniards' struggle to define their country's historical identity, and Spanish imperialism in the Maghreb has left a deep impression on popular culture.[19]

Of course, there were considerable differences between the historical arguments employed by military writers for or against expansion in northern Africa. The disparity was much less pronounced, however, in their works on a closely related area in which they also shared a strong mutual interest: that of war itself. Not surprisingly, considering their profession, they viewed war as inevitable and as an agent of historical progress, dismissing pacifists as hopelessly misguided. Yet, even more significantly, the military thinkers I examine largely concurred in their portrayal of warfare as an overwhelmingly "moral" and spiritual affair. Only the self-proclaimed advocate of Enlightenment reason, Enrique Ruiz-Fornells, argued that science should continue to play a major role in preparing for and waging war. To the others—and even to Ruiz-Fornells to a certain degree—war was an irrational, uncontrollable phenomenon that could easily assume a dynamic energy of its own. In fact, the tendency common to Spanish military writers—even those of dramatically different outlooks and mind-sets—to employ the same "language of war" represented the Spanish counterpart to a practice widespread among leading intellectuals elsewhere in Europe. As Daniel Pick writes, influential European pacifist as well as militarist thinkers employed the same evolutionary and degenerationist terms when discussing war, which they often portrayed as a manifestation of evolutionary naturalism.[20] Hence even as bellicose a writer as Burguete could find much of value in the writings of an antimilitarist such as Herbert Spencer, whom he frequently cited. And in Spain the increasing popularity of such language and imagery within the officer corps had important consequences for the civilian world as well. For if, as scholars of the French Revolution have argued, language and semiotics serve as the principal tools with which people interpret, articulate, and shape political culture, the transformation of much Spanish military rhetoric and imagery from a largely rationalist and scientific character to a more mystical and spiritual emphasis represented a shift of considerable consequence.[21]

* * *

All of these themes—from education to history to militarist rhetoric—heavily influenced what was probably the most important component of Restoration military thought: ideas of national identity and nationalism. Neither Spanish literary regenerationism, often associated with the Generation of '98, nor its military counterpart was unique in Europe. Instead they formed part of a general trend in which Europeans increasingly turned to new forms of nationalist ideology as they lost faith in liberal political institutions and culture. And, as Hobsbawm and others have observed, this nationalist thinking often came to acquire a markedly rightist tone as the twentieth century progressed.[22] By studying Spain during this period, and in particular the role played by military culture, one can better understand not only the process by which nationalist thought in general evolved, but also why radical right-wing forms of nationalism could prove so much more effective than their liberal counterparts.

John Breuilly has convincingly argued that modern nationalism should be understood above all as a political phenomenon in which the state plays a central role.[23] My study demonstrates that such an understanding is especially appropriate to Spain and, in particular, to Spanish military nationalism. For even if the fundamental tenets of nationalist ideology are inherently flawed, or even irreal and "imagined,"[24] the Spanish nationalism of the late nineteenth and early twentieth centuries was in the end a product of very tangible political crises and interests. This is not, of course, to deny the importance of culture and ideology; modern nationalism derives much of its appeal and strength from irrational, often emotional, forces and the cultural and ideological contexts from which they stem. But in modern Spanish society it was primarily political necessity that gave rise to their construction and use as ideological tools.

Many writers have traced the origins of modern Spanish nationalism to the "War of Independence," and the armed struggle against Napoleonic occupation, in fact, served as a starting point for much subsequent nationalist mythology.[25] But Spanish nationalism was of negligible effect overall until the latter part of the nineteenth century. Some intellectuals may have attempted to define the Spanish "nation" and Spanish identity, but at the time they were relatively scant in number and influence.[26] And the Catholic right remained suspicious of or openly hostile toward Spanish nationalism until well into the second half of the nineteenth century.[27] It was only after the revolution of 1868 that economic and social changes, the corresponding rise of socialism and anarchism, and colonial difficulties led a powerful group—the officer corps—to begin to employ nationalism on a regular basis as a tool for political change. Scholars have certainly not ignored the ways in which military interests, from the *pronunciamientos* of the nineteenth century to the Civil War of the 1930s, weakened constitutional government, but they have written surprisingly little about how notions of national identity and even nationalism itself could provide officers with ideological support for their political behavior.[28]

The only scholar to examine this issue in any significant depth, Sebastian Balfour, argues that military nationalism emerged in the Spanish officer corps during the early twentieth century. Balfour correctly relates the nationalism of the officer elites to "the needs of modernisation," but his argument that military officers then sought "to modernise the nation through an authoritarian state" cannot be applied to many army elites with considerable influence in military culture.[29] Enrique Ruiz-Fornells, for instance, whose illustrious career I examine in depth, explicitly embraced what he perceived as liberal, progressive Enlightenment values throughout his life. Although the economic hardships associated with Spain's painful process of modernization helped push some officers toward authoritarianism, a significant self-described liberal, republican segment of the officer corps also continued to thrive well into the advent of the Second Republic.

Yet Balfour's explicit acknowledgment and analysis of the role of military nationalism in Spain—although brief—is of much value, not the least because it recognizes the importance of a phenomenon that remains ignored by most Spanish historians. Of course, scholars of nationalism in general have neglected the armed forces in their analysis altogether—an omission of similar import. Nevertheless, in the case of the Spanish officer corps the methods of these same scholars and their observations on society, culture, and ideology often prove apt. Anderson, for example, has shown how what he calls "print capitalism" can foster the development of national identity. His observation that the concept of "the French Revolution" did not acquire meaning as a tangible "'thing' . . . with its own name" until it "entered the accumulating memory of print" can be modified to apply to a similarly pivotal event in Spanish history.[30] For in Spain it was the work of intellectuals writing about the war against Napoleon that invested the experience with significance as a concept, and finally as a sort of symbol representing the values and character of an "imagined political community" or nation. Military writers, moreover, drew numerous lessons from their perception of the conflict. Among the more intellectually oriented officers, references to the nation and national interests became increasingly characteristic of the ideological struggles—in which the memory of guerrilla warfare against the French often figured prominently—between the "Krausists," the "utopian militarists," and other such schools of thought within the officer corps.[31] These developments manifested themselves in the still-emerging military print culture, which would explode and reach its most advanced stage during the Restoration. Military periodicals, academy lesson plans and textbooks, and the many works of history penned by army officers all functioned together in this first phase of development of the "accumulating memory" of nationalist ideas and myths. They would combine, moreover, with the growth of military social and intellectual clubs to form what Karl W. Deutsch calls the "communicative facilities of a society," which foster the development of nationalism.[32]

Nevertheless, military nationalism was not a significant force in Spain until after the Restoration of 1874, and it was precisely because of the relationship of officers to the state that it strengthened. Cánovas's Restoration system made it substantially more difficult for officers to turn to their customary method of altering their relationship to the state—the coup d'état or *pronunciamiento*. Although such extralegal attempts to intervene in politics by no means disappeared during the late nineteenth century,[33] their lack of success shows that the national political system was now better equipped to deal with such threats. Indeed, it was above all this new situation that changed the ways officers tried to alter the state and their relationship to it. Now they turned more than ever before to ideology and culture in addition to, if not instead of, the traditional method of the *pronunciamiento*. As a result, the military print culture began to "accumulate" to an unprecedented degree.

In addition, the same basic problems of modernity facing other countries—such as changing economic conditions, the decline of traditional social relations and of a sense of community, and the seemingly widening gap between state and society—were exacerbated in Spain by colonial crisis. In other European powers the "new imperialism" could serve at least somewhat successfully to bridge the separation between the state and modern society, as was the case in Britain, where even members of the working classes succumbed to jingoism and "social imperialism."[34] In Spain, however, regardless of any strong initial popular support for the war in Cuba, the loss to the United States in 1898 and the subsequent policies regarding conscription for service in North Africa weakened the state's legitimacy in the eyes of many citizens. Furthermore, for the officers the loss of empire, a new hostility from the formerly friendly forces of civilian liberalism, increased deployment of the army to suppress social unrest, and the seeming lack of adequate support for military activities in Morocco all facilitated disillusionment with the state and construction of the ideal of the nation as an alternate object of loyalty and a means of advancing corporate interests. Thus nationalist rhetoric flooded the growing number of institutions that promoted such interests, thereby helping to create a sense of community—both imagined and real. The instruments of the nationalist officers included the military press, academies, and clubs. Like the four men on which this book focuses, officers who assumed leading positions within the army and Spanish politics were frequently tied to these institutions that promoted nationalism, especially as the twentieth century progressed.

The Spanish military writers also fit the general pattern of European nationalism in terms of their social status, professional aspirations, and strong interest in pedagogical matters. Hobsbawm's contention that schools and universities are good measures of the progress of nationalism may be appropriate for nineteenth-century Europe, but its validity for other places and times is doubtful.[35] In Spain, of course, the poor condition of the educational systems corresponded to a lack of strong nationalist sentiments. But by the end of the century and thereafter civilian schools and universities were not always the best places to seek out signs of nationalism—especially in Spain. Admittedly, it is easy to link new programs of education to modernity in general, and the same is of course true for modern nationalism. If one accepts such associations, Spain's hesitant path to modernity corresponds well to the underdeveloped state of its educational system and the weakness of civilian nationalism at the time.

But such weakness was not so characteristic of a significant portion of Spanish society: the officer corps. Army officers in Spain experienced social and professional conditions broadly analogous to those of the sectors of the European middle classes from which nationalist thinkers often arose, and they too had a keen interest in the topic of education. As Breuilly writes, the "typical nationalist intellectual can be seen as an unsuccessful professional," even if the apparent lack of success of such a professional is always "relative."[36] In the case of Spanish military writers, fairly regular promotions and long-term assignments to serve as academy instructors or in other relatively stable positions were not always perceived as enough to constitute social and professional success, especially by the many officers who had to take second and third jobs and engage in a considerable amount of political maneuvering just to receive the benefits they felt corresponded to their worth. By equating themselves with "the nation" and employing nationalist rhetoric, these disgruntled officers were expressing their dissatisfaction with their relationship to the state in essentially the same manner as the middle-class civilian nationalists all over Europe. And, like the European middle class in general, military writers could go so far as to reject liberalism altogether in favor of the ideology of an authoritarian and modernizing state—although such an outlook was anything but universal.

In the Spanish army, moreover, there was a direct link between social status, professional aspirations, and the production of nationalist rhetoric. As is the case for scholars at universities today, for officers in the Spanish army publications counted toward promotion. The plethora of books and articles written by officers may have served the primary purpose of increasing their chances of professional advancement, but they had as a significant side effect the accumulation of a nationalist print culture. For in many cases these publications relied on or reinforced, at least implicitly, notions of national identity and nationalism.

* * *

What forms of nationalism did officers embrace? What kind of national identity proved most useful to them? Despite the wide variety in the major schools of thought within the Spanish military intelligentsia, these schools all shared a similarly romantic and "historicist" approach to Spanish nationalism.[37] Even officers like Enrique Ruiz-Fornells, who explicitly promoted what they perceived as progressive Enlightenment values, reason, democracy, and their country's liberal historical legacy, paradoxically relied on a more romantic, historicist notion of national history that stressed the alleged peculiarities of the Spanish nation and national character. For such historicists, as Breuilly writes, history is "the only way to understand a society" and to "apprehend the spirit of a community."[38] Ruiz-Fornells fervently believed that history vindicated his belief in Spain's inherent and natural liberal condition and destiny, and he cited the Constitution of Cádiz, the liberty supposedly characteristic of medieval Spanish society, and other such historical examples as proof. Influential civilian intellectuals, moreover, made similar arguments.[39]

Yet despite the popularity of this approach, it suffered from its inherently contradictory nature, which in turn limited its effectiveness. After all, the liberal officers who openly praised Enlightenment reason were at the same time relying on a historicist—and therefore essentially illiberal—vision of history. Of course, to cite Breuilly, "ideology is not a logical mode of thought and history is not logic." One should not, he continues, be surprised by the many Europeans who claimed to be both liberal and nationalist.[40] Similarly, he cautions against assuming that this ideological incompatibility inevitably led to the replacement of liberal nationalism by its "logical culmination," fascism.[41]

Within the Spanish military community, however, liberals *did* promote a form of nationalism that would serve the twentieth-century authoritarian right—whether fascist, traditionalist, or a combination of both—more effectively than it would serve their own liberal republican interests.[42] For example, the textbook of the liberal officer Ruiz-Fornells on "moral education," which was assigned to infantry cadets during the late nineteenth and early twentieth centuries, may have praised democratic values and the primacy of constitutional, civilian rule, but it also left readers with a rather irrationalist and romantic impression of Spanish history.[43] And within Spanish military culture, at least, it is difficult not to believe that this vision of history, which was introduced to generation after generation of teenage cadets and came to permeate military culture, did not contribute to the efficacy of subsequent right-wing nationalist ideology. The officer corps was, moreover, the sphere of Spanish society in which the tools, motives, and social preconditions of this nationalist thinking could come together in the most dynamic fashion. And, needless to say, the powerful role played by the military in subsequent Spanish history only reinforces the importance of the turn-of-the-century military nationalist projects.

* * *

Finally, it is important to understand how commonalities in age, experience, and professional interests linked the four primary subjects of this book. All were infantry officers of roughly the same age and career path, although some rose to much higher ranks than others. Indeed, all four men, born between 1868 and 1879, belong to the category a leading Spanish military historian has designated as the "military Generation of '98," having completed their academy training and served as young officers in Cuba or the Philippines by around 1898. The elite members of this generation would achieve considerable status, entering the generalship around 1917, reaching the apex of their military and political careers with the establishment of Primo de Rivera's dictatorship in 1923, and then assuming the status of the "residual elite" after the declaration of the Second Republic in 1931.[44] Hence, when the Civil War broke out in 1936 the three figures of my study who had achieved notable professional success—Generals Ruiz-Fornells, Burguete, and Millán-Astray—were all overshadowed by a new group of principal protagonists in Spanish military affairs. In fact, the generation whom they had educated as cadets and young officers had come to gain far more influence over Spanish society as a whole than they had ever enjoyed themselves. But Burguete, García Pérez, Ruiz-Fornells, and Millán-Astray had helped create the nationalist climate in which the new protagonists would work so well, having supplied their successors with much of the ideological material they would employ with such success.

Chapter One

Liberalism, Tradition, and War
The Spanish Army in the Nineteenth Century

Already master of much of Europe in early 1808, Napoleon Bonaparte saw no reason to fear his neighbors to the south. Through a combination of threats and deceit, he had stripped the Spanish royal family of power and occupied much of the Iberian Peninsula with his troops. His armies, having achieved notable victories elsewhere, expected no significant opposition from their Spanish counterparts. With his brother Joseph installed as the new king of Spain, Napoleon was seemingly free to direct his attention to new challenges.

By early spring, however, it became apparent that Spanish submission might not be so easy to maintain. Popular resistance to the French presence was clearly building, although it would not take its most dramatic form until May. By the first day of that month the atmosphere in the main square of Madrid, the Puerta del Sol, finally reached a critical point. A large, threatening crowd had gathered there, and during the night peasants armed with knives, cudgels, and primitive firearms joined it. The following day violence finally erupted, and mobs attacked and killed the isolated French soldiers they encountered. The French acted to regain control quite quickly, ruthlessly crushing the uprising and executing hundreds of Spaniards. But by early June rebellion had swept much of Spain.[1] Subsequently recorded by Goya in his famous painting and by numerous monuments and written works, the Dos de Mayo uprising had evolved into the full-scale people's war that would form the basis of one of contemporary Spain's most important myths. And the "Spanish ulcer," as Napoleon regarded the Spaniards' resistance to his will, would contribute decisively to his eventual downfall.

Writers have since made much of the way in which the war brought the Spanish nation together by fostering widespread resistance to a foreign threat. Indeed, the "War of Independence," as Spaniards came to call it, subsequently became a key element in attempts to forge and propagate a sense of Spanish national identity.[2] As in many modern nationalist movements elsewhere, armed struggle against a common enemy thus figured prominently in contemporary Spain's first national myth. The memory of the war, moreover, complemented the more general interpretation of history that many nationalists would propagate. To them, the heroics of the medieval warrior the Cid, the "discovery" of America by Christopher Columbus, and the conquest of Mexico by Hernán Cortés all revealed the same inherently Spanish characteristics of bravery, strength, ingenuity, and impetuousness that so aided Spain in its struggle to expel the Napoleonic armies.

Like many myths, the nationalist memory of the War of Independence was by no means a wholly artificial creation. Admittedly, Spain's geographical and social divisions did not suddenly disappear in 1808, and the Napoleonic invasion and occupation elicited a wide variety of responses all over the country. In more than a few cases, class warfare *between* Spaniards was the precondition of the "national" endeavors against the intruders.[3] And conspiracies hatched for varying personal and political reasons fomented popular resistance. But a common goal—expulsion of the French—was shared by individual groups of insurgents acting wholly independent of one another, and the combination of their actions with public xenophobia and crowd behavior can be viewed to at least some degree as genuine patriotism.[4] Through their repeated use during the war, moreover, patriotic expressions began to acquire popular meaning. As one writer observed, "The word patria was new to the mouths and ears of Spaniards, and if a term used only in books came to be part of popular acclaim, it could not have come into use without the accompaniment of the ideas that it awakened and encompassed."[5]

Ironically, however, the very war that nationalists later found so appealing also hindered subsequent attempts at nation building. After all, the efficacy of the Spanish freedom fighters had depended to a large degree on the highly decentralized manner in which they operated.[6] In certain respects the popular rebellion against the French may indeed have signaled, as some historians have argued, the emergence of nationalist sentiments.[7] But in other ways the war reinforced rather than curbed Spain's long tradition of localism in government and society, which had thrived even during the country's most ostensibly "absolutist" periods.[8] The various juntas established throughout the country, moreover, could show more interest in building their own respective empires than in working together in the name of the "*patria,*" or Spanish nation.[9] And even in its mythical form, the War of Independence may actually have done more to hinder the development of a viable form of Spanish nationalism than to foster it.[10]

Furthermore, the traditional institutions of armed force, often key elements in nation-building endeavors, had failed to take a leading role in the war. Instead, they had shown themselves profoundly lacking in skill and organization, as General Sir Arthur Wellesley—later the first duke of Wellington—would bluntly observe.[11] Hence after the war the Spanish army lacked both the means and the legitimacy to serve as a consistent, reliable, and unified body around which a strong and viable nation could be built. Because neither the monarchy, the church, nor any other national entity succeeded in this regard either, the "institutional weakness of modern Spain," as Stanley G. Payne described the condition in his classic work, would persist for well over a century.[12]

Of course, the Napoleonic Wars were by no means the sole cause of Spain's subsequent problems, and the character and consequences of this tumultuous period are in any case far too complex to receive full treatment here. But the Napoleonic conflict can serve as an apt point of departure for a discussion of the military world of nineteenth-century Spain, especially with regard to the political and nationalist aspirations of army officers. For even during this period of ostensible national unity, wartime opposition to the foreign occupiers tended to fall into two major camps. And, as one would expect during wartime, the conflict was particularly apparent with regard to the issue of military policy. Whereas some liberal deputies at Cádiz made utopian plans to abolish the regular armed forces and create a citizens' militia, more conservative elites viewed the popular rebellion as something to be brought under control through institutional measures, such as incorporating a larger segment of the population into the ranks of the regular army.[13] After the expulsion of the French, this kind of tension between liberalism and traditionalism—in civil as well as military spheres—would plague Spain until well into the twentieth century.

For a large part of the population, opposition to the French stemmed from a desire to protect traditional rights and the values of the church and the monarchy from the perceived threat of foreign liberal and revolutionary elements.[14] Many peasants, clergy, and other more provincial members of society joined or at least lent their support to the *guerrilleros,* whose actions gave birth to the use of the English word *guerrilla*—literally "small war" in Spanish—to describe the irregular methods they employed. Later the ideological legacy of these forces of reaction would assume its most extreme form under the banner of Carlism, a rival dynastic movement formed around Don Carlos—pretender to the throne of Isabella II—and his descendants. The desire of the Carlists to impose their traditionalist vision on Spain led to several bloody civil wars in the nineteenth century, and these ultraconservatives surfaced again as a major political force in the 1930s. In fact, many of their ideas would eventually find a place in the Franco regime's ideological front, which in certain ways represented the final manifestation and triumph of the reactionary outlook of the original *guerrilleros.*

Yet along with the term *guerrilla,* another, very different, linguistic innovation emerged during Spain's Napoleonic period that would later enter the vocabulary of the entire Western world. The term *liberal* was employed for the first time in its modern political sense to describe those Spaniards who, while also supporting the expulsion of Napoleon's forces, wanted to create a very different kind of regime than did their conservative Catholic counterparts.[15] The famous 1812 constitution of Cádiz, at the time one of Europe's most progressive documents ever, lay the foundation for modern Spain's long tradition of political liberalism. Although Ferdinand VII would temporarily bring the liberal movement to a halt upon the restoration of his monarchy in 1814, it would soon resurface as a formidable political force, with army officers often serving as its most influential proponents.

The officer corps, however, was hardly a homogenous body, and plenty of conservative and politically apathetic men joined the liberals in its ranks. Spain's strong tradition of praetorianism—the tendency of the military to intervene in civilian politics—thus came in various shades during the nineteenth century. This penchant for political activism existed in large part because no single faction had emerged from the War of Independence strong enough to impose its will in a definitive fashion.[16] Because the same divisions that characterized civil society extended through the military world as well, the army was anything but a source of political stability. The highly politicized state of the officer corps, moreover, marred the organization and performance of the army itself. Spain sustained, as the regenerationist Rafael Altamira observed, more years of war in the nineteenth century than France, Germany, and many other European powers,[17] yet the country's armed forces paradoxically suffered from a profound lack of professionalism, efficient organization, and—perhaps most important—military effectiveness.

The roots of many of these problems lay in the transformation the officer corps began to experience with the eighteenth-century Bourbon reforms. During this period soldiering at the lowest level began to undergo a gradual shift from lifelong occupation of the few to temporary duty of the masses, a change with implications related to class and nationality. By the time foreigners were expelled from the continental Spanish army in 1835, the seeds of the "citizen soldier" ideal had been firmly planted. Conversely, those who led the soldiers came to expect to make careers out of their military activities, and the position of officer began to acquire the status of a "profession." In the nineteenth century fewer men with titles served in the officer corps, because manpower needs had led to the relaxation of the requirement of noble status to obtain a commission. Of course, the growth in the number of officers who depended on their military salaries as their only sources of income brought with it increasingly powerful corporate interests in favor of expanding the military bureaucracy.[18] Many military men soon became aware that, in the absence of viable electoral means of change, civilian politicians depended on their support to gain power and implement their programs. Hence the officer corps periodically succeeded in exacting material benefits from the governments in power, and the increasingly officer-heavy Spanish army exerted greater demands on the national budget. The ideological counterpart to these economic-corporate interests was the tendency of officers to think of the army only in terms of themselves. From there the next step would be to blur the distinction between their own needs and those of the nation as a whole.

Ideologically speaking, however, the decline in the aristocratic character of the officer corps came to an abrupt halt with the restoration of 1814, when Ferdinand VII encouraged young nobles to enter the armed forces. These men joined officers of middle-class backgrounds to form a collective body that thrived on "aristocratic" values. As Thilo Jens Wittenberg convincingly argues, Ferdinand VII's strong reaction against the corps' increasingly bourgeois character, which had become apparent by the middle of the eighteenth century and then accelerated during the war against the French, had significant ideological ramifications. According to Wittenberg, Ferdinand's dissolution of the general staff, his purging of liberal officers, and his creation of the Guardia Real all served to weaken the "corporative tradition of enlightened absolutism" that had previously characterized the officer corps. Moreover, the king's "intellectual decapitation" of the army contributed to the more individualist and "moral" vision of warfare that had grown naturally out of the experience of guerrilla fighting.[19] For purely political reasons, guerrilla leaders associated with liberalism suffered professionally under Ferdinand.[20] But Spanish military thought in general remained receptive to antirationalist approaches to war, rooted in the "guerrilla myth" and valuing courage, heroics, spirituality, and morale over material resources, tactics, and strategy.[21] Even if, as one historian argues, the king deserves credit for creating an army that was later capable of withstanding the threat of Carlism,[22] royal military policies had the long-term effect of strengthening the irrationalist and anti-intellectual component of Spanish military thought.

On the surface, the officer corps' most significant role in nineteenth-century Spain lay in its seemingly unceasing intervention in politics. Although the military activists were in fact relatively few in number, officers of various political persuasions were commonly leaders of the periodic rebellions against existing governments. Such risings in general became known as *pronunciamientos* after Major Rafael de Riego used the term in a speech to troops before rising against the absolutist regime of Ferdinand VII in 1820.[23] *Pronunciamientos* took a wide variety of forms, but almost always involved the use of force—either threatened or real—against a regime that had alienated various political factions. Sometimes the *pronunciamientos* consisted of nothing more than barracks revolts that sufficed to panic the government or to inspire other units to join in the risings; on other occasions they more closely resembled the classic coup d'état. In any case, a general pattern soon emerged in which liberal officers and civilians would "pronounce" and create a government more to their liking, which itself would fall when their more conservative counterparts later resorted to the same tactic. Although the *pronunciamientos* often failed, they succeeded frequently enough to become a common method of effecting governmental change. And, as would be the case over a century later when General Emilio Mola launched the revolt that sparked the Civil War, personal, career-related considerations often lay behind the political ideologies that ostensibly motivated the officers to act. After Ferdinand's return to the throne, for example, poor working conditions, economic hardship, and the threat of an uncertain future in the Americas fueled the growth of liberalism in the officer corps that culminated with the *pronunciamiento* of 1820.[24]

Spanish praetorianism persisted for much of the century, even as the army pursued war against the Carlists at home and against insurgents in Morocco and the Americas. And the same ideological conflicts that had marked the War of Independence survived in the officer corps as well, manifesting themselves on a purely political level between traditional parties and on more philosophical levels in the debates over military service, organization, education, tactics, and strategy and over approaches to war in general.[25] These conflicts culminated in the revolutionary and counterrevolutionary period of 1868–75, with the restoration of the monarchy under Alfonso XII as the end result. Although often overlooked by the historians who have focused overwhelmingly on political figures and their ideas, military corporate interests contributed decisively to the events of 1868.[26] The question of military service was particularly important, which helps explain why it would figure so prominently in the writings of so many officers. Although debates over universal military service have been common in modern times, such as in Prussia's responses to Napoleon and in Bismarck's later attempts to lengthen the period of service required of all young men, in Spain the issue had a particularly strong impact.

After the death of Ferdinand VII in 1833, it had soon become clear that some form of constitutional monarchy was the only real alternative to the threat of Carlist absolutism. Along with the rights, albeit quite limited at times, that Spaniards grew to expect as part of constitutional rule came an increasing acceptance—at least in theory—of a corresponding *contribución de sangre* that the government could demand of them. Thus arose the liberal-romantic notion of the Spanish "citizen soldier," which was not unlike what liberals in the Cortes had advocated during the war against Napoleon. Like his predecessors in the French revolutionary armies, the citizen soldier was to take up arms in defense of national sovereignty and liberty.[27] And just as the French socialist leader Jean Jaurès would later embrace this idea, in Spain politicians and military thinkers—including Enrique Ruiz-Fornells—would emphasize the ostensibly close relationship between universal military service, social equity, and liberal democratic values.

For the masses, however, the liberal ideal of obligatory military service had little to do with reality. The citizen soldier may have served as a plank in the liberal political platform, but bourgeois interests also ensured that in practice the brunt of military service fell squarely on the poor. Young men who were conscripted had the legal right to hire substitutes or make payments, known as "service in the form of cash," to avoid having to serve themselves. An early outgrowth of this sort of inequity was the growing disenchantment of the poor with liberalism and the corresponding growth in popularity of political movements of a more radical democratic bent. Indeed, the issue of the military draft became so explosive that it contributed decisively to General Juan Prim's *pronunciamiento* and overthrow of Isabel II in 1868.

The revolution of 1868—"revolutionary" in the contemporary Spanish sense that it signaled a shift toward stronger constitutionalism—grew out of the economic crisis that had hit the country two years before. Not the least of the many negative consequences of the crisis was the bankruptcy of insurance companies, many of which actually sold protection against the military draft. Families could buy policies that, should their sons one day be called for service, afforded a second chance at the draft lottery or even paid the full price of exemption. Needless to say, the financial failures of these insurance companies only worsened the social crisis, thus contributing to the growing rejection of Isabeline liberalism. Other army-related causes of the revolution of 1868 included the state of the military profession in general, which suffered from budgetary constraints and provided officers few opportunities for advancement.[28] These professional interests of officers continued to influence their actions throughout the turbulent period that followed, undoubtedly playing a more important role for most of them than did political ideologies.

Yet a smaller, intellectually oriented group of military men responded to the officer corps' poor social situation by formulating, debating, and promoting reforms that, although undeniably products of special interests, also aimed to improve Spain's condition in general, often transcending the purely practical and entering the same ideological, philosophical, and even spiritual milieu that would soon interest Spain's literary regenerationists. Organizations devoted to writing, learning, and discussing the "social question" and other such affairs were not new to the Spanish military; cadets in Toledo, for example, had formed a Sociedad Literaria in the 1850s, in part to address such matters. In that tradition, in 1871 an article appeared in the *Correo Militar* calling for the establishment of an institution that would act as a sort of military think tank and help foster Spanish regeneration. Shortly thereafter a group of like-minded officers founded the Ateneo Militar.[29] The founders of this center were reacting in large part to the many flaws they perceived in Prim's regime, but international events had also made their mark. Like Europeans everywhere, they were impressed by the recent demonstrations of Prussian military might. "Let us imitate those studious and intelligent German officers, who have conquered so many pages of glory for their patria," wrote Captain Eduardo López Carrafa, an early advocate of the center.[30] Although ostensibly "apolitical," the Ateneo Militar intervened heavily in the turmoil of the next few years. It also, however, resembled its civilian exemplar, the Ateneo Literario y Científico, in its function as a center for liberal education and debate.

The assassination of General Prim in late 1870 initiated a surge in republican sentiment within the officer corps. Prim may not have adequately addressed the conditions behind the dismal career prospects and shortage of active postings for officers, but with his charisma and other valuable leadership qualities he nevertheless had alleviated strong military opposition to the regime. After his death the amount of antigovernment plotting surged, with the Ateneo Militar often at the center of the conspiracies. In the eyes of many of the regime's leaders, republican military activists posed a greater threat than the forces of conservative reaction. At this point, in fact, the government viewed the Ateneo Militar as a largely united front of opposition. Yet any such unity would soon dissipate after Ruiz Zorrilla and the Radical Party took over the government in June 1872. Of particular interest to the Ateneo Militar was Zorrilla's program for extensive military reform, which made good the promise of the revolutionary generals of 1868 to abolish the draft (*quintas*). Intense debates ensued over this and other issues, such as how personal service records and "merit" should influence promotions, policies regarding the artillery, and so on.

This new, unmistakably political orientation of the Ateneo Militar soon had significant ramifications. The civilian press began to voice concern over the center's praetorian potential, thus driving a wedge between military and civilian republicanism. At the same time a majority, of officers grew to oppose the Ateneo because of its politics, an early example of the separation between the "military-intellectual elite," which was at times intensely concerned with its corporate interests, and the vast majority, subalterns and other officers, who had their own, very different, corporate interests—a usually ignored but crucial social and ideological distinction within the corps.[31] Finally, in 1874 the crisis of another civil war against the Carlists caused the Ateneo Militar to close its doors.[32] But the breach in military intellectual orientation would persist through the outbreak of the Civil War, separating the mass of officers from their more politically and ideologically influential colleagues, such as Ruiz-Fornells and Burguete.

The Spanish army's next notable institution of this sort, the Centro del Ejército y de la Armada, was founded in 1881 with, like the Ateneo Militar before it, notable support from the military press. The Centro also resembled its predecessor in its involvement in political conspiracies, although its much longer life has allowed it to sponsor far more debate in the form of lecture series and publications.[33] Even during the first decade of the twentieth century, when the Centro actually converted itself into a gambling center in order to augment its previously small income,[34] it also continued to sponsor intellectual debate. Throughout the Restoration period Burguete, Ruiz-Fornells, García Pérez, and Millán-Astray all contributed in one way or another to the Centro's more scholarly activities. And in addition to political and administrative discussions and seemingly endless speculation on such esoteric subjects as the nature of Spanish identity, the center sponsored social functions as well as gymnastics, fencing, and other forms of physical activity.

Not the least of the Centro's many contributions to the Spanish military world was its extensive library, the records and catalogue of which offer a revealing view of the culture of the officers living in the capital city. By 1918 the library held over 22,000 volumes covering a wide variety of subjects, and readership levels were surprisingly high. Although many of the books were devoted to technical military matters, a careful examination of the 433-page catalogue of 1917 reveals more variety than one might expect. The subject catalogue, based solely on words taken from book titles, includes entries under such headings as Philosophy, Modernism, Nationalism, Poetry, Regeneration, and Love, the latter two including works by the likes of Max Nordau, Henrik Ibsen, and Arthur Schopenhauer. Of course, Tactics, Strategy, and the Art of War were also headings, but works under those headings by no means overwhelmed the less technical works. Under Poems (*Poesías*), for example, the reader would find well over one hundred titles, roughly the same number as all the listings under Tactics and related categories in all languages (such as *Táctica de Infantería, Tactique d'Artillerie,* and so on).[35]

And, as Appendixes 1 and 2 illustrate, the books more concerned with liberal arts than with technical military matters did not remain unread. In addition, officers also made extensive use of the library's collection of novels (*novelas*), which numbered more than 2,500. According to the Centro's library records, the novels circulated at a very rapid rate; in one year alone each was checked out over a dozen times on average. As a service to its patrons the library actually allowed readers to take the novels home with them, a service still fairly unusual in much of Europe. The other books, moreover, could be browsed in open shelves, with recent acquisitions prominently displayed.[36] The officers of Restoration Spain, then, enjoyed easier and more extensive access to literature of all sorts than most civilians. Also revealing is the high number of French books among the library's holdings, especially in comparison to those of other languages besides Spanish. In light of this aspect of Spanish military reading habits, it becomes clearer how in Spain the perception of the German armed forces so closely resembled that of the French, even in the case of relatively well-educated officers such as Burguete and Ruiz-Fornells. Most of the Spanish military world, it seems, viewed Germany through Germanophile French lenses.

The other major institution shaping the intellectual environment of the Spanish military world was the Academia General Militar. Founded in 1882, this institution was intended to diminish the traditional rivalries between the infantry, the artillery, and other branches of service and corps. In 1893, however, the Academia closed its doors, ostensibly having failed in this important goal.[37] And in fact the subsequent behavior of Burguete, Ruiz-Fornells, and García Pérez, who had all been there as cadets, seems to demonstrate that the institution did little to alleviate political resentment and infighting.[38]

Despite its relatively short life, the Academia affected subsequent Spanish military culture in several important ways. Most visibly, it served as a sort of old-boys' club, providing political and economic benefits to the officers fortunate enough to serve on its teaching staff on a long-term basis. As I make clear in later chapters, the business of military education in Spain thus helped sustain the corporate interests of an influential group of officers. After the Academia's closure, similar corporatism would thrive within the Infantry Academy, where the likes of García Pérez would spend large portions of their careers.

Yet the Academia General, created in part in reaction against the technocratic and scientific thinking promoted by the corps of engineers and the artillery, played its most important role in helping develop new notions of nationalism and national identity. Like the Centro, the expanding military press, and other institutions of military education, it helped form an important part of the discursive space in which leading military thinkers formulated and debated issues of Spanish nationalism.[39] Because the Academia General was explicitly inspired by the Prussian military model, what Spanish officers understood as a "German" concept of military honor figured heavily in their nationalist ideas. But whereas Prussian norms had already been applied to the Spanish army since the Seven Years' War, Spaniards now looked more for inspiration to the army Moltke had used to defeat the French in 1871 than to the model of Frederick the Great's Prussia. Thus a more modern notion of military honor, which had played a role in Spanish military culture in the eighteenth century, now figured heavily in officers' nationalist ideas.

Betraying a distinctly historicist outlook, the officers argued that Prussian military leaders had fostered a vigorous sense of military honor grounded in inherent national psychology, which in turn had helped them attain success on the battlefield at Sedan. Spaniards, then, needed to follow the Prussian lead and look to the history of past Spanish military glory in order to identify and cultivate their own, specifically Spanish, concepts of military honor and nationalism. Hence cadets learned to equate nationalism with military values.[40] The

Academia General's instructors and the authors of its textbooks, moreover, were often inclined to reject the liberal forms of nationalism that sometimes surfaced at the Centro in favor of more conservative and traditionalist discourse. The nationalism embraced by twentieth-century military thinkers—and eventually by the Franco regime's ideologues—thus grew out of a mixture of the Academia General, other academies, books and journal articles by individual officers, avant-garde intellectual and political movements abroad, and the more general context of concurrent developments in civilian culture.

This civilian culture mirrored its military counterpart in its dominance by elements from competing political ideologies—especially those of liberalism and traditionalism—that clashed and coalesced to help shape the emerging notions of national identity and nationalism. And because military elites were far from isolated from the ideological developments of the literary and political intelligentsia, an understanding of Spanish military nationalism requires analysis of the origins and emergence of ideas of national identity and nationalism among leading writers, historians, and political figures.

* * *

To a certain degree, for most of the nineteenth century Spanish liberals enjoyed a less ambiguous relationship to nationalism than did conservatives. Embracing a self-serving perception of the Enlightenment and the French Revolution, liberals would eventually look to the ideal of "the nation" as an alternative to traditional monarchical loyalties and conservative conceptions of the state. Until well into the period of the Restoration, however, most liberal nationalism was tempered and unrepublican. Restraining its enthusiasm for "the Spanish people" as a collective historical agent, the nationalist historiography that served the moderate liberal cause portrayed the Isabeline liberal monarchy as the natural culmination of Spain's historical evolution. Hence the leading nineteenth-century "general histories of Spain"—including the volumes Burguete and other officers would study and criticize—tended to praise the periods of Spanish history ostensibly characterized by liberal state building and consolidation. Of course, nationalist discourse was anything but uniform, and progressives criticized the conservative nature of the moderate liberal (*moderado*) conception of history. In its place they offered their own interpretation of the national past, which emphasized the relative religious freedom and municipal liberties of the Middle Ages and criticized the absolutist Hapsburg dynasty that followed.

Nevertheless, the dominant historiography of the nineteenth century was basically conservative. As Carolyn P. Boyd writes, historical production rested "on an eclectic methodology derived from Enlightenment philosophy, Romantic idealism, and empiricism."[41] But even the liberal methodology it employed—

with its emphasis on documentary evidence and "scientific" empiricism in general—served conservative ends. Using much the same rhetoric as their ideological opponents, liberals responded to charges by traditionalists of "foreign" influence not by rejecting the essentially xenophobic premise of their critics, but by arguing that liberalism was in fact an important part of Spain's historical legacy.[42] Like their conservative opponents, liberals thus embraced an essentially romantic, historicist interpretation of Spain's supposedly unchanging national character—but for them that character was liberal. And military officers were not, of course, isolated from the civilian writers.

Thinkers of the political right, whose rejection of historical positivism made them more likely to believe in the Spanish people's supposedly unchanging "national character," actually remained wary of nationalism as such for much of the nineteenth century. During the first half of the century, Spanish nationalism was almost exclusively the property of liberals. The shunning of nationalism by the political right, common throughout post-Napoleonic Europe until the likes of Bismarck finally coopted nationalism for more conservative purposes, was especially pronounced in Spain because of the strong link between conservative traditionalism and Carlism. The Carlists equated nationalism with the values of the Isabeline monarchy that they so fervently opposed and of a liberal, secular state in general, interpreting nationalist rhetoric as a threat to local rights and privileges and to the traditional authority of the church. Hence at first the post-Napoleonic Spanish traditionalists were anything but nationalists in the modern sense, and they rejected the political term *nation* in favor of the more spiritual concept of the "*patria.*" At the same time, the disorder and threat to the legitimist state and army created by the Carlist wars reinforced the liberalism of many army officers. Only during the upheaval that accompanied the arrival of the First Federal Republic did the Carlists finally adopt the language of nationalism.[43]

Yet Spanish neotraditionalists—a term that refers to the subsequent non-Carlist promoters of traditionalism—had slowly begun to embrace nationalism several decades earlier.[44] As was often the case, war—this time in North Africa—helped induce rightists to begin employing the language of nationalism. In particular, the 1859–60 Moroccan conflict first made nationalism respectable in the eyes of the Spanish right. Conservatives had understood the role that some idea of the nation as an inherently Catholic entity could play by discrediting secular ideologies as "anti-Spanish," but the imperialist pretenses of Spain in Africa pushed them toward a full embrace of the language of nationalism.[45]

Not surprisingly, the leading military historians of nineteenth-century Spain—all officers themselves—made full use of nationalist rhetoric as well. In a book published in 1862 Francisco Villamartín, one of modern Spain's leading military historians, endeavored to identify and analyze the national character of the typical "Spanish soldier" who had determined the course of his country's history. Villamartín did not, however, deny the strong regional differences and provincial loyalties of the Spanish people in the manner of many subsequent Castile-centered military historians. Instead he stressed the way the opposing forces of provincialism and nationalism in Spain came together to create something positive: "a great impulse toward independence." The "spirit of the province," he wrote, may sometimes appear to threaten the Spanish nation, but in fact "this same provincial spirit serves as a stimulus to the nation, lending it powerful force." Describing his country's people as "provincialists in peace" but "Spaniards in war," he maintained that their strong love for the *patria* revealed itself fully only at times of national danger. For him, geographical, cultural, and racial diversities were integral and praiseworthy elements of the Spanish national character.[46] His views were echoed in the massive and very nationalist history of the war against Napoleonic occupation written by fellow historian and career military man José Gómez de Arteche. According to Gómez, provincialism was a destructive, "incurable cancer of the Spanish nationality" and the "eternal obstacle of unity," but at the same time it paradoxically served as "the germ of force and the strongest foundation for the enlargement of the patria!"[47]

More extreme, traditionalist nationalism also found its way into schools of nineteenth-century military thought. Although expressions of moderate and liberal outlooks appeared more frequently in the writings of army officers, Miguel A. Espina's 1886 *La civilización y la espada* (Civilization and the sword) demonstrated how neotraditionalism could surface in nineteenth-century military thought. For Espina, a lieutenant colonel in the Spanish infantry, "the sword" represented the best of humanity's qualities, a tool to be used for the *patria,* honor, king, God, and empire. War was an essential instrument of civilization, an unavoidable yet praiseworthy product of the natural discord between nations. Espina's perception of war was largely vitalist, with a strong dose of religion thrown in. Implying that religion and the fatherland were inseparable, he praised the church for its "profound knowledge of the art of war" and portrayed war itself as a means to achieve national regeneration. "War is divine in the mysterious glory that surrounds it and in its irresistible attraction," he wrote, also describing armed conflict as "an atonement" and "a means of purification."[48] Although he—like most other traditionalists of his day—tended to favor the word *patria* over *nation,* he anticipated the sentiments of many subsequent military nationalists in Spain by equating military power with national greatness. The country, he lamented, had generally ignored military heroes in favor of civilians when constructing public monuments, and the military profession in general did not receive the national respect it deserved. In his eyes, sacrificing sons of the *patria* to military service had as its most valuable consequence the strengthening of the entire *patria* itself.[49]

* * *

Thus Espina's romantic and vitalist traditionalism, although not characteristic of most nineteenth-century Spanish military writers, shared a preoccupation with what were essentially the same issues of nationhood and regeneration that so preoccupied many civilian conservative and liberal writers. Although there is no evidence that he had an impact on military culture anywhere comparable to that of Villamartín or the officers discussed in the following chapters, his writings foreshadowed certain aspects of the peculiar ideological mixture of religion, vitalism, and war that would reach its apogee under Franco. In addition, the context of this early discourse on the nature of the Spanish nation served as an important backdrop to the institutional and ideological developments within the pre-1898 officer corps described in the first part of this chapter. Although scholars have largely ignored the role of military culture in the origins of the nationalist currents that would gain greater prominence in the twentieth century, it was this surprisingly literate, intellectually dynamic, and varied community that made some of the most forceful contributions to early Spanish nationalism. Even the undeniably unique figure Ricardo Burguete, to whom I turn next, betrayed some influence of the military nationalists who had come before him.

Chapter Two

The Nietzschean Warrior

A popular officer who looked to Nietzsche for inspiration, Ricardo Burguete is undoubtedly one of Spanish military history's most colorful figures. His long, distinguished, and controversial career began in 1885, when—as the fourteen-year-old son of an infantry officer—he became a cadet at the Academia General Militar. By the time of his country's defeat in the War of 1898, the Zaragoza native had already earned praise for his actions in Morocco, Cuba, and the Philippines.[1] Upon his return to Spain at the end of century, he soon made a name for himself both within and outside the military community with his firsthand accounts of Spain's attempts to crush the Cuban and Philippine separatist revolts and his historical, philosophical, and military studies. A member of Spain's Royal Academy of History and the author of countless books, pamphlets, and periodical articles, Burguete was the subject of much attention from the Spanish press, and he even joined discussion circles with such acclaimed and influential writers as Ramiro de Maeztu, Miguel de Unamuno, and Pío Baroja.[2]

Burguete was, moreover, one of the most prolific writers of early-twentieth-century Spain to attack the "bourgeois" values of capitalism, industrialism, and scientific progress with the same arguments employed by the modernist intellectuals from elsewhere in Europe who, as one critic writes, expressed their disgust with contemporary civilization and morality "through the most diverse means, ranging from rebellion, anarchy, and apocalypticism to aristocratic self-exile."[3] And Burguete, who contributed briefly to the editorial endeavors of an anarchist periodical, was clearly willing to consider extreme measures. Traditionalist responses to the problems of a rapidly changing society were common, especially within the military community, but Burguete sought solutions in anarchist ideas as well as in the works of such thinkers as Nietzsche and D'Annunzio. In fact, Burguete's writings demonstrate that many of the same views promoted by the better-remembered writers who helped set the stage for modern radical right-wing political movements elsewhere in Europe had a powerful spokesman in Spain as well.

Of course, Burguete's rejection of the turn-of-the-century liberal status quo was not a purely political response, and to characterize the new outlook officers like Burguete adopted as "rightist" is to neglect an important dimension of what they felt. For in some cases neither their rejection of the current state of affairs nor the solutions they embraced fall squarely into the category of right or left. Instead their ideas stemmed more from the same cultural disenchantment common to many European intellectuals, thus defying easy political classification. In particular, Burguete's views on anarchism blurred customary political divisions and represented an early Spanish form of the "reactionary modernist" synthesis that played an important role in many contemporary European political movements.[4] Above all, Burguete's merging of aristocratic values, military interests, populism, and ostensibly anarchist ideology resembled the ideas of the diverse antiliberal political movement that had formed in France around the war minister General Georges Boulanger in the 1880s. Not surprisingly, then, Burguete was active in the subsequent regenerationist campaign behind Spain's answer to Boulanger: the "Christian general" Camilo García de Polavieja. Susceptibility to this sort of influence from abroad was typical of the young Burguete, who even acquired the growing fascination with the occult seen all over Europe in figures as diverse as the German emperor Wilhelm II; the renowned British military theorist J. F. C. Fuller, who was also very much a self-educated man; and the French artist Odilon Redon. An intellectual gadfly, in some ways Burguete resembled the French literary fascist Pierre Drieu La Rochelle. Embracing Nietzschean elitism and rejecting liberal capitalism, parliamentarism, and even the kind of "science" frequently associated with biological racism, the young Spanish officer anticipated the "third way" approach to politics Drieu would advocate in his 1934 *Fascist Socialism* and later writings.[5] And Burguete's swing to the left later in life, when he called himself a pacifist but still clung to much of his earlier vitalism, invites comparisons with the political journey of Georges Valois from anarchism to fascism to libertarian socialism.[6]

Burguete's military and political activities also appear to have had more in common with radical modernist thinking than with the traditional Catholic conservatism espoused by many of his colleagues. He employed, for example, the techniques of modern mass politics following an attempted *pronunciamiento* in 1905, making a victorious national tour of cities with significant garrisons in order to bolster his public image and propagate a heroic but self-serving vision of military nationalism and sacrifice.[7] When he led the military's brutal suppression of the Asturian labor unrest of 1917—which was harsh even by the standards of the Spanish army—he gained a considerable amount of national attention as an iron-fisted ruler with little sympathy for the masses. And after Spain's horrible military defeat near Anual, Morocco, in 1921, Burguete launched a well-publicized attack on the high commissioner for Africa, General Dámaso Berenguer, interpreting the debacle as proof of the superiority of Nietzschean qualities over rationalist science. Burguete's actions led the government to try to placate him with the post of military governor of Madrid, and one year later he himself assumed the position of high commissioner for Africa.[8] In

1925 he became the head of Spain's notoriously harsh rural military force, the Civil Guard. At this point his career and philosophical outlook seemed a perfect match for those of the rightist dictators whose leadership was on the rise all over Europe.

Yet Burguete soon left his seemingly radical right-wing path. By the late 1920s his politics had become noticeably more liberal, and he died an ardent republican. In 1930, as president of the army's high court, his open support for the conspirators of a failed republican coup led to his brief imprisonment and helped pave the way for the establishment of democracy in Spain one year later. By the time the Civil War broke out in July 1936, he had publicly announced his affinity to the Spanish Socialist Party and the principles embodied by the Popular Front, having already gained further attention in 1931 by addressing pacifist rallies in Germany. Even as an antiwar activist, however, he still cited Nietzsche as a source of inspiration, thus revealing the same sort of contradictions that had characterized his entire career.[9]

* * *

Probably because of the republican and anti-Francoist sentiments he openly expressed during the later years of his life, Burguete received surprisingly little attention from Spanish historians for most of the twentieth century. Although scholars have not ignored his professional and political activities, his historical and philosophical works have been largely forgotten.[10] Burguete's virtual absence from histories of Spanish military thought during the period is especially striking in light of the attention given to the writings of some of his colleagues. Many historians of the ideological history of the Spanish officer corps after 1898 have at least mentioned Joaquín Fanjul's *Misión social del Ejército,*[11] but the same scholars have said nothing about the works of the much more prolific Burguete.[12] And Burguete, who actively sought the attention of civilian politicians and the press, was undoubtedly the better-known figure at least through the outbreak of the Civil War. Espasa-Calpe's *Enciclopedia Universal Ilustrada,* published during the first two decades of the twentieth century, included a description of Burguete's military and literary accomplishments. Fanjul, on the other hand, remained overlooked by the classic Spanish reference work even in the appendix it published in 1931.[13] Pío Baroja, a onetime companion of Burguete who came to pen some acerbic criticism of his literary endeavors, had to acknowledge that Burguete enjoyed considerable prestige as a writer, and in 1917 a representative in the Spanish parliament commented on "the truly inexplicable success" Burguete's writings had enjoyed.[14]

In this case, then, the Franco regime largely succeeded in its efforts to preserve the memories of a "hero" while forgetting a figure whose otherwise noteworthy actions as a military officer were tainted by his failure to support the rebel cause in the Civil War. After all, even anti-Francoist historians have had to take note of Fanjul, who became an important martyr in Franco regime propaganda when he died in support of the 1936 military rebellion that launched the war.[15] And it is hardly surprising that most scholars have not looked to Burguete, who died a prominent republican, as an intellectual precursor to Spain's radical right-wing movements.

* * *

Burguete's writings have not, however, completely escaped the attention of scholars of Nietzsche's impact on the Spanish literary community. After all, he openly modeled his first book, which appeared under the pen name "El Comandante ***," on one of history's most influential works of philosophy: *Thus Spoke Zarathustra* by Friedrich Nietzsche. According to Gonzalo Sobejano's extensive study of Nietzsche's reception in Spain, Burguete's *Así hablaba Zorrapastro,* along with several of his other works, fits the mold of more well-known Spanish Nietzscheans such as Ramiro de Maeztu and Azorín. For Sobejano, Burguete's early-twentieth-century "anarcho-aristocratic" mind-set resembled that of the famous literary figures.[16]

In this book, published around the turn of the century,[17] the young officer introduced many of the ideas he would later return to repeatedly in his search for the right path to Spain's regeneration. Like the better-remembered writers associated with the "Generation of '98," he strove to identify and understand the causes of Spain's decadence, and his analysis centered more on spiritual than on practical matters. The product of Burguete's first significant literary endeavors, *Zorrapastro* offers a fascinating glimpse into the mind of one of the period's most influential military figures, many of whose ideas remained popular among Spanish officers even after he himself no longer adhered to them.

The work, which serves as the primary subject of this chapter, centered around the rhetoric of Zorrapastro, a character whom Burguete presented as a sort of Spanish counterpart to Nietzsche's Zarathustra. It was above all an attack on the failure of Spain's leaders and system of government, but it also leveled harsh criticism at many other elements of contemporary society. Through Zorrapastro, Burguete revealed his own thoughts on nationalism, morality, capitalism, democracy, the armed forces, and war itself—all matters of utmost concern to his regenerationist contemporaries. Like Nietzsche, he rejected the idea of "progress" as representative of little more than corrupt politics, inept government, foolishly blind liberalism, capitalist greed, a hypocritical bourgeoisie, and "scientific" denial of the natural forces he believed to drive history. Although his book's title and construction appear at first glance to parody those of Nietzsche's famous work, Burguete clearly thought highly of *Thus Spoke Zarathustra.* His book included numerous quotations from the German philosopher and his contemporaries, although it often failed to attribute them. Such incessant quoting of texts would become characteristic of Burguete's later works.

Nevertheless, Burguete's book was not just a parroting of Nietzsche's aphorisms or a crude interpretation of his thinking from a Spanish perspective. His reading of Nietzsche may have profoundly shaped his thinking, but *Zorrapastro* was very much his own invention. Although this obviously self-educated officer misinterpreted aspects of Nietzsche's thought and sometimes revealed rather muddled reasoning on his own part, there is no doubt that the scope and depth of the book's vision of Spanish history and regeneration were fairly unusual for a military man of his day—even though an increasing number of his colleagues would adopt similar views as the century progressed.

Moreover, *Zorrapastro* exemplified and fostered the nascent reaction against the technical and scientific side of the Spanish military and its general staff. The work represented both the decline in influence of the officers who were strong in science and engineering—fields in which they often surpassed their civilian counterparts—and the rise of more antirational, vitalist views on strategy, tactics, and even politics and society. Burguete would develop many of these notions further and express them more clearly and directly several years later in the book that earned him the brief praise of Unamuno: *Mi rebeldía*.[18] And in his later works he would return repeatedly to many of the same themes, although he would also temper some of his more radical views as he grew older and his power and prestige increased. But although *Zorrapastro* and *Rebeldía* both revealed their author's views in particularly extreme forms, in many ways the former displayed his early mind-set and wit most fully. In his musings on topics as varied as democracy, Catalan nationalism, and the place of women in society, Burguete expressed himself so candidly through the words of his character Zorrapastro as to expose the strengths and weaknesses of his thought quite clearly.

* * *

In the subtitle to *Zorrapastro*—a variation of the Spanish adjective *zorrapastroso*, roughly equivalent to "badly soiled"—Burguete introduced his protagonist as an "ex-government minister, ex-senator, ex-deputy, ex-chairman [*ex-presidente*], ex-liberal, ex-democrat, ex-philter [*ex-filtro*], ex-banker, ex-moralist [*ex-moral*], and ex-bastard [*ex-puto*]." Zorrapastro was, the subtitle continued, "*in-hábil*, impolitic, impugning [*in-pugnador*], improper [*in-proprietario*], indecent and unclean [*in-mundo*], and imputative." The reader soon learned how, after achieving considerable success in the political and financial world, the protagonist had turned against conventional standards to become a frank and "indecent" critic of the society he had abandoned.

The prologue began with the retreat of the protagonist, age sixty—twice as old as Nietzsche's Zarathustra—into the mountains. At this time Zorrapastro also dismissed his two lifelong "*inseparables compañeros,*" thereby symbolically breaking with his past. These two creatures, a pig and a *zorra* (literally "vixen," but the word can also mean "whore"), had served as his "spiritual counselors." The "virtues" of his mother and sisters, all prostitutes, had also helped shape the moral code that had served him so well in life. Later the reader learned how Zorrapastro's father, a lawyer, had raised him with "healthy bourgeois morals" until a bookshelf of legal codices fell and crushed him to death with "the legal weight of many murderous laws." Thereafter Zorrapastro, now a corrupt lawyer himself, had worked his way into parliament and eventually become a government minister.[19]

After descending from the mountains, Zorrapastro—like Nietzsche's Zarathustra—entered a village where he found a crowd gathered to watch a tightrope walker. Here Burguete followed the German philosopher's famous story line quite closely, although his metaphors were more explicit and he made several modifications so that the account better introduced the main themes of his own book. Upon seeing Zorrapastro the people greeted him as "the cleverest and most dexterous [*el hábil entre los hábiles*]" and begged him to "perform on the tightrope as in earlier times." But he refused and instead lectured the crowd on the "*hombre inhábil*" (roughly equivalent to "misfit" or "impudent man"), who essentially served as Burguete's version of the *Übermensch.* "*Habilidad* [cleverness, or dexterity]," Zorrapastro told the crowd, "allows crookedness to flow through your morality" and is "the product of the wonderful union of the seven deadly sins." You can achieve true happiness, he asserted, only by following the example of the misfit, or "*hombre inhábil,*" whose power could destroy "the unhealthy products of my old moral code." But the crowd mocked Zorrapastro, just as the first words of Nietzsche's Zarathustra regarding the *Übermensch* elicited nothing but incomprehension and laughter from the people gathered to watch Nietzsche's tightrope walker (11–12).

Zorrapastro then faced the performer on the tightrope and warned him that the crowd would turn against him if he failed to come up with a "new *habilidad,*" or cunning trick. Soon the people indeed began to jeer, but they scattered when a second tightrope walker caused the first to lose his balance and plunge to the ground. With his last words the fallen man explained that he had performed "to give comfort to the multitude and to satisfy its demands." The crowd had weaved a safety net called "suffrage" with the strings of "democracy," he continued, but the people had let the pig and the *zorra* gnaw at the net. It would have withstood his fall anyway, the dying man insisted, "if they all hadn't turned into pigs and *zorras* as they fled in terror" (12–14).

This account of the tightrope walker introduced the reader to Burguete's notion of *habilidad,* or skill, and in many ways foreshadowed the arguments of the book's following pages. His protagonist, Zorrapastro, had come to realize that contemporary society allowed "the skilled man," or "*hombre hábil,*" to rise above others by relying on talents rooted in hypocrisy, greed, and denial of the "natural" differences between superior and inferior men. The story also forecast an eventual collapse of the current political system, symbolized by the fall of the tightrope walker after the *habilidad* of its leaders no longer sufficed to keep the masses under control. Then the *hombre inhábil,* or misfit, who as an *Übermensch* was impudent, violent, passionate, free, and brutally honest, would forge a new aristocracy to regenerate society.

After the tightrope walker died, Zorrapastro dragged the body away from the crowd. Eventually he left it elsewhere to be eaten by vultures, which, "more compassionate than people, took elements from the dead out of necessity as the people had taken them from the living." Burguete would repeat this description of vultures living from the sustenance of the dead—another emphatically "natural" occurrence of the kind that so appealed to him—in his other books. His firsthand accounts of the fighting in Cuba and the Philippines, for example, occasionally broke into descriptions of plant and animal life and their supposed social-Darwinist lessons for humanity. For example, he recounted how, while en route to Cuba, he had seen several dolphins in pursuit of a school of fish, which had turned his mind to thoughts of Darwin, the "struggle for existence," the supremacy of force, and even war (18).[20]

In the body of the book Zorrapastro described in much greater detail the notions put forward in a more general and metaphorical fashion in the prologue. His speeches—aimed in the first place at the military establishment—began after he had arrived in the city of Cabron Pelirrojo, literally "Red-Haired Goat" or "Cuckold," a prosperous, industrious, and populous city. Like the name *Zorrapastro, Cabron Pelirrojo* was a play on words based on a Spanish version of the name that Burguete created for the Nietzschean original—in this case "*Bunte Kuh,*" or "Motley Cow." Again making ample use of puns and double meanings, the narrator described the city's major sources of wealth, the horn (*cuerno*) and the fig (*higo*) and the behavior of the citizens in such a way as to portray all the women as promiscuous and the men as cuckolds. Upon seeing Zorrapastro, the people gathered to greet him, and the women even offered him "their tastiest fruits" (25). He was too old to accept, however, and he also turned down the men's offer to drink a toast from their horns. In his later writings Burguete would frequently employ gendered—and often misogynist—rhetoric when describing Spain's downfall and the vitalist, "masculine" strength its regeneration would demand, exemplifying the link between military values and the sort of gendering of Spanish national identity later fostered by the

Franco regime. Here his protagonist, Zorrapastro, in acceding to the people's request for advice on what to do about their corrupt governor and the decadent—and implicitly "feminine"—character of their society, foreshadowed such thinking in the series of discourses that constitute the body of *Así hablaba Zorrapastro.*

Zorrapastro began with one of his favorite topics, urging his listeners to renounce "the cult of *habilidad.*" According to Zorrapastro, the blame for society's corruption by the *hábil* lay largely in a mistaken devotion to "progress," a term he associated with the ideas and developments that had descended from the Enlightenment to replace older beliefs and ways of life. He was particularly critical of the notion of human equality. People once knew to differentiate between "superior and common men," he said, citing the legal distinctions drawn between them in the constitutions of ancient Crete, Carthage, and Sparta as examples. But "progress," in a misguided attempt to follow the "laws of nature," erroneously dictated that all men be put in a single category. This attempt to use "science" to justify democratic values was now failing, he claimed, paradoxically pointing to recent discoveries by natural scientists regarding nature's "aristocratic laws" and the hierarchies inherent to the animal and plant kingdoms as proof (28–32).

Burguete's early attack on science, which he strongly associated with liberal, democratic values, represented his first significant contribution to a debate that had raged among Spanish intellectuals for several decades. As Spaniards witnessed industrialization and the concurrent rise of the middle class, they voiced doubts with increasing frequency about the positivist, scientific values that underlay the transformation of their society. According to many, the casting aside of spiritual values in favor of their materialist counterparts brought with it the decline of the true metaphysical forces upon which Spanish civilization had traditionally rested.[21] As I will show, Burguete clearly adhered to this view, adopting much of the regenerationist nationalism made popular in his day by the likes of Ganivet, Miguel de Unamuno, and Rafael Altamira. Even when Burguete came to advocate economic expansionism and industrial growth, he did so without renouncing his antimaterialist views—an apparent contradiction he shared with Ramiro de Maeztu.[22] Together these elements of Burguete's antirationalist mind-set would shape his concept of Spanish nationalism, even in its later republican form.

According to Zorrapastro, the belief in the equality of men had allowed the cleverest (most *hábil*) "*percebe*" (literally "goose barnacle," but it can mean "idiot" or—as Burguete uses it—"leech") to rise above the masses, who themselves donated their essence (*substancia*) to the *hábil.* Leaders thus rose "not through their own merits, but through the gift of others who revere the quality of *habilidad.*" Undoubtedly alluding to Restoration Spain's political system, the so-called *turno pacífico*, Zorrapastro described how citizens formed groups that then took turns letting the most *hábil* among them take charge. Sovereignty was always "conventional and pacific," and no one could use force—"even with the intention of improving the conditions of the oppressed"—to command. "Under the current system all of you believe you rule," he said, "and the greater your slavery, the more you believe in your sovereignty" (33–34).

This disenchantment with parliamentary government was, of course, an increasingly popular sentiment in Spain, especially after the military "disaster" of 1898. And a growing number of intellectuals elsewhere in fin-de-siècle Europe also viewed their constitutional monarchies as weak and inherently flawed. Many of these regimes, such as Giolittian Italy, resembled Restoration Spain in their designed intent to maintain the status quo by allowing limited, "controlled" suffrage.

Like many other intellectuals, Burguete traced what he saw as the inherent hypocrisy and corruption of Spanish parliamentary politics to more profound cultural causes. He drew attention to the assertion by the German philosopher Eduard von Hartmann, whom he—like his French contemporary Georges Sorel[23]—often cited, that Catholicism was linked to the principle of authority and Protestantism to the "critical negation" thereof. Spain's liberalism, he said, represented "a shameful Protestantism" that had grown out of "the debris left over after the encyclopedists finished their destructive task." He viewed liberal ideology as more appropriate for Protestants, because they were "accustomed to follow their conscience" and respect written law. A liberal education for Catholics, however, produced only "victims of absolute radicalism who know their rights, but not their duties." Such "Pseudo-Catholic liberals" lived for "vulgar, earthly prosaism," showing respect only for money. And they labeled all who rebelled against them as either reactionaries or anarchists, which meant that the two extremes—"creative reaction and destructive anarchy"—actually unite (109–11). Openly questioning the traditional political boundaries associated with "left" and "right," the young Burguete thus perceived the potential for a rather unorthodox merging of ostensibly opposite political forces in order to combat parliamentary liberalism. As will become clear, he often promoted such seemingly unnatural ideological unions. Characteristic of political movements such as Boulangism in France, these unions also resembled those of the reactionary modernist thought subsequently associated with elements of the radical right and fascism.

Rather ironically for someone with such a strong interest in history himself, Burguete also attacked liberals for looking too much into the past for the doctrines they promoted. Liberalism's attachment to the ideals of the encyclopedists and the French Revolution, he said, was analogous to "having such a large pretension as to want to transform a foul-smelling cadaver into a new and living man." In the nineteenth century many "Latin peoples" had suffered from this tendency to look backward, demonstrating that Protestants were "spiritually and cerebrally stronger than we *pseudo-católico liberales,*" he concluded (111). Such references to the alleged differences between Catholics and Protestants fit well within the broader genre of books that had appeared on the supposed decadence of the "Latin races."[24]

Curiously, Burguete never reconciled his own fondness for history with his condemnation of liberals for looking to the eighteenth century for lessons. Instead he continued to denounce the intellectual legacy of the Enlightenment and the French Revolution while embracing the study of medieval history and its morals. For him the epoch of the Enlightenment was decidedly "anti-Spanish," unlike what he perceived as the true source of national identity: the Middle Ages. Zorrapastro's explicit rejection of the philosophes' ideas anticipated the viewpoint adopted two decades later by many of the most important right-wing intellectuals who supported Primo de Rivera's dictatorship and later formed *Acción Española*—a journal that helped lay the ideological foundations of the Franco regime.[25] In fact, Burguete undoubtedly derived many of his arguments against the French Enlightenment from the same source as *Acción Española* writers: the renowned historian Marcelino Menéndez y Pelayo. In his multivolume *Historia de los Heterodoxos Españoles,* which began appearing in its first edition in 1880, Menéndez y Pelayo had described the 1700s as "history's most perverse and heretical" century.[26] Burguete would continue to espouse such opinions, openly citing Menéndez—who would be lavishly praised by radical right-wing Spanish nationalists in the 1930s—in some of his later works.[27]

Burguete's disdain for the intellectual legacy of eighteenth-century France also resembled the outlook of Charles Maurras, his much better-remembered contemporary from the other side of the Pyrenees whose political and literary endeavors would also provide some inspiration for *Acción Española.* At the same time that Burguete began to spread his views, *Action Française* spokesman Maurras—one of Europe's most important promoters of radical right-wing nationalism—was launching his own attack on the democratic and liberal heritage of the French Revolution and the Enlightenment. Just as the thinking of Maurras was, in Eugen Weber's words, "grounded in the overwhelming mood of decadence and disgust that followed the French defeat of 1870,"[28] Burguete took part in the collective soul-searching of the fin-de-siècle Spanish intellectuals who were so profoundly affected by the national shame of their own "Sedan" of 1898.[29] And he clearly came to many of the same conclusions as Maurras. Like the French thinker, Burguete did not appear to base his support for Catholicism on personal religious faith; he seemed to value the church primarily for its defense of traditional national values against the threat of "progress." Furthermore, Burguete's vision of a society based on royalty and social hierarchies, brought about by anarchist violence if necessary, was also quite similar to that of Maurras.[30]

Burguete, however, held a much more positive view of the anarchists than did Maurras. In *Zorrapastro* he even went so far as to support Maurras's critique of liberal parliamentary government by drawing from the writings of Peter Kropotkin, a leading Russian advocate of anarcho-communism. Burguete's protagonist recounted how his first experiences in parliament brought to mind Kropotkin's call to the voters to visit Congress and observe the " 'awful vices of your representative government.' " Another citation from Kropotkin covered over two pages—by far the longest attributed quotation in the book. In it the Russian libertarian derided the parliamentary system for requiring its members to decide on matters about which they knew nothing. All they cared about was whether their vote would serve in the interest of their party, he maintained. Zorrapastro would return to anarchist doctrine later in the book, this time borrowing its apocalyptic vision of the violent downfall of the establishment and the creation of a new society (103–6).

Zorrapastro also attacked the government's system of criminal justice, harshly criticizing the widespread corruption of judges and lawyers and what he perceived as the travesty of jury trials. Capitalism, he believed, had perverted the sacred principles of justice, so that jury members considered the protection of property—itself practically an untenable concept in the Proudhonian mind of Zorrapastro—as their most sacred value (91–95). Burguete's overwhelmingly negative perception of the Spanish judicial system, made clear in his descriptions of the legal adventures of Zorrapastro, was typical of a turn-of-the-century army officer. The military's distrust of jury trials was especially strong, and its members shared this sentiment with many civilians. Indeed, when a Spanish law of 1900 had limited the jurisdiction of military courts over offenses committed by the press, the law's authors had attempted to stymie the inevitable negative reaction of officers with a clause denying jury trials to those accused of slandering military authorities.[31] And when officers responded in 1905 to a derisive cartoon by storming the offices of the Catalan humor weekly *¡Cu-cut!* and the regionalist newspaper *La Veu de Catalunya,* Burguete's open support of their violent insubordination helped the military gain permanent exemption from the civil judicial code through the 1906 Law of Jurisdictions. Therefore, although Zorrapastro may have criticized the civil justice system as an institution of capitalism, in practical terms the objections of his creator, Burguete, clearly stemmed from the limits it imposed on military authority. And Burguete's actions demonstrated that despite any intellectual affinity he may have felt toward Unamuno and other leading writers, he in no way shared their openly expressed distaste for the new law.[32]

* * *

Burguete based his criticism of capitalism itself on overwhelmingly moral grounds. Once again painting a rather simplified and rosy picture of the past, his spokesman Zorrapastro described Spain's agricultural tradition of communal relationships, in which property and material were shared by all and quantity of labor served as the basic unit of value. Burguete's praise for precapitalist communal rural life in Spain echoed the writings of the influential regenerationist Joaquín Costa, who advocated basing agrarian reform in part on traditional collective practices.[33] But Burguete, rather than examining the development of Spanish agricultural systems in the detailed manner of Costa, simply focused his criticism on the growth of capitalism. Problems arose, Zorrapastro stated, when money came to represent units of labor. People could then save their funds, creating an imbalance between production and consumption that enabled one to satisfy "his greed at the expense of his necessities—to enrich himself in exchange for degenerating. Gold used for exchange and commodity impoverished the race and promoted idleness, pity and, among other things, a glut of merchants" (85).

These words stood in sharp contrast to those of many of Burguete's colleagues, who, instead of condemning capitalist values, sought to foster in soldiers and officers an explicitly bourgeois mind-set.[34] They also illustrate how Burguete, despite his rejection of phrenology and other such positivist methods of racial study, resembled his many European contemporaries in believing in at least some concept of "racial degeneration." But his attack on Catalan biological nationalism—examined later—suggests that for him, as for many Spaniards, the idea of "*raza*" always remained imprecise and in any case more cultural than biological.[35]

Zorrapastro described the ideas behind his historical perception of "this brutal capitalist regime" as rooted in "Aristotelian doctrines and thereafter taught to our unfortunate workers by Karl Marx," and it is clear that Burguete's economic views, like those of the young Maeztu, owed much to Marx's writings on protocapitalist society and the revolutionary potential of industrialization. The French socialist thinker Pierre-Joseph Proudhon, an intellectual ancestor of the anarchists whom Zorrapastro later cited explicitly, clearly influenced Burguete's social vision as well (86).

The future was not without hope, Zorrapastro insisted, because capitalist society—"like all putrefaction"—contained the seeds of new life. For among death, vileness, and misery lurked the "vital energy" that would give birth to "the new era of force." He warned his listeners that the chambers of commerce, industry, and agriculture they had founded in defense of the status quo could do little to prevent the inevitable. For how could they expect to unify themselves, he asked, when, as he put it, "the sources of your wealth grow from common hatred and disunity?" The number of poor people and the demands for labor would both continue to grow. Eventually, then, the "era of the *inhábiles* will have sounded." Zorrapastro supported this apocalyptic vision of a coming revolution by quoting Carlyle, Aristotle, Quevedo, and Mirabeau on the evils of merchants, usury, and—in the case of Carlyle—the coming uprising of the impoverished masses. "Prepare yourselves, dear citizens!" he concluded, "to receive with dignity the moral severity of your new redeemers. At last you shall reach paradise!" (86–90).[36]

Burguete's belief in the eventual collapse of capitalist society did not, however, prevent him from speaking freely against the hardships the working classes had to endure in the meantime. Referring to the resistance of Gijón's workers to the attempts by their employers to lengthen the working day to twelve hours, his spokesman Zorrapastro harshly criticized the modern state for supporting "free and unlimited exploitation" of workers (133). Here again Burguete's sentiments resembled those of Maeztu, who wrote very sympathetically about the hardships faced by miners in northern Spain.[37] As will become clear, Maeztu's early writings strongly colored Burguete's thought in many ways.

Curiously enough, years later Burguete would appear to forget the compassion he had once expressed for the Asturian working classes. In August 1917, having risen to the rank of general, he led the army's brutal suppression of the Asturian strike, issuing a harsh military decree that characterized the labor unrest as "treason," forbade public gatherings, and increased the military's legal jurisdiction. "I will be inexorable with the instigators and with my means of repression," he vowed, warning that insults to the forces of order " 'can receive summary judgment' when the circumstances demand such an example."[38] He also promised to fight the rebels by hunting them down "like wild beasts," a phrase he may have borrowed from a tract by Thomas Carlyle on the limits of acceptable behavior by strikers. Interestingly, it was under Burguete's command of the Asturian repression that future dictator Francisco Franco, who headed the infantry battalion at Oviedo, gained his first experiences dealing with civil disturbances.[39]

Yet despite how reactionary Burguete may have appeared in 1917, his compassion for the plight of the poor and his animosity toward capitalist interests appear to have been genuine when he expressed them at the turn of the century. After all, in 1917 Burguete was reacting to a very different set of circumstances than those he had described nearly two decades earlier, because well-organized and ideologically defined union federations had grown out of the earlier, less threatening workers' groups of late-nineteenth-century Gijon.[40] The context of World War I as well as the widespread social upheaval throughout Spain also influenced Burguete's actions. Like most of his colleagues during the Great War, Burguete was a Germanophile, and he detected British and other Allied interests behind the nationwide wave of strikes. His suspicions seemed to be confirmed when Melquiades Álvarez, the prominent Reformist who took a leading role in the 1917 strike movement, expressed an openly pro-Allied and possibly even interventionist stance. Burguete would subsequently reveal to his family that he believed Álvarez had coordinated the strike in Asturias with the goal of installing a republican government that would lead Spain into war against Germany.[41] In fact, the Socialists probably chose to support the ascension of Álvarez to power at least in part because they wanted the spokesman of the new regime to be moderate enough not to alarm the Allies,[42] but it is far from indisputable that they wanted Spain to go so far as to declare war. Furthermore, the labor unrest of 1917 may have initially been provoked by Restoration leaders themselves in order to scare the bourgeoisie, to provide an excuse to crush the opposition, and to discredit the politically troublesome officer corps in the repression that would ensue.[43]

At the time, however, Burguete clearly believed that the strikes were the product of Allied agents. When he publicly made charges to that effect he triggered a minor crisis among Allied diplomats, who strongly objected to his remark about the "English gold" that had supposedly helped finance the labor unrest. As a result of the controversy, the Marquis de Lema, the pro-Allied Spanish foreign minister, may have subsequently endeavored to remove Burguete from his Asturian post. In any case, Lema immediately contacted British diplomats and attempted to reassure them when Burguete stepped down at the end of August.[44]

Hence Burguete's ostensibly anti-working-class actions in 1917 were shaped more by the international context of the Great War than by any strong affinity to capitalist interests. But, needless to say, the sympathy for the workers revealed in *Zorrapastro* had its limits. In spite of his tendency to parrot "modern" notions as he understood them, in certain ways Burguete's vision of the perfect society was more traditional, especially with regard to the social position of the working classes. Like his colleague García Pérez and leading traditionalist thinkers, he came to favor a more humane, paternalistic attitude toward the masses as a way of countering liberal doctrine and the brutal social consequences of unbridled capitalism.[45]

The qualified sympathy that Burguete displayed for the workers was fairly common among military officers. Although they did not hesitate when ordered to quell civil disturbances, they were clearly uncomfortable with the increasing frequency with which they were called upon to act against the workers. And they often seemed to view the increasing radicalism of the labor movement as an inevitable if regrettable by-product of the social injustice that went along with industrialization.[46] Even the infantry captain Francisco Barado y Font, a more conservative military writer and historian, argued explicitly against excluding the "inferior classes" from the military's task of regeneration. And he was willing to acknowledge at least one advantage of the poor over the higher levels of society: they were under no obligation to act as "a mirror of the law."[47] Like Burguete, Barado also cited Nietzsche, but he viewed the philosopher's maxims much more critically than did Burguete. In a speech at Spain's School of Military Studies, for instance, he voiced criticism that must have been aimed at Burguete, dismissing the assertion by "the emulators of Nietzsche" that "valor . . . is the foundation of morality" as a "rather arbitrary judgement."[48]

Yet Burguete and Barado agreed in their rejection of any notion of true social equity. Like Spanish traditionalists, Burguete based his ideal of society on a hierarchically arranged, preindustrial model. He took the somewhat more unusual route in Spain, however, of employing popular fin-de-siècle arguments—based on the principles of social Darwinism and Nietzsche's rejection of democratic ideals—toward decidedly unmodern ends: a future world based on the aristocratic values of the Middle Ages.

Therefore, although Burguete did not advocate a truly corporate, Catholic state along the lines envisaged by some Carlist thinkers and the Spanish advocates of Leo XIII's social Catholicism, the differences between the Nietzsche-, D'Annunzio-, and Kropotkin-citing Burguete and his more traditional contemporaries were not always as great as they first appear. It is not so surprising, then, that Burguete's penchant for the views currently at the vanguard of Spanish society—such as regenerationism at the turn of the century and republicanism three decades later—did not prevent him from occasionally supporting the arguments of the more traditional forces in Spanish society, especially as he grew older. For example, he enthusiastically sponsored a priest's lecture series for soldiers on the dangers of revolutionary social movements, the wisdom of Leo XIII, and the virtues of the Catholic trade unions, even writing a laudatory epilogue for the speeches, which were subsequently published as a book.[49] As I will show later, Zorropastro's advice to workers at the turn of the century differed from the docile attitude recommended by the priest, whose book was published two decades later. But the condemnation of contemporary capitalism by Zorropastro and the priest and their glorified conception of the past were very much alike.

Zorrapastro's words on the decline of the church and its replacement by the new "religion" of money, however, were even stronger than those of the priest. As with his criticism of parliamentary government, his views on capitalism and religion relied more on cultural and spiritual values than on concrete arguments. Burguete's philosopher blamed modernity's "optimist culture," which he equated with "materialist culture," for discarding traditional religion and replacing it with the new sanctified cult of labor. "In the old regime men were enslaved with divine mandates," Zorrapastro explained, but now men had to follow the even more "perverse" mandates dictated by capitalism. In the end, however, the forces of progress had to admit that religion was a necessity—"an immanent law, as strong as the law of attraction." Progress had thus learned, "through its sense of conservation," to accept religion as a "necessary evil." After all, he reasoned in the tradition of Marx, it allowed the exploited "to dream of their compensation in another life" (142–43).

Yet even the forces of Catholicism eventually realized that they had to break with progress, he continued, and all other forms of Christianity would soon follow suit. Thanks to "pessimist philosophy," which served as Zorrapastro's antithesis to the misguided complacency promoted by "modern optimist culture," people had begun to reject the staples of progress and return to nature. Progress would thus self-destruct; by rejecting religion it had left most of humanity with only pessimism. The poor would rise and put an end to "this wretched and vile paganism, which by producing nourishment from trash and dung, degenerates the race and impoverishes the spirit." His listeners had neither "great vices nor sublime virtues," he told them, saying that their "deeds are only large enough to be embraced by your crude corporal senses." He concluded by referring to the anecdote that Voltaire died eating his own excrement. Although he claimed that he never believed the story, he said, "even if it were true, your healthy appetite would still be more abnormal than that of the poor, sick Voltaire" (147–48).

* * *

Throughout his life Burguete would often turn to his understanding of medieval history when he addressed the problems of his day, a practice he initiated with *Zorrapastro.* His assignment to the Majorcan city of Palma, where he served as aide-de-camp to the captain general during the first decade of the twentieth century, apparently stimulated his strong interest in this period of Spanish history. It was there, where the "great ramparts, now near death, transude the iron taste and ancient vigor of a past nobility," that he wrote many of his books with a new comprehension of the role history played as "the true genealogical tree of spiritual affiliations" (127). In *Zorrapastro,* for example, Burguete could not resist relating his analysis of the exploitation of the masses into a discussion of the fifteenth-century revolt of the *remença* peasants of Catalonia. Zorrapastro's simplified account described how the peasants had risen heroically "against the monopoly of capital by the privileged," eventually persuading the king to exercise his "redeeming authority" and join their side to lead them to victory. He lamented that peasants of his day did not resort to their "natural right of action" in the manner of their urban counterparts, and he viewed industrial workers' recourse to physical force as a natural response to "the force that civilization and material progress grants the bourgeoisie, through the free use of capital and government, over those who do not enjoy such powerful means." But the best solution to contemporary social ills, he believed, would require the masses to follow the example of the *remenças* and turn to "the justice of God and king." Unfortunately, however, "Today's kings," he said, "have abandoned the force of their peoples to be slaves of money, and until the hour of Redemption men will perish in hunger strikes or by the swords that they themselves constructed for the use of their sons" (134–37).

Zorrapastro interpreted the summoning of a cavalry squadron to repress the Asturian strike as a typical development in contemporary Europe, where fearful capitalist interests now supported obligatory military service as a means of achieving social discipline and reassuring the bourgeoisie. Anticipating the arguments of Action Française, he emphasized the need for a new monarch who, like the medieval king, would unite the disenfranchised and enlist them as soldiers in the struggle against the power of capitalism.

Yet in the end responsibility for the character and actions of a monarch lay with the people themselves, Zorrapastro believed. He viewed constitutional and monarchical forms of government as essentially alike, arguing that they differed only in that "one is hereditary and the other elective." For just as monarchs hand down power to their descendants, in the electoral system the leaders take turns in order to transfer power to their offspring "through the laws of property and heredity respected by all." It was up to the people, then, to discard their heads of state as "useless arms" and concentrate on improving their king. Whereas monarchs had once forged their offspring in their image, they now had to educate their children to be "adaptable to the law," he lamented. To illustrate the superiority of the Middle Ages, when "the people could make demands on their monarchs" if the latter failed to produce the right offspring, Zorrapastro referred briefly to the fabled influence of the subjects of James I on the Aragonese king's actions, a legend Burguete would return to later. Clearly alluding to the Carlist Wars, he also charged his listeners with having "waged two wars to ensure the triumph of females and thereby sustain your despotic laws." His listeners' legal tyranny, he claimed, represented a desire to "take revenge on the woman-monarch for the terrible slavery that almost all of you felt under the woman-citizen." He also lamented his listeners' unwillingness to tolerate "an energetic regency" or allow it to "educate its offspring to rule." Such mutual subordination, whereby the monarch submitted to the laws of the people and the people to the king, clearly offended Burguete's belief in the superiority of elitist, "vital" rule. His spokesman Zorrapastro thus harshly criticized the confusion to come out of the contemporary system of government, and he viewed most of its laws as inevitably asinine—given that "such absolute docility can reside only in idiocy" (34–38).

Zorrapastro's words undoubtedly reflected Burguete's desire that Spain's young king Alfonso XIII, who was to begin ruling when his mother relinquished her regency in 1902, would act promptly and unflinchingly to regenerate his country. This longing for strong leadership from the king was common among Spanish officers of the day, many of whom hoped he would take Wilhelm II's "soldierly values" and his unbending support of the German military as models for his own behavior. Although the creator of Restoration Spain, Antonio Cánovas del Castillo, had succeeded in placating most officers by emulating Bismarck and basing his system of government on the figure of the soldier-king,[50] by the end of the century many Spanish officers wanted a leader who would advance their interests even further by strengthening the military's say in domestic and international affairs and by promoting military values.[51]

Behind Zorrapastro's idea of the leadership qualities a monarch needed lay his more abstract vision of the transformation he believed society must undergo. Although on the one hand he urged the king to repeat the actions of his forefathers and harness the powers of the oppressed, he also devoted a considerable amount of attention to describing the "new aristocracy" he believed would rise to regenerate the nation. Harshly criticizing the aristocrats who had exchanged their role as "the king's strong-arms" for positions as "equerries and lackeys," he accused them of having become "effeminate and ungainly" and therefore easy targets for the forces of the Enlightenment. Whereas the nobility of the sword had once served the nation valiantly, aristocrats now believed it better to serve their own interests as members of parliament. And as a result of their "bourgeois behavior," Zorrapastro charged, they failed to "hear the cries of an oppressed class that had remained faithful to you throughout history—until you abandoned it." But the fateful hour would arrive, he promised, returning to his apocalyptic vision of a coming revolution. Only the aristocrats who repeat the honorable behavior of their ancestors would survive the collapse of "this new bourgeois Jerusalem" (122–25).

Yet, like many advocates of revolutionary social change, Burguete never came up with a precise picture of the society that was to arise after the anarchist apocalypse he envisaged. But the descriptions that he provided of his ideal future world drew explicity from anarchist doctrine. Like members of the intellectual vanguard both within and outside of Spain, he espoused a social vision that stemmed in part from an idealistic interpretation of the preindustrial past. A romanticized representation of former times was, of course, an undeniable component of some anarchist thought, even if the practical anarchism of the rank and file and their leaders was based on rationally based political objectives.[52] After all, the European elites who flirted with anarchism rarely had any ties to practical parliamentary or social politics. In general, the political movements they found most attractive rejected the liberal status quo of the late nineteenth century but failed to formulate concrete, practical alternatives.[53] The proposals that radical intellectuals embraced tended to represent syntheses of ideological stances associated with the entire political spectrum.

Burguete attributed his vision of a "new aristocratic era" to his stay in Palma de Mallorca, where the archeological ruins of former aristocratic greatness taught him to appreciate the writings of Proudhon with "Carlylian sincerity." He claimed that the "logical anarchy alive in the pages" of the French philosopher's *What Is Property?* transformed him simultaneously into "a *libertarian* and *aristocratic* spirit." He found no contradiction in the concept, for in every hero of the glorious past he saw what he described in *Zorrapastro* as "an anarchist who, striving for the empire of the ideal, tried to re-create the world" (126–28). Clearly he shared what Gonzalo Sobejano calls the "anarcho-aristocratic individualism of the men of 1898, who were so absorbed in Nietzschean ideas."[54] Through his spokesman Zorrapastro he proclaimed: "I sincerely believe that only the conversion of anarchy and all its consequences into spiritual doctrine will be capable of sustaining the peremptory aristocracies of the future, which will flourish in the same manner as the past aristocracies and religions flourished from the heat of bloodshed. . . . Anarchy of dynamite and anarchy of the sword have the same goal. It is the revolt of nature, sometimes by force and sometimes by intelligence, against the unhealthy domination by others" (129).

Burguete's positive portrayal of "propaganda by the deed," which foreshadowed the praise that the fascist thinker Ernesto Giménez Caballero would direct three decades later at the "truly Hispanic" qualities of anarchist assassins, reached considerable extremes in *Zorrapastro*.[55] Burguete's philosopher even went as far as to characterize both Jesus and "his imitator Mohammed" as anarcho-aristocratic, since both men understood that aristocracy grew naturally out of anarchy, originating in "germs of death" in order to transform species. But as a firm believer in the sanctity of God, Zorrapastro explained, he did differ markedly from Proudhon on the issue of religion. He equated God with all that is good ("*el bien*") and viewed him as the cause behind creation ("*causa de la creación*")—a universal truth without which anarchist rebellion would have no legitimate purpose. According to Zorrapastro, "Only anarchy can serve as the new Jordan of past and present aristocrats" (129–31).

Although Burguete never satisfactorily explained exactly how anarchy and aristocracy were to coalesce, he offered some clues as to which elements of each he found attractive. Besides adopting Costa's ideas on the communal organization of precapitalist Spain and Kropotkin's notions of "propaganda by the deed," he clearly departed from anarchist orthodoxy in his emphasis on the need for a strong leader to unite the disenfranchised and enlist them as soldiers in the struggle against modern liberal capitalism. Comparing such a leader to a medieval king, he sounded like a Spanish version of Maurras, whose *Action Française* espoused an extreme form of royal authoritarianism that drew from France's supposed past glories. And although Maurras may not have gone as far as Burguete and embraced anarchism, one should not assume that his position as a radical royalist precluded sympathy toward anarchism. As one historian of the cultural politics of French anarchism has written, "There was in fact an aristocratic and elitist species of anarchism in the fin de siècle that may have enticed the royalist reactionaries." Similarly, the French thinker Maurice Barrès transcended conventional political categories by moving from Boulangism to anarchism to anti-Dreyfusism.[56] Indeed, this seemingly bizarre mutual attraction between royalism and revolutionary anarchism even had practical consequences for politics in France, and the French prototype served as an exemplar for the sort of synthesis that Burguete proposed.

In the late 1880s a wide variety of groups violently opposed to the parliamentary regime of the Third French Republic united in a populist and often radical front that formed around the figure of Boulanger. Although scholars continue to debate the relative strength of the conservative right and the revolutionary left in the Boulangist movement, its most noteworthy general characteristic was the peculiar and unnatural relationship it fostered between differing political philosophies. Sternhell has emphasized the "prefascist" quality of this merging of nationalism, racism, and independent socialism. His interpretation hardly comes as a surprise to anyone familiar with his work, since it corresponds well to the "neither right nor left" definition of fascism that he has espoused for years.[57] Other historians, however, have taken issue with Sternhell, focusing on the conservative component of Boulangism and of later fascist movements all over Europe.[58]

Regardless of the merits and weaknesses of Sternhell's view, however, the way in which otherwise very different groups of intellectuals and elites found unity in their political, economic, and spiritual discontent is crucial to understanding both Boulangism and European fin-de-siècle political culture in general. In France anarchists were the subjects of overtures from various groups of the political left and right, including royalists, anti-Semites, Boulangists, and representatives of the church. The contacts were especially strong between the more elite group of intellectual and cultural anarchists and other radical opponents of parliamentary liberalism. But in the Boulangist episode the well-documented collusion between anarchists and other enemies of the Third Republic also had a significant popular element.[59] Hence it was not as strange as it first appears for Burguete to overlook the contradiction between his elitist, aristocratic social vision and the antiauthoritarian principle of anarchism. For if French anarchists could invest their hopes in a populist movement centered on a military figure, such a synthesis was hardly unthinkable for someone like Burguete.

Of course, contemporary Spanish writers undoubtedly played a major role as well in stimulating Burguete's interest in anarchism, even if their fascination with anarchist tenets remained at a far more intellectual and abstract level than that of French royalists or Boulangists. People such as Azorín, Maeztu, Unamuno, and Baroja were all attracted to aspects of anarchism at one time or another, in some cases interpreting its supposed vision of the distant past as an alternative to the culture and ethics of modern industrial society.[60] Even if none of their ideas actually had much tangible impact on formal or practical anarchism in Spain, the wide variety of themes they explored, which often transcended traditional political boundaries, represented a Spanish form of the same eclectic intellectual synthesis arising elsewhere in Europe. By sharing an interest in thinkers as disparate as Nietzsche, Darwin, Ibsen, Stirner, Spencer, Marx, and Bakunin, Burguete injected elite military culture with many of the components that found a place in the social vision later propagated by opponents of liberal democracy.

* * *

The final section of Burguete's book, "El ocaso de Zorrapastro," began with the philosopher attacking the press, a move that led to his expulsion from Cabron Pelirrojo. In typically extreme and gendered terms, Zorrapastro equated the press to "a wretched prostitute so destroyed by men that she kills with the only virtue she's allowed to employ" (156). Ironically, years later Burguete would contribute regularly to the civilian and military press. His hero Zorrapastro, however, succeeded only in offending the reporter in the book as well as the army, the local magistracy, parliament, merchants, students, and their teachers, all of whom demanded that he leave.

Zorrapastro yielded to their wishes and headed for a city clearly meant to be Barcelona, where his adventures provided a revealing glimpse of the young Burguete's strong distaste for Catalan nationalism. Upon his arrival the people were in an uproar over the recent "scientific" discovery of a racial distinction between themselves and the inhabitants of the "mother country [*metrópoli*]," by which Burguete meant Castile. According to the researcher who made the discovery, the Catalans were of "Aryan origins," whereas their Madrid-based counterparts descended from "Semites." His findings, based on "the examination of a few moth-eaten skulls," had proved that "centuries of history have been nothing but a lamentable mistake," the narrator commented sarcastically. In order to make these physical differences visible, the most enthusiastic nationalists had even taken to growing shaggy beards and wild, unkempt hair, the reader learned. Yet the "scientific" discovery was not enough for separatists, who also felt they needed the support of their own art form. They therefore "adopted the exaggerated manifestations of modernism, replacing originality with extravagance" (158–59). Burguete, it seems, had no great fondness for the biological racialist thought popular at the time or for the flamboyant architecture so characteristic of the Catalan capital. This passage of his book was undoubtedly inspired in part by a well-publicized speech that the mayor of Barcelona, Bartolomeu Robert, had delivered in March 1899. In the speech Robert had alleged the racial superiority of Catalans over Castilians, implying a relationship between the latter's cranial features and Spain's supposed degeneration.[61] Within the world of the Spanish military, some officers, especially those associated with the Medical and Sanitary Corps, also pursued the "science" of phrenology and biological notions of race in general.[62] But Burguete was unwilling to devote too much time to such endeavors—which was unsurprising in light of his rejection of positivism and liberal science—and this view seems to have been characteristic of most infantry officers.

Burguete therefore strongly criticized the separatists' attempts to employ this ostensibly scientific proof along with their own "artistic ideal" in order to engender mass support. Interestingly enough, however, he focused more on the hypocrisy and class base of the overwhelmingly bourgeois nationalists than on the "treason" the movement represented to most army officers. Although Burguete undoubtedly shared at least in part the fear of many officers that Catalonia would become a "second Cuba,"[63] his dislike of Catalan nationalism seemed to stem, above all, from the social character of the movement. Given its strong association at the time with the capitalist interests of the Barcelona bourgeoisie, the Catalan nationalists had little hope of winning over someone like Burguete. And he was undoubtedly disgusted by their support of tariffs, which he objected to on principle for weakening his country's economic and spiritual health.[64]

Predictably, then, Zorrapastro began his stay in Barcelona in a provocative fashion, charging his listeners with basing their nationalism on falsehoods. The enthusiasm with which they sang their anthem, "Bon cop de fals dels segadors," prompted him to describe what he believed to be the true history behind the song. Quoting Victor Balaguer, a leading figure of the nineteenth-century Catalan literary renaissance, he recounted the brutal assassinations of the wives and daughters of Castilians by the legendary *segadors,* or reapers, during the revolt of the Catalans in 1640. He then cited the author of the most celebrated contemporary history of the revolt, Francisco Manuel de Melo,[65] on "the horrors that the hymn commemorates," describing in great detail the atrocities the *segadors* joyfully committed against the bodies of those they killed. Zorrapastro also contrasted the enthusiasm with which a crowd in the Liceo, Barcelona's famous opera theater, sang the Catalan hymn with a similar crowd's reaction in the same establishment to a speaker who warned them of the dangers posed by the masses. At first dead silent, their fear of the oppressed classes had caused them suddenly to become delirious and call for "blood and revenge." They wanted nearly enough blood, he recalled, "to fill the moats of Montjuich" (160–61).

The castle atop Montjuich, the Barcelona hill now home to the city's Olympic Stadium, had been the sight of the torture and execution by military authorities of numerous individuals accused of anarchist terrorism. Burguete's views on the matter clearly differed from those of the many other military officers who supported the harsh measures meted out by the authorities. Zorrapastro did not, of course, display complete and unqualified support for the prisoners of Montjuich; he referred to their many vocal supporters—in part the product of a vigorous press campaign to convert the issue into a Spanish Dreyfus Affair[66]—as the "foolish comrades of those misfortunate ones." But, like the many Spanish intellectuals who wrote extensively on the matter, he nevertheless sympathized with the prisoners' plight. He sardonically described "the disinherited descendants of the Berenguers,"[67] who, unlike the more radical workers, who resorted to violence to claim "their rightful inheritance from Adam," worked all night in the factories while the nationalists celebrated and cheered on the Ramblas in the name of an independent Catalonia. As the resigned factory workers toiled faithfully but without enthusiasm, Zorrapastro commented bitterly, they heard the heavy machinery around them make a "monotone, rhythmic noise reminiscent of the stanza, '*Bon cop de fals! Bon cop de fals! Bon cop de fals!*'" (161–62).

With these words Zorrapastro once again succeeded in provoking his listeners to drive him away. Shortly thereafter a group of industrialists, bankers, and businessmen attempted to win him back to their side, hoping to convert him into the corrupt *percebe* he had been in earlier times. But they failed, and the industrialist and former friend of Zorrapastro whom they enlisted to further their efforts had no luck in winning him over to separatism or even to "the cause of civilization and progress" (163). Burguete, in fact, portrayed the industrialist as a vile and selfish hypocrite who violently lashed out at his employees for daring to demand their rights. The book ended with a brief description of a failed "libertarian" rising of the masses, whose leaders Zorrapastro faulted—this time in a manner more akin to that of Lenin than to that of Bakunin—for not adopting the principles of discipline and hierarchy he had advocated. In Burguete's eyes, then, it seems that only an institution like the army, with its requisite hierarchy and order, had the potential to successfully force the regeneration of Spain.

* * *

Burguete's suggestive but in many ways unsatisfactory conclusion to his book resembled that of his exemplar Nietzsche in its failure to provide an explicit explanation or synthesis of the many disparate, multilayered, and sometimes contradictory arguments found throughout the text. Nevertheless, several major themes linked the various ideas discussed earlier.

Above all, Burguete's reaction against the nineteenth-century cult of reason revealed itself quite clearly in Zorrapastro's discourses on a wide variety of topics, from the "*inhábil*" man to capitalism, progress, history, and Catalan nationalism. In virtually all of his diatribes, moreover, he used methods and language of scientific reason not always unlike those he so vehemently attacked. He may have reacted against the dominant intellectual movements of the nineteenth century, but, like Nietzsche, he could not avoid employing many of their tenets to support his own arguments. As I will show, in his later writings he would continue to reveal a similar adherence to the antirational, Nietzschean ideals of will and passion, but he would also remain fascinated with the biological, psychological, and sociological theories typical of rationalist science. In fact, he would join the many other European intellectuals of his day who paradoxically used notions associated with nineteenth-century "scientific" thought to attack its very foundations. Even Nietzsche, when describing human nature and history in largely Darwinian terms of struggle, had revealed such a contradiction, and in Burguete's less subtle and more simplistic writings the same philosophical inconsistency surfaced even more readily. In *Zorrapastro* Burguete also introduced his illiberal, intensely vitalist, and very masculine conception of national strength, and he explicitly linked this vision of nationalist regeneration to mystical values of war and military sacrifice, thereby foreshadowing the ideological synthesis subsequently used by Spanish radical rightists.

Several years later Burguete expressed the same basic arguments regarding liberalism, nationalism, and Spanish regeneration in general in a more lucid fashion in *Mi rebeldía,* the book that seems to have most enhanced his position in Spain's early-twentieth-century literary community.[68] As in *Zorrapastro,* he lashed out in vividly militarist terms at the established forms of politics, society, and military organization in Spain. The pages of this book, he proclaimed in his typically histrionic and immodest manner, were "replete with convictions and sealed with blood; a rebellion of the spirit, which flees the prosaic and the intellectual in order to raise willpower as its only triumphant banner."[69] As I will show later, Burguete would cling to his belief in the supremacy of Nietzschean will over reason and intellect until his death. The book also made clear the degree to which he believed that sacrifice was a supreme act by which one could demonstrate reverence for the *patria* and that a soldier's death in battle was the most sublime form of sacrifice for which one could strive. "The nation [*pueblo*] with the greatest moral capacity is the one with the greatest number of men willing to sacrifice themselves for it," he wrote. "Moral capacity is the exclusive determinant of victory in war, even though this capacity is also subject to the requirements of the art of war."[70] Several decades later, such vitalist nationalism and idealization of sacrifice would come to merge fairly easily with the Catholic-conservative military mysticism of Millán-Astray and Franco.

Burguete's ideas, moreover, did not always remain in the purely theoretical realm, even at the turn of the century. In fact, not long before *Zorrapastro* was published, Burguete had played an active role in the regenerationist movement centered around the "Christian general" Camilo Polavieja. Like Boulanger in France several years earlier, Polavieja had attracted a wide variety of supporters who were hoping to join him in regenerating a country suffering from political malaise and colonial crisis. Although his manifesto of September 1898 was primarily a call for what one historian calls "a purification of democracy," some of Polavieja's followers had a decidely more authoritarian outlook than the manifesto implied.[71] After returning from his tours of duty in Cuba and the Philippines, Burguete was soon swept into the movement, even joining Baroja, Azorín, and other famous writers and political figures in various discussions among themselves and with Polavieja in person on creating a new, regenerationist government. At about the same time, Burguete associated regularly with at least some anarchists, secretly participating in discussions in the editorial office of the anarchist periodical *Aurora roja*.[72]

With time, however, the young officer's radicalism and his strong distaste for contemporary politics, the press, democratic ideals, and other increasingly important elements of Spanish society would become more moderate. Eventually, in fact, he himself would play a prominent role in the world of politics and the press, even advocating the empowerment of Spain through capitalist industrial growth. His earlier homage to Nietzsche had revealed the mind-set of a young, relatively radical officer who, not surprisingly, would temper his views with the growth of his power, prestige, and position in the very status quo that he had once so fervently attacked. In matters of his profession, however, his basic philosophical outlook remained largely unchanged, as the following examination of his ideas on war and the military makes clear.

Chapter Three

Spiritual Combat and the Aesthetics of War

Burguete's interest in metaphysics, so clearly evident in *Zorrapastro,* strongly influenced his writings on strategy, tactics, and other ostensibly more straightforward aspects of war and the military. Most strikingly, his vision of war as an overwhelmingly spiritual and mystical affair—not to be understood or pursued with the tools of rationalist science—stood in sharp contrast to the views of the traditionally liberal and technocratic segments of the Spanish army, and it even colored his ideas on the conduct of battle. In the manner of many European military thinkers during the years before World War I, Burguete believed in the dominance of Clausewitzian "moral" forces in combat, and he allowed this belief to shape the sweeping programs for tactical reform he endeavored to make part of official Spanish military doctrine. Like his nationalist rhetoric, in a sense this romantic and antimaterialist understanding of warfare was intellectually inconsistent with the liberal republican politics he would embrace as his career progressed, although he never attempted to reconcile this incongruity. As his career advanced he wrote with increasing frequency on military affairs, tending to orient his books toward a more general readership as he grew older. The shift from detailed studies such as that found in his tactical program to less specialized, more philosophically oriented examinations of war and the armed forces stemmed in part from his frustration over the army's refusal to embrace his technical ideas completely; in 1911 he would complain bitterly that many aspects of his manual on tactics remained ignored or had been cast aside.[1]

Yet in certain respects Burguete's popular works on war and the military merit more attention than his technical and specialized studies anyway. On their most basic level these writings reveal that Burguete shared the strong interest of many of his colleagues in proposals regarding universal military service and educational reform in Spain, which they linked to the more general goal of strengthening Spanish national identity. And, like many officers, he carefully studied the history of the Franco-Prussian War, although he differed markedly from most Spanish military observers in the lessons he drew from Moltke's victory. In his view the conflict was anything but a vindication for the advocates of universal conscription and the pedagogical potential of military service; instead it demonstrated the limited value of mass conscription and national education as advocated by the leading advocates of reform. He concurred with many military writers in Spain and elsewhere, however, in interpreting the war as proof of the dominance of moral forces in battle, and he would find in the Russo-Japanese War further confirmation of this view. Such thinking not only reflected Burguete's strong distaste for the rationalism typical of the nineteenth-century European intellectual world, but it also represented his rejection of what he perceived as the doctrinal hegemony of positivist thought in the officer corps. When waging his intellectual battles in the theater of military thought, he continued to employ the same language of war that he and many fin-de-siècle writers elsewhere in Europe had used in their attacks on the cultural status quo. Promoting a mystical vision of armed conflict and attacking the cult of reason, Burguete joined these writers in paradoxically grounding many of his arguments against reason in social science theory itself.

As will become clear, many of Burguete's ideas bore a striking resemblance to those of the renowned British military theorist J. F. C. Fuller, a prolific and often highly insightful thinker who wrote pathbreaking tracts on armored warfare before falling into disrepute during the 1930s, when he became a supporter of British fascism.[2] Both men were self-taught, voracious readers with very eclectic interests, about which they were usually more than willing to express their opinions. It is doubtful that Fuller even knew of the existence of the Spanish military writer, and the name Fuller probably meant nothing to Burguete until the 1920s—if even then. But the similarities between their writings reveal that they were products of common intellectual and cultural influences. Antimaterialist in outlook, the two men shared a strong interest in crowd psychology and a seemingly bizarre fascination with the occult and with the cosmic forces that they believed lay behind everything from Pythagorean and Platonic teachings to world religions.

Although Burguete does not appear to have pursued many of these matters with as much enthusiasm as Fuller, both men interpreted historical change in general in terms of broad cyclical or spiral processes, and they both betrayed much admiration for the writings of Carlyle and Spencer. On the more concrete level of strategy and other military affairs, both men were severe critics of their countries' institutions of military education and doctrine, and both related tariffs and other instruments of national economic protectionism to the poor health of Western civilization as a whole. Azar Gat, a historian of modern military thought, has observed that Fuller could reach "dazzling heights and embarrassing lows" in the content and style of his writings. At first reading, he continues, Fuller's works reveal a "wealth of tantalizing ideas, brilliant insights, original flashes of inspiration, and extremely suggestive historical interpretations which flow incessantly from Fuller's untamed, self-taught, and amateurish but ingeniously creative mind."[3] To at least some degree this assessment could apply to Burguete as well, although Burguete was not as brilliant or original a thinker as Fuller. And in spite of the many undeniable differences between the two, in many ways the thinking of both shared much with that of leading modernists to whom protofascism and fascism held much appeal. Such an intellectual climate can, as Gat and others have written, inform ideas on the strategy, conduct, and future of war.

* * *

Not surprisingly, Burguete's combat experiences as a young officer heavily influenced his later writings on the nature of war. After completing his studies at the Academia General Militar in 1891, he took up arms for his country on the peninsula and in Morocco. In 1894 he earned praise for the "*levantado espíritu, valor, abnegación y disciplina*" he displayed in northern Africa, and the following year he was promoted to the rank of captain on the basis of combat merits and sent, via Puerto Rico, to Cuba. By May he had joined the Spanish forces in their efforts to suppress the Cuban separatist revolt. He led his men in several bloody attacks, losing many of his troops and even suffering a light machete wound to his face in hand-to-hand combat. He received the decoration of the Red Cross, First Class, for his military feats in late April 1896, only two weeks before receiving word that the war had taken the life of his brother Luis. Upon learning of the loss, he requested and received permission to return to Madrid for two months. After this leave he found himself on a ship headed for the Philippines, where he again played an active role in the fighting before receiving serious wounds in February 1897 and then returning to Spain with the newly acquired rank of major and the much esteemed Cross of María Cristina, First Class.[4]

Once back on the peninsula, Burguete immediately began writing, and *Zorrapastro*, his early works on tactics, and his firsthand accounts of Spain's most recent colonial debacles were all in print by 1902. He clearly aimed his books about Cuba and the Philippines at a general audience, including vivid descriptions of his journeys from Spain, of his stops at exotic port cities along the way, and of the countryside and native inhabitants on the islands where he saw combat.[5] Indeed, many of the readers of his book on the war in the Philippines must have found his depiction of Port Said, the Suez Canal, Colombo, and Singapore at least as interesting as his firsthand accounts of battle. This work also included historical and political analyses undoubtedly written as much for civilian readers as for his fellow officers.

During the remainder of the decade Burguete wrote prolifically while serving on the peninsula and in the Balearic Islands, but his literary productivity tapered off after he was named lieutenant colonel in 1909 and sent to join the fighting in Morocco. He was already well enough known to attract a crowd of well-wishers at his departure for Africa, including the famous "Christian general" and regenerationist Camilo Polavieja.[6] Burguete continued to publish after becoming a brigadier general in 1913, but by the time he was named major general in 1918 he had largely ceased writing and devoted most of his time to politics and his profession. Although he completed another book after his trip during the First World War to observe military campaigns in Serbia and Romania,[7] he attracted considerably more attention for publicly attacking his colleague General Dámaso Berenguer following Spain's horrible military defeat near Anual, Morocco, in 1921—characteristically invoking Nietzsche in his diatribes.[8]

* * *

Nietzsche's strong influence was apparent in Burguete's turn-of-the-century writings on one of the most frequently debated political issues of Restoration Spain: military service. The issue provided Burguete with the opportunity to draw attention to himself by publicly opposing the proposals regarding mandatory service supported by many of his older, respected colleagues, and it clearly revealed his intense dislike of "democratic" and "progressive" programs for restructuring the armed forces.

As in many countries both in Burguete's time and today, in Spain the demands of military service fell almost exclusively on the poor. The situation was especially tragic for the great number of young Spaniards unable to pay their way out of service during the periods of intense fighting in Cuba, the Philippines, and Morocco, because being drafted then was often tantamount to a death sentence. Desertion rates were particularly high in poorer regions, where the young men who refused to serve could not afford to hire substitutes or offer "service in the form of cash" as allowed by Spanish law. Moreover, the government only enraged its critics further by sending young and volunteer troops into combat in place of more "expensive" career officers, arguing that the country's financial hardships left it with no alternative. The magnitude of the problem was clear to many, and officers publicly protested against the injustice of the system and its detrimental effect on troop morale and combat efficacy. Some officers, adopting the vision of many of their French colleagues, also wrote of the potential they saw in universal military service for uniting young men of various social classes.[9]

Burguete, however, rejected the argument that obligatory military service would help unify the various segments of Spanish society. Resting his argument largely on a Nietzschean distinction between different types of men, he argued that a professional army composed of a select few was far superior to an army of the masses whose composition was based on democratic principles. In a typical failure to interpret Nietzsche's writings beyond their most explicit and superficial level, Burguete had his spokesman Zorrapastro point to the "profound veneration for professional soldiers" that he saw in the section of *Thus Spoke Zarathustra* titled "On War and Warriors" and in the assertion by Nietzsche's protagonist that a true *Übermensch* could emerge from their ranks.[10] Quoting the conquistador Cortés on the inferiority of "soldiers without will," Zorrapastro argued that many men were unfit to take up arms. He also cited the admiration for the professional soldier he believed Tolstoy had expressed in his writings.[11]

Burguete attributed enthusiasm for the notion of the "nation in arms," which in fact found considerable backing from a variety of circles both inside and outside of Spain, to a faulty understanding of history. Whereas many of Burguete's colleagues believed that the wars of the French Revolution and Napoleon had marked a definitive transformation to the age of large national armies, he, like Fuller, maintained that modern warfare—with its increasing dependency on new technology and skills—actually demanded a smaller, highly trained, and well-motivated group of soldiers and leaders.[12] Like his denial of human equality in general, his argument that only certain types of men were fit to be soldiers also rested in part on his understanding of ancient history and the ideas of such thinkers as Socrates, Plato, and Aristotle. These philosophers and many of their contemporaries, he maintained, understood that civilians were quite different from soldiers.

At first glance the wars of the nineteenth century may appear to vindicate the advocates of mass armies, Burguete reasoned in *Zorrapastro,* but closer examination revealed otherwise. Zorrapastro claimed that Bismarck's memoirs attributed Prussian victory over the French exclusively to the better quality of the German soldier, and he cited the Prussian chancellor on the many problems his army of the masses posed. On the French side military leaders had also complained that the large number of troops hindered the performance of the good soldiers, was difficult to control, and contributed to the high number of deaths by friendly fire, according to Zorrapastro. He admitted that harsh discipline might help keep troops under some control, but—as the Spanish campaigns in Cuba and the Philippines demonstrated—it did not create the fighting, patriotic spirit necessary for victory. And he mentioned the logistical difficulties posed by overly large armies, which even their strongest advocates could not deny.[13] Demographic realities probably shaped Burguete's objections to the nation-in-arms principle as well, since it implicitly conceded that Spain—with a small population—would be at the mercy of larger states.

Like so many European military thinkers, Burguete believed the cavalry would serve as "the arm of the future," largely through its ability to spread enough panic and terror to overwhelm even large armies that were subject to relentless discipline.[14] Although he conceded that a true "*patria* of the strong" could overcome the inherent defects of a nation in arms, he also made it clear that he did not believe Spain belonged in that category. "Our nation, like no other, should have learned its lesson with the blood that ought to have purged it of such stupidity," he wrote. "We had 300,000 men in Cuba and 30,000 in the Philippines, but the number of real soldiers in each colony was extremely low. . . . The current army doesn't serve the *patria*—it consumes it." Through his protagonist, Zorrapastro, he urged his listeners to discard "the stupid conventionalism that all citizens are always under obligation to shed blood for the *patria*." After all, he reasoned, everyone should serve in peacetime through taxes, and when Spain really needed an army of the masses one would form. "The art of war and warriors is like religion and its prophets," he argued. "The hero accomplishes everything, and—just like Carlyle says—the hero inflames his people with the fire of his heroism." If the people of his day who hated the military allowed it to continue to swell its ranks, they did so only because they thought it would thereby become like "a wafer without any substance, easily blown apart by a single puff."[15]

In his later works Burguete would continue to base his case against universal military service on the same arguments he had first expressed in *Zorrapastro*. Throughout *Mi rebeldía*,[16] for example, he expressed his objections to universal military service, and in 1905 he presented his most detailed and concrete ideas for reforming military service in an entry submitted to *El Imparcial*, which was sponsoring a contest for the best proposal to rectify the country's much debated "military problem." Given the predominant role the armed forces and their actions played in society, the interest of a leading civilian newspaper in military affairs was not at all unusual or surprising; shortly after the Spanish defeat of 1898 *El Liberal* had sponsored a similar competition.[17] Burguete did not win *El Imparcial*'s prize, but his entry is nevertheless valuable because of what it reveals about his ideas and their place in the national debate over the organization and purpose of the Spanish army.[18]

In Burguete's entry he portrayed universal military service in Spain as financially and militarily undesirable, suggesting instead that the country maintain a standing army of 200,000 men based on a five-year period of service. According to Burguete, the increase in the number of troops from the existing total of 60,000 would actually save the country money if implemented correctly, and, unlike plans to make Spain a true nation in arms, it would ensure that only the right kind of men became soldiers. Rather than abolishing the provision for "service in the form of cash," he wrote, the government should make the system more equitable and profitable by using a graduated scale to link the fee for exemption to individual income. Offering a tangible alternative to the plans for universal service he had attacked in *Zorrapastro*, he even included a table defining ten categories according to personal or family income and the amount the members of each would have to pay if they did not wish to serve.[19]

* * *

On a more general level, Burguete's perception of "civilization" and "progress" as the underlying causes of Spain's so-called military problem also found its first expression in *Zorrapastro,* but was developed more fully in his later works. Again basing his observations largely on his understanding of the Franco-Prussian War, Burguete strongly criticized the preponderance of "scientific" approaches to war. Like so many military thinkers elsewhere in Europe, he believed that too much attention to new technology and improvements in firepower had overshadowed the moral qualities most important in determining the outcomes of wars. In the words of his spokesman Zorrapastro, "The truth is that one doesn't learn the rudiments of the art of war by memorizing rules and regulations; like all arts, you learn it by feeling, and the feeling for war is learned at home or—at the least—in school."[20] In this brief passage the young Burguete revealed how the Franco-Prussian War had made a strong impact on his thinking in two important ways: he clearly concurred with his many European contemporaries who interpreted the conflict as a vindication of the Clausewitzian belief in the dominance of nonquantifiable "moral" factors in combat, and he shared the closely related interest that grew after Prussia's victory in the role education should play in preparing a country for war.

After his victories the Prussian general Moltke had, in a widely repeated statement, attributed much of his success to what he had learned from the military theorist Clausewitz. Hence Clausewitz soon replaced Jomini, who was inclined to reduce war to a learnable set of rules and principles, as the most fashionable military writer in Europe. And his new followers, as part of the fin-de-siècle reaction against the rationalist legacy of the Enlightenment, emphasized his views on the "moral" qualities necessary for victory in warfare, such as a superior fighting spirit. Although this segment of Clausewitz's thinking was hardly his best, it offered the day's military planners the intellectual support they most wanted. Moreover, it related closely to Clausewitz's notion of "friction," which influenced Burguete as profoundly as it did so many of his European counterparts.[21] For Clausewitz the term referred to the inevitable elements of uncertainty and chance present in all military action. Friction, he wrote, "distinguishes real war from war on paper," and it made moral qualities all the more important for those forced to confront the many unforeseeable elements of combat.[22]

Not all European military thinkers, however, were willing to forsake the use of scientific studies in forecasting the character of future wars. The Boer War and the studies presented by the day's leading theorist of war and peace, Jan Bloch, and other researchers at The Hague Conferences of 1899 and 1907 had offered strong empirical evidence that new technology and greater firepower spelled disaster for even the most "morally fit" soldiers who staged a frontal attack, and many Europeans, including some Spanish officers, were receptive to Bloch's findings.[23] But the Russo-Japanese War of 1904–5, in which the well-trained and highly motivated Japanese troops had overcome heavy losses to defeat their enemy, seemed to prove otherwise. Burguete therefore joined the many Europeans who interpreted the war as proof that even great advancements in defensive weaponry were no match for a spiritually strong offensive effort. After all, they reasoned, a defensive posture was morally inferior to an offensive one, and moral qualities were the bottom line in warfare.[24]

Burguete devoted much of his 1905 book *Ciencia del valor* to the Japanese victory over the Russians in the battle of Mukden, which he believed validated his views on friction and the supremacy of willpower on the battlefield. In this work he relied primarily on Luigi Barzini's account of the war for its descriptions of how the fighting unfolded.[25] He probably also gleaned a fair amount from the reports of Colonel Luís Fernández de Córdoba, better known as the Marquis of Mendigorría, who had joined more than eighty representatives from fifteen countries in observing the war.[26] In a later book Burguete would explicitly refer to the writings on the war by the Marquis, who himself had penned an oft-cited report on Burguete's proposal for reforming tactical doctrine.[27]

As its title suggests, *Ciencia del valor* focused on the role of the less tangible and more spiritual elements of warfare such as morale and valor, and it relied heavily on examples from the Russo-Japanese War for support. The lessons of the conflict had particular relevance for Spain, Burguete argued, since the country resembled Russia in its lack of spirit, of willpower, and of "collective moral value." Both the Spanish and Russian peoples had assumed "defensive" attitudes and organizations, he wrote, which meant that both remained

> in a state inferior to that of savages, since they suffer from the effects of modern life and all its corporeal frailty. And they continue to lose their qualities of valor, which require bodily or spiritual hardships in order to maintain themselves.
>
> A people in such a state is like uncultivated soil: it has neither the lushness of virgin soil nor the capability to grow the superior species of cultivated soil.[28]

For, Burguete continued in the vein of Clausewitz, "uncultured peoples [*pueblos incultos*]" were unlikely to produce great leaders. Returning to the terminology of Zorrapastro, he described the best that could rise from their ranks as an "*hombre hábil*" who desired only "to resist all dilemmas by eluding them and who believes, like his people, that to live is to evade struggle." This disdain for "defensive" attitudes, which Burguete claimed often manifested themselves in an "aggressive" posture meant to mask a fear of fighting, was to color his views on matters as varied as history, biology, and military strategy and tactics, as his discussion of the Russian and Japanese peoples and their performance in war illustrates.[29]

According to Burguete, the Japanese military successes demonstrated that the nation had experienced the conflict as "a heartfelt sentiment and the product of a natural desire for expansion," whereas for their opponents the war had been little more than an "idea." As I will show later, his belief in the inherent superiority of the forces of sentiment over intellect strongly influenced his view of world history. Moreover, in his eyes both Russia and Spain suffered from misguided attempts to "Europeanize" their armed forces. Rather than borrowing ideas from countries to the west and then modifying them to serve "the historical sentiment of the Russian people," the Russian state had crudely imposed foreign notions on the country without making the appropriate alterations. And Spain's "recent disasters" represented the same fundamental truth as Japan's victory over the Russians: "in the struggle between a sentiment and an idea it was only natural that the former won, as the structural disposition of nature dictates that it always will." The general staff played an insignificant role in the Japanese army, he claimed, whereas its Russian counterpart could take advantage of that army's "cerebral predominance" to force its ideas on war over the whole organization—a process that led to pitiful defeats at the hands of the Japanese.[30] As will become clear later, he held similar views regarding the form and function of the Spanish general staff.

Burguete shared his fascination with Japan and the Japanese people with Ramiro de Maeztu, whom he lauded for attributing the defeat of Russia to the superior "spiritual potency" of its enemies.[31] He also cited Maeztu's praise for Bushido, a code of unquestioning obedience and loyalty that bound samurai warriors to their lords, which the famous writer believed underlay the Japanese victories. Invoking the Spanish literary canon, Burguete explained that Bushido was "a religion of oaths to heroism; a warrior ethic made dogma: it is *the religion of upright men* of which Calderón spoke and so many speak without understanding."[32] This reverence for Bushido philosophy, as first popularized in Spain by Maeztu and introduced to the military community by Burguete, left an imprint on Spanish society that lasted well into the Franco dictatorship. Most remarkably, José Millán-Astray would subsequently claim that he had made use of Bushido values as founder of the Spanish Foreign Legion, even promoting their teaching to Spanish youth.[33]

Burguete's respect and admiration for Maeztu, which was especially prominent in his discussion of Japan but also surfaced elsewhere in his writings, suggests that historians who have stressed the anti-European and anti-intellectual bent of the officer corps in Restoration Spain have unjustly ignored the smaller but clearly significant group of figures like Burguete who openly admired such thinkers as Nietzsche, Unamuno, and Maeztu. Andrée Bachoud, for example, emphasizes the harsh criticism that the *Correspondencia Militar* directed at Maeztu, Unamuno, and other leading Spanish intellectuals in 1909, writing of the continuity she perceives between these verbal attacks and Millán-Astray's famous cry of "Death to the Intelligentsia!"[34] But although her appraisal may be accurate for many readers of the daily paper—whose editor tended to sympathize with the concerns of lower-ranking officers[35]—it fails to acknowledge the importance of a more intellectually oriented and elite group of officers, many of whom exercised a disproportionate influence within the military community and within Spain as a whole. The opinions expressed by the two different kinds of Spanish military press, the professional journals and the politico-military dailies, in fact differed markedly from one another.[36] Indeed, in 1904 Modesto Navarro, a much decorated colonel and prolific writer, informed his readers that he had thought it more appropriate to submit his manuscript to a specialized professional journal than to a military or civilian daily, because only in the former "can one conscientiously and with the necessary depth discuss the matters treated here."[37] Moreover, the officers who later rose to prominent positions in the Second Republic and the Civil War were more likely during this period to express themselves in specialized and scholarly journals such as *Revista Técnica de Infantería y Caballería, Memorial de Infantería,* or *Estudios Militares;* in books; or in speeches at the Spanish military's think tank of the day, the Centro del Ejército y de la Armada, than in the daily military newspapers.[38] Even avowedly antirationalist officers such as Burguete and Millán-Astray made use of these media, often explicitly acknowledging that—in spite of their professed hatred for the forces of intellect—they paradoxically read and thought highly of works by leading Spanish and foreign intellectuals.

Of course, the opinions of the mass of officers and noncommissioned officers who read the military dailies undeniably played key roles in shaping Spanish history as well, as was demonstrated by the clear influence of the Juntas de Defensa in the weakening and eventual collapse of the Restoration political system.[39] But the ideas of their more intellectual colleagues merit more detailed and profound attention than they have received, because they influenced political and military elites of their own day as well as those of the subsequent regimes of Primo de Rivera and Franco. The military periodicals Bachoud cites may indeed have attacked Unamuno and other leading thinkers, but Burguete and many of his colleagues actually thought quite highly of the famous intellectual. And their good words were sometimes reciprocated. In a 1904 essay, for example, Unamuno briefly praised Burguete's book *Mi rebeldía,* describing it as "worthy of lavish elegy" and concurring with its criticism of democracy, and Maeztu, writing during World War I, commented respectfully on Burguete's post-1898 reflections on technology and valor in warfare—referring to no other Spanish military figure in his entire article.[40]

* * *

Like his views on the moral qualities of warfare, Burguete's focus on the role of education in preparing a nation for war also stemmed in part from his understanding of the Franco-Prussian War. As he first revealed in *Zorrapastro,* he concurred with the large number of officers in Restoration Spain who looked to European—especially German—models for their programs of military education, although he often viewed these models differently than did his peers.[41] Above all, a desire to foment a mystical, almost religious, form of Spanish nationalism and spiritual regeneration determined his considerations of military education. Although his opposition to national armies of the masses prevented him from going so far as to join the many Spanish advocates of using military service as a true "school for the nation," he clearly believed that priming a man for war and the fostering of patriotism that goes with it should begin long before one became old enough to take up arms. When Moltke had said that schoolmasters deserved credit for the success of the Prussian army—a remark commented on by Joaquín Costa and widely repeated in the Spanish military press[42]—Burguete had undoubtedly taken notice. In fact, he would use choice quotations from Moltke and his ostensible mentor Clausewitz to illustrate the value of military education to members of modern society. Through Zorrapastro he praised an unspecified golden age when "ferocity and love for the *patria* were learned at home, and they endured even through transformations in the *patria,*" and in a subsequent book he asserted that the soldierly qualities that Clausewitz believed existed naturally in "savage or semi-savage peoples" had to be fostered through formal military education in the leading nations of his own time.[43]

Burguete's spokesman Zorrapastro lamented that young men entering the military in his day had to try to forget the basic rules and values they had been taught at home. Suddenly they were expected not to live carefully, but to risk and even sacrifice their lives if necessary, and they had to be willing to kill the same neighbor whom they previously had been admonished to respect and forgive. As Spanish soldiers they were also expected to conform to uniform standards of behavior, because "he who wants to distinguish himself through advancement runs the risk of being shot by his colleagues," Zorrapastro claimed. "What would Zarathustra say?" he asked rhetorically.[44]

For Burguete the term *education* encompassed far more than formalized instruction; it referred to the much deeper process of developing a strong love for one's country and instilling the values of a warrior. "Military instruction without education is like a body without a soul and only serves to make robots and mechanical soldiers," he asserted.[45] In a later work Burguete would repeat the same analogy and argue that "instruction serves to develop the brain while education serves to develop sentiment."[46] The distinction he drew between "instruction" and "education" resembled the viewpoint of his colleague Enrique Ruiz-Fornells—examined later in this book—and of the founders of the Institución Libre de Enseñanza, a progressive organization devoted to the development of modern pedagogical methods free of church and state interference. The Institución's leaders strove to make education truly meaningful for students and saw the organization as an alternative to the country's Catholic schools, which they accused of teaching little more than rote memorization.[47] The Institución influenced quite a few officers, and Joaquín Fanjul would even reproduce most of its 1883 report on the army's potential role in educating the Spanish masses.[48] Although Fanjul did not agree with every aspect of the report, he—like so many of his colleagues—shared the Institución's interest in using military service to educate the largely ignorant populace. Burguete, however, did not share its views on the educational potential for the masses of obligatory military service. But he was aware that many others did, and Zorrapastro's views on education served as an important contribution to the discussions on pedagogy that already raged within the military community.[49] Burguete's ideas were, of course, considerably less rationalist than those of the *institucionalistas,* and his spokesman Zorrapastro even concluded his discourse on the matter by emphasizing the role he believed mothers should play in preparing their sons to be soldiers. Although he did not provide any practical advice on child rearing, he forcefully advocated instilling military values at home beginning at a very early age. "I can practically say," he advised mothers in typical hyperbolic fashion, "that when you discipline your womb you will bear soldiers."[50]

Burguete's subsequent writings on education reiterated and expanded on his initial call for "discipline" in raising children. Interestingly, ten years later Fuller would voice similar views, suggesting that boys and girls begin to receive patriotic and semimilitary education beginning at the age of four.[51] Writing at the turn of the century, Burguete—as usual—pushed the argument to dramatic extremes, advocating teaching children "to endure pain and to confront life" in order to foster their self-confidence, describing the level of self-confidence as a degree of "elasticity." Although "excessive severity breaks the coefficient of elasticity, excessive tenderness will make it atrophy," he thought.[52] He also reproduced a passage by Clausewitz on the need for *"pueblos cultos"* to prepare their soldiers physically and spiritually for the hardships of war, attributing to the famous military thinker a strong belief in the function of military education in instilling the "qualities of resistance" necessary to make man into " 'a useful instrument for war' "—namely, " 'moral and physical vigor *and a little common sense.*' "[53]

Burguete lamented that the instructors of his own country's military academies had failed to heed Clausewitz's advice and continued to teach little more than highly technical knowledge and rote memorization skills,[54] which he equated to imposing "the impressions and mechanical tracks of phonographic records" on students. This process, he wrote, acted "at the expense of moral and physical strength and is comparable to filling an attic with fragments of inarticulate formularies, abstract formulas, and historical deductions and judgments of little force and no more value than junk. Yet all is expertly classified, since the attic is held together with algebraically squared abscissas and ordinates, upon which a trigonometric graph has been imposed and which—because of all the effort spent preparing the brain for infinitesimal errors—can handle only infinitesimal acts."[55]

Burguete's critical view of what he perceived as the overly positivist bent of military education in Spain, which was revealed quite clearly in the exaggerated and bitter words of this passage, stood in stark contrast to that of many other military writers of his day. Even those who shared his distaste for the mathematical and technical components of the typical academy curriculum rarely launched such bitter attacks on the institutions. After all, in many ways the academy system supported the very livelihood of military writers in Spain. The men who taught in these institutions enjoyed good prospects for promotion and the chance to supplement their income by writing new (and often superfluous) editions of military textbooks, which—like all published works—could help them rise professionally. In this practice they followed the lead of the civilian *catedráticos* who wrote and assigned their own textbooks for extra money and merits for promotion in the civil list.[56] Many of the leading Spanish military writers—including virtually every officer besides Burguete mentioned in this book—spent at least several years teaching at the Infantry Academy in Toledo. It is hardly surprising, then, that so few officers criticized the system of military education in Spain as vehemently as Burguete, because the very officers most likely to articulate their complaints in writing depended on that very system for professional and financial gain.

The most notable critique of military education in Restoration Spain to appear after that of Burguete was published in 1917 under the pen name "Captain X."[57] The book echoed Burguete in its vehement criticism of the academies as self-serving institutions of deeply entrenched corporatism with little value except to the largely incompetent group of officers who enjoyed careers teaching there. Supporting his accusations with charts and lists of the curricula, daily schedules, and budgets of the institutions, Captain X supported Burguete's criticism of the pedagogical methods and mathematical orientation of the academies. His book also exposed the "blind mercantilism" behind the system of textbook writing, publishing, and other requirements at the academy, from which many military writers profited.[58]

Burguete, who did not share the corporate interests of the academy's instructors and the authors and publishers of its textbooks, described the academy directors as men who, "because they don't know or haven't memorized the scientific formulas that are supposed to adorn the good soldier as an expression of his culture, pretend to revere these formulas in order to hide their own moral misery or physical weakness." He praised the type of soldier he called the "*troupier,*" or rank-and-file soldier, who may have lacked the type of education supposedly promoted by the academies, but nevertheless enjoyed true physical and spiritual strength. "In the judgment of the *super-intellectuals,*" he wrote, "the *troupier* is primarily to blame for our blunders, while in my judgment, in the judgment of a sincere and humble soldier, it is he who endured all the weight of the campaign and saved us from complete embarrassment." For Burguete, then, the crucial lesson of the Franco-Prussian War lay not simply in its supposed demonstration of the importance of schools, but rather in its demonstration of the *kind* of education most necessary to cultivate soldiers. By emphasizing intellectual qualities over their spiritual counterparts, he wrote, Spain was committing "the same error made by the French after the War of 1870. We are following the trend set by the Nation that praised the teacher without understanding that in that war as in all others, the schoolmaster molds other attributes before molding the mind."[59] Moreover, Burguete was far from certain that the Franco-Prussian War had great relevance for Spain on a practical level anyway—apart from its demonstration of the superiority of Clausewitzian willpower in battle.[60] Instead he advocated studying historical examples of more use to the immediate needs of the Spanish forces in Morocco, strongly criticizing the Spanish military academies for not teaching cadets about the nineteenth-century French campaigns in Algeria.[61]

Similarly, Burguete cast doubt on the wisdom of blindly adopting the model of the British Boy Scouts as an institution useful for instilling military skills and values, a move then under discussion in many European countries. Joining the many Spaniards who argued that the guerrilla skills employed so successfully against Napoleonic troops were inherent to Spanish national identity, he believed that any Spanish version of the Boy Scouts would require fundamental alterations from the British model. He even questioned the need for such an institution in Spain in any form, given that "the aim is to make the boy scout into an excellent guerrilla fighter, which comes naturally to the man of Spain's countryside." All a Spaniard needed was knowledge of "typically Spanish tactics and a bit of allowance for his nature [*una táctica castiza y un poco acomodada á su naturaleza*]."[62] Once again, Burguete's views differed fundamentally from the Eurocentric ideas on education expressed by so many of his colleagues. They also echoed, like so many of his ideas, the reasoning typical of Ganivet's *Idearium Español,* which argued that the Spaniard was an inherently better guerrilla fighter (*guerrero*) than military officer (*militar*).[63]

* * *

Burguete also strongly opposed the blind application of "European" ideas to the Spanish general staff, an institution he criticized for many of the same faults he perceived in the country's system of military education. Above all he attacked the mathematical and scientific orientation of staff officers, blaming them for the growing "bureaucratic infection" of the armies of the modern age.[64] In this case as well, Burguete's comments fit squarely within the context of the reforms proposed for European armies in the wake of the Franco-Prussian War, as many Spanish officers now favored modeling the Spanish general staff on its Prussian counterpart.[65]

Burguete's ideas were already quite clear when he penned *Zorrapastro,* in which his Nietzschean protagonist defined the general staff as the "spirit and nervous system" of the large army and faulted it for emphasizing natural science and laboratory research over the virtues and instincts of a warrior. People of his day believed that a general had little need for willpower or true leadership qualities, Zorrapastro had told his listeners, as war "has reduced itself to mathematical formulas." Therefore, "the spirit [*genio*] of the soldier is no longer necessary." Not surprisingly, he linked the faults of the current general staff to his listeners' "democratic creed," describing it as a function of "your spiritual misery and your physical poverty."[66] But the general staff nevertheless had a place in Zorrapastro's vision of the impending revolution of the *inhábil,* which he believed would return the institution to its rightful place. But this would happen, he said, "not before we torch its laboratories and hurl its desk chairs and research instruments over a cliff." As an afterthought he suggested that they throw the *hábil* over as well.[67]

Burguete's rejection of the Spanish general staff's scientific focus and of more positivist and rationalist approaches to war in general was of considerable importance, because it exemplified the growing division between two schools of thought within the officer corps. As the century progressed, the more technically and scientifically minded segment of the officer corps found itself increasingly at odds with officers whose emphasis on the spiritual and moral aspects of warfare led them to discredit the contributions of military engineers, artillery officers, and mathematicians to strategic and tactical planning. As a prolific writer and highly visible figure, Burguete lent important support to the reactionary, antiscientific side of the conflict.

The military of the last quarter of the nineteenth century still held its traditional place in Spain as a leading promoter of scientific advancement and new ideas. This was especially true for military engineers and artillery officers, who were well represented in Spanish mathematics and physics circles. As Thomas F. Glick notes in his study of the reception of Einstein's ideas in Spain, the character of Don Carlos in Clarín's 1884 novel *La Regenta* represented "a type of military engineer who was a devotee of physics and mathematics, and through them, philosophy."[68] Clarín's own brother, Genaro Alas, undoubtedly provided some of the inspiration for the character of Don Carlos. A military engineer with an interest in journalism and politics, Alas actually presented one of the clearest expositions in nineteenth-century Spain of Darwin's ideas and their importance.[69] Half a century later, when Darwin was "virtually proscribed" by the Franco regime, it would be almost unthinkable for a military officer to give a series of presentations on such a topic, especially in a military casino.[70]

Alas also praised the military's well-attended technical speeches on subjects such as the Franco-Prussian War and advancements in explosive powders, fortifications, and cavalry tactics, and he spoke considerably more positively than Burguete of the general staff. He referred to the organization as the "military or strategic lobe of the military brain" as well as "the advisor of the political lobe and, simultaneously, the inspector and financial head of the military organism in its entirety."[71] The "strategic lobe" he praised was clearly at the forefront of Spain's scientific community; the general staff's artillery officers, engineers, and geodesists were better scientists than their counterparts working at Spanish universities, which were struggling through a considerable crisis at the time.[72] Even as late as Einstein's visit to Spain in 1923, many military officers displayed a strong interest in the latest developments in theoretical physics.[73]

Despite its leading position in the Spanish scientific community, however, the general staff clearly failed to win the respect of many combat-oriented military officers. Moreover, the low level of participation in the last Cuban war by officer-scientists had increased the animosity that the veterans of the campaigns there, such as Burguete, felt toward their research-oriented colleagues. In this case Burguete was probably also betraying the lingering effects of his days as a young cadet at the Academia General Militar, the only institution of military education in Spain about which Burguete seemed to have at least some positive feelings.[74] It had been founded in part to combat the elitism of the technical corps, especially the artillery and the general staff. The latter's existence as a separate corps, with an overwhelmingly technical and bureaucratic focus and its own academy and promotions list, further fueled the resentment of its critics. Moreover, although its bureaucratic nature may have been typical of its European counterparts, it differed fundamentally from the German general staff, which functioned as a "service"—not a separate entity—and took its officers primarily from other branches for periods of temporary duty.[75]

Of course, the reaction against the technical side of the military that Burguete's writings both articulated and promoted also stemmed in part from the reaction of intellectuals all over Europe against rationalism and positivism. In Spain, Ganivet had even made a point of including a bitter attack on "scientific" and "mechanical" approaches to war among his broader objections to science in general.[76] But the officers who constituted the older school put up a noteworthy resistance to young mavericks like Burguete. Colonel Modesto Navarro, an older, highly decorated officer and the author of many books himself, wrote a 388-page critique of Burguete's controversial infantry tactical manual, which had first appeared in 1900.[77] Navarro's well-written and intelligently argued work focused on what he correctly identified as "the main idea [*la idea madre*]" behind Burguete's tactical thinking: the principle of the offensive.[78] Although Navarro saw value in offensive doctrine, he believed that considerations such as terrain, recent improvements in firepower, and even political and social circumstances made Burguete's blind faith in the spirit-driven frontal attack inappropriate for the Spanish army.

Navarro's work was lavishly praised by many officers and even earned him a strong recommendation for promotion from the general in charge of the Escuela Central de Tiro del Ejército,[79] but it also met considerable resistance from Burguete's defenders. Some officers believed that the more cautious tactical ideas promoted by Navarro had no place in modern Spanish military thinking. Equating a defensive posture with weakness and defeat, they strongly supported Burguete's proposals. An official report on Burguete's work took a more moderate position, stressing the degree to which it radically modified the fundamentals of the current tactical program. It quoted from an earlier critique of the proposal by the Marquis of Mendigorría. Although the report praised Burguete's work and his "powerful intelligence and high professional culture," the author also rather conservatively warned against implementing such sweeping reforms without further study.[80] Another evaluation repeated the same general sentiments, noting the controversy that surrounded the work but concluding that Burguete nevertheless deserved official recognition and promotion on the basis of his proposed tactical program.[81]

Quite clearly, then, the attack Burguete launched shortly after 1898 on the established tenets of Spanish military thinking proved no serious detriment to his professional advancement. Although he would complain loudly about the "Europeanizing" tendencies he sensed in the army as the century progressed, he himself had played a considerable role in introducing Spain to the increasingly popular belief in the inherent superiority of offensive doctrine in war that was arising from the other side of the Pyrenees. And, like many of his colleagues elsewhere in Europe, he based much of his thinking on strategy and tactics on a broader antirationalist and "spiritual" philosophical outlook.

* * *

Burguete's lifelong belief in the inherent superiority of moral forces over their material counterparts did not, however, prevent him from drawing on the latest "scientific" theories when convenient. Like so many of his contemporaries elsewhere in Europe, he paradoxically employed the social sciences in his attacks on "progress" and reason. In France leading writers such as Henri Bergson had also invoked the name of science in their antirationalist tracts, making use of Italian political sociology's theory of elites and other trends in the field of social research. According to the intellectual historian Zeev Sternhell, this use of "rational explanation of the irrational" actually helped weaken democracy and foster the rise of fascism.[82] Yet regardless of whether these attacks on reason grounded in the realms of psychology, biology, and anthropology actually constituted a "fascist"—or even "protofascist"—threat to democratic ideals, it is undeniable that they had become fairly popular in Europe by the turn of the century. And Burguete's writings on war revealed that he strongly promoted similar thinking even when writing specifically about his profession.

Burguete was especially interested in theories of collective psychology, and he made references to the works of French and Italian specialists such as Gustave Le Bon, Pascal Rossi, Gabriel Tarde, and Scipio Sighele. He came to believe that the subject merited further study simply because of the rise of democratic forms of government all over the world, and he even advocated teaching about individual and collective psychology in military academies. After all, he reasoned, such knowledge could be of great utility in war.[83] León Fernández Fernández, a military officer and prolific writer who spent much of his career teaching at the Infantry Academy in Toledo, had also stressed the importance of understanding collective psychology in a 1903 book devoted to the subject.[84] Some military authorities, however, had viewed an interest in such matters suspiciously, apparently because of their political implications. They even used an author's desire to write a book titled *Sociología de las muchedumbres* as evidence against him in the Montjuich trials of the late nineteenth century.[85] But Burguete trod on safer ground by stressing how military leaders could make use of crowd psychology.

Turning again to his very gendered conception of national identity, Burguete based much of his discussion on the premise that crowds were inherently "feminine" in nature. He even went so far as to argue that the gender of Spanish terms for large groups of people reflected "the feminine concept" that each word implied. According to Burguete, the notable exception to the rule was the masculine word for "army"—*el ejército*—which stemmed from its definition as "troops organized, trained, imbued, and commanded by a man who, as a 'caudillo,' was clearly of a 'masculine condition.'" For Burguete the inherently feminine character of crowds explained why the "collective spirit" shared the "predominance of heart over intelligence" with the "feminine spirit." Similarly, he made the Freudian comparison of the vulnerability of crowds to the "hypnotic power" of suggestion with the role played by "amorous suggestion in sexual relations." The "passional instability" of crowds explained their natural inclination toward the inherently feminine sentiment of apathy, although by taking advantage of their "suggestibility" a strong leader could unleash their passion and energy. The crowd *(muchedumbre)* had the "feminine mental predisposition" toward synthesis instead of analysis, responding best to elementary concepts and ideas of "energetic" character. Referring to a passage by Nietzsche, Burguete argued that crowds resembled women because they "respect and admire force and harshness and scorn the kindness that comes from weakness or softness." In his view the ideal military leader also knew how to use the power of imagination when leading troops, and he cited the argument he attributed to the sixteenth-century Spanish philosopher and physician Juan Huarte in his classic *Examen de ingenios* that imagination served as a caudillo's most important quality. The ideal warrior was "a soldier-poet and a poet-soldier," and "artists and warriors, thanks to their imagination, will always better understand and better make themselves understood by women than reflective, reasoning, or calculating men."[86]

Given the rise of mass political campaigning in Spain at the time, the interest of a nationalist like Burguete in the writings of Gustave Le Bon and in the Freudian notion of the "hypnotic" power of suggestion was hardly surprising. As José Álvarez Junco demonstrates in his study of the populist Republican Alejandro Lerroux, the age witnessed the growth of mass rallies in which a great speaker could "seduce" his listeners very much along the lines suggested by Le Bon and Freud, and contemporary newspapers frequently commented on Lerroux's ability to render his audiences "*sugestionado,*" or spellbound.[87] Moreover, the perceived lessons of the Franco-Prussian War and Clausewitz's writings on the "total" character of modern warfare contributed to Burguete's interest in crowd psychology as well, and he explicitly tied the notions of Pascal Rossi on the power of suggestion over crowds to Clausewitz's words on how a successful military leader could make good use of "strong feelings [*animo fuerte*]."[88] Such a reading of Clausewitz was widespread outside of Spain; the author of the 1908 English translation of *On War* pointed to contemporary crowd psychology as proof of the growth of Clausewitzian thinking in Europe.[89]

Burguete not only shared Clausewitz's interest in crowd psychology and mass politics with many of his contemporaries, but he also held ideas on gender relations in general that were similar to those of many leading thinkers in and outside of Spain. Like many of his contemporaries, he equated national strength with masculinity, arguing that feminization hindered the development of strong nationalism. And the influence of such notions extended well beyond his views on the supposedly masculine qualities of military leaders and the feminine characteristics of the masses they led. In *Zorrapastro* he condemned modern male society in general for its "enslavement" by women, at the same time charging that men of his day pursued their mates more through force of habit than through true passion—"practically the same instinct that makes a dog feel a stupid obligation to relieve itself on every spur stone and corner it passes." Schopenhauer, he argued, had been right to state that real pleasure comes only from the satisfaction of "true necessities," but the behavior of men toward women in modern society showed that men no longer understood this.[90] He continued this line of reasoning in his prologue to Carmen Eulate Sanjurjo's book dedicated to shedding light on the role women have played in significant historical events. In the modern world of "progress," he wrote, women no longer "rule the hearts of men," and without "pasión amorosa" there can be no heroism. Suffrage movements represented misguided resistance to the "natural law" that "woman was born to submit herself to man, and the multitude, the crowd, the society, was born to submit to the ruler."[91]

Burguete's notion of "natural law" was also shaped in part by his understanding of biology and anthropology, and he even wrote of the "Spanish cadaver" and the need to "better study the physiological and psychological phenomena of the organism of the army."[92] His tendency to apply the same thinking to countries as to individuals and his portrayal of the nation as a living organism were, of course, very much in fashion both in and outside of Spain in Burguete's day. In 1902 the famous regenerationist writer and "father" of the Generation of '98, Joaquín Costa, had called for an "iron surgeon" to restore Spain's health by cutting out its cancer, a metaphor future dictator Primo de Rivera would use to justify his seizure of power in 1923. Miguel de Unamuno made similar biological analogies, referring to Spain and the other neutral powers of World War I as "eunuchs," which implied that they were incapable of regeneration. And in perhaps the best-known use of a biological metaphor to describe the Spanish condition, the title of José Ortega y Gasset's *España invertebrada* referred to the author's belief that his country lacked a backbone.[93]

The interest of so many Spaniards in biological interpretations of Spain's condition resulted in part from the influence of the nineteenth-century French philosopher and historian Hippolyte Taine. The ideas of Taine, who strongly influenced many writers associated with the Generation of '98, clearly left their mark on many aspects of Burguete's thought as well. Like the Spaniards who began their intellectual soul-searching after their country's defeat at the hands of Cuban rebels and the United States in 1898, Taine had become interested in his country's history and "illness" as a result of the French "disasters" of 1870–71.[94] And Taine's determinist views of the psychological, geographical, and biological forces behind national character and history were echoed in the writing of countless Spaniards, prompting Ortega y Gasset to lament in 1908 that a whole generation of Spanish intellectuals had been "badly educated by Hippolyte Taine."[95]

A large number of Burguete's ideas betrayed at least the indirect influence of Taine, and he explicitly cited the French thinker in several of his books.[96] Burguete argued in his 1913 *Teoría y práctica de la guerra* that Taine's division of the life of an artist into two periods also applied to military leaders. The first period, based on natural, true sentiment and inspiration, would eventually give way to a final stage devoid of inspiration, when the artist fell into a life of "affection and decadence" and relied only on laws and formulas derived from previous experiences. Burguete described the process as a transition from "art" to "science," whereby "calculations and routine come to replace the observations of nature."[97] Michelangelo's early masterpieces therefore corresponded to the feats of the great caudillos, he wrote, whereas the artist's "decadent" works, such as the *Conversion of Saint Paul,* the *Crucifixion of Saint Peter,* and the *Last Judgment,* had their equivalent on the battlefield of Waterloo. His primary purpose lay in arguing that the European art of war had progressed well into its final, decadent state, and he wrote long, technical descriptions of how changes in tactics, firepower, and strategy reflected this.

Burguete based his argument in favor of the "art of war" over "military science," however, more on a mystical vision of war itself than on his technical observations, and he actually shared this mysticism with many European intellectuals and even with his more traditionalist colleagues from within the Spanish army itself. At the turn of the century he had already become convinced that war was a beautiful, mystical, and inevitable manifestation of "the supreme will of nature," as he wrote in *Zorrapastro.* In this work he dismissed the popular antiwar movement—which he would embrace shortly before his death—as driven largely by capitalist interests, and he charged that the "modernist" condemnation of war for its anti-aesthetic nature was simply wrong. After all, he reasoned, "few natural phenomena possess the beauty of war."[98]

Although their conception of *modernismo* may have derived largely from the influential literary figure Rubén Darío's use of the term to describe a growing movement of aesthetic renovation,[99] the Spanish intellectuals of 1898 tended to view it as a rather amorphous concept linked to industrialization, new social theories, and other manifestations of modernity.[100] At a 1902 banquet in honor of Pío Baroja attended by Burguete, Galdós, Valle-Inclan, Maeztu, Azorín, and other well-known writers, a fight erupted between representatives of the younger and older generations when a member of the latter described the event as "a banquet of modernists" and charged that "all modernists are pederasts."[101]

Burguete, himself a member of the younger generation of writers, did not question the premise of aesthetic modernism; he merely criticized the Spanish "modernists" for failing to perceive the beauty inherent to warfare. In typical fashion, his spokesman Zorrapastro attempted to support this point by citing various figures from outside Spain: "Fortunately, Nietzsche and his disciples—with d'Annunzzio [*sic*] at the forefront—exalt force as one of the primary attributes of beauty, and they never tire of stressing the important role of war and warriors in the formation of the Übermensch. Even Tolstoy, in all his inspiration, contrasts absolute peace with war envisioned as a natural and superhuman occurrence of immense beauty. . . . Carlyle, as spiritual father and spiritual saint—if the English genius will pardon me for using this modernist expression—sings praise of war and believes that the superhero can come only from the ranks of warriors." Through Zorrapastro, Burguete himself contributed to the mystical vision of war by employing religious terminology, urging that "we bless war as a fruit of heaven."[102] He made similar references to the religious nature of warfare in his later writings, stressing the value he perceived for Christians and warriors in the qualities of sacrifice and stoicism. In his book about his experiences in the Philippines, for example, he praised the "holy blood of sacrifice" spilled by the Jesuit missionaries working to convert the native inhabitants of the archipelago to Christianity. In the same work Burguete also wrote positively of how the Norse people regarded war as a religion in itself, citing Carlyle's writings on the subject.[103]

Burguete later asserted that, like "the image of Christ, the idea of the moral greatness of sacrifice lies at the bottom of our hearts," and he claimed that only "love and war" had the ability "to purge man of egoism and ruin."[104] As he had revealed in *Zorrapastro,* his dislike of ultramontanism and the Vatican's policies did not prevent him from embracing the mystical qualities he perceived in Christianity, and his writings anticipated many aspects of the reverence the Franco regime would display for Saint Ignatius Loyola and sixteenth-century mysticism in general.[105] Burguete once wrote, "I have felt the intense emotion of the wounded on more than one occasion; the moral voluptuousness that sweetens and surpasses the acuteness of pain. Previously I had felt envy for the heroically wounded, whom I believed superior to me because of the blood he shed. In military campaigns I had the same reverence for hospitals as for temples, and when I was completely alone and infected with gangrene myself, I could not have endured the intensity of the material pain without the joy it also brought me."[106] Although Burguete claimed to believe the Clausewitzian maxim that "war is no more than an instrument of politics," he clearly found it easy to praise war for its own sake as well. Finding redemption and regeneration in the horrors of combat, he thus anticipated the observations the famed German writer Ernst Jünger would make after World War I. In fact, other Spanish officers with relatively modern and progressive views would openly embrace Jünger in the 1920s—the same period in which Burguete came to advocate republicanism—and they translated and published Jünger's works for reading by military officers.[107] Well before World War I, therefore, Burguete had experienced in the former Spanish empire and North Africa the same spiritual, romantic, and irrationalist qualities of warfare that some writers north of the Pyrenees would first perceive after the Great War's outbreak in 1914. "I am a soldier in love with the army and in love with war," Burguete wrote.[108]

Thus the manner in which Burguete professed his love for the aesthetic beauty and regenerative qualities of war fit within a more general philosophical trend throughout Europe that predated the influence of Jünger. In his writings Burguete employed what one historian describes as the "language of war" that developed out of evolutionary naturalism during the last part of the nineteenth century. Even some of militarism's fiercest critics among the European intelligentsia, from Spencer to Tolstoy, tended to share the perception of Burguete and other militarist writers of modern war as a product of intangible forces beyond the control of human reason, and they often portrayed it in mystical terms.[109] The Catholic traditionalist writers of the Spanish military who had little else in common with Burguete, such as Antonio García Pérez and the others I discuss later in this book, shared his notions of the regenerative and spiritual values of war.

* * *

As the twentieth century progressed the vitalist, mystical, and social Darwinist voices within the Spanish army became louder in comparison to the views of the more rational, cautious, and technically oriented officers exemplified by the officer-scientists of the general staff. Zorrapastro's words had ushered the growing reaction against the scientific and technical side of the Spanish military into the twentieth century, and Burguete's later writings further promoted such thinking. Although the armed forces would continue to include highly competent scientists, engineers, and scholars among their ranks, a clear shift would occur in the military's overall intellectual orientation. The growing antirationalism of writers like Burguete clearly influenced the academies, general staff, intellectual societies, libraries, and other traditionally more liberal and rationalist institutions of the Spanish military. In *Zorrapastro* a belief in the superiority of "natural" forces over the power of reason had linked the protagonist's discourses on war and the armed forces to the otherwise disparate topics of his other speeches, and the application of the same thinking to civilian as well as military affairs had revealed that Burguete's generation of officers did not fit the outwardly more apolitical mold of the officer-scientists. Thanks to the prominent positions army officers would play in later Spanish governments, the language of war and antirationalist ideas disseminated through the military community during the first part of the twentieth century would have significant, long-lasting ramifications for society in general, becoming an integral part of Spain's official national self-identity.

Chapter Four

History, Destiny, and National Regeneration

Even if images of war—from guerrilla impetuousness to battlefield aesthetics—figured prominently in Burguete's conceptions of Spanish national identity and regeneration, they by no means overshadowed his broader and more fundamental interest in history and historical destiny. As in the works of nearly all nationalist writers, history figured prominently in Burguete's literary endeavors, from his studies on military affairs to his philosophical essays. His views on history—expressed in a wide variety of forms—formed the principal foundations for his interpretations of Spain and its people. Like so many other Spanish writers of his day, he wrote extensively on history, and he repeatedly emphasized its supposed uses for the present and the clues he believed it revealed about his country's destiny. In particular, he stressed the lessons of history for the Spanish actions in Morocco, although he later found it more difficult than he had imagined to apply these lessons with success. And as a member of the Royal Academy of History he even contributed to some of the major discussions of his day on Spanish historiography, writing an extensive study on several of the most frequently debated issues among scholars of medieval Spain.

Burguete's fascination with history and historiography was hardly unique to a member of the Spanish army. Besides the many officers who wrote books and articles on Spanish history, some even published studies on the writing and philosophy of history.[1] The pages of the more specialized and scholarly military journals of fin-de-siècle Spain, such as *Revista Técnica de Infantería y Caballería,* included frequent references to histories by Francisco Villamartín, José Almirante, and other leading military writers of the previous century. Burguete, moreover, followed a long line of officers admitted to Spain's Royal Academy of History; four officers had actually presided over the organization during the nineteenth century, and more than thirty career military men had become members during the same period and the first three decades of the twentieth century.[2]

The officers' interest in history stemmed to a considerable degree from the widespread debate over the nature of Spanish identity, which itself reflected the country's crisis of political authority and extended well beyond the ranks of the military. In many cases the appraisals of different periods of Spanish history expressed by leading Spanish writers, educators, and politicians easily betrayed their political positions. Burguete's writings on history, however, did not lend themselves to such straightforward assumptions about his politics. His historical writings reveal that although he shared some of the same concerns and ideas as conservative Spaniards, he could also embrace interpretations of history that even self-proclaimed liberals rejected as too radically leftist and anti-Spanish. Above all, he differed significantly from his contemporaries in his reluctance to contribute to the growing myth of Castile as the historical and spiritual heart of Spain. Castile-centered historiography, which represented an important element in the attempts by intellectuals to identify a Spanish national culture, coincided with the emergence of regional nationalist movements in Catalonia and the Basque country.[3] Given the obvious distaste for Catalan nationalism that Burguete revealed in *Zorrapastro,* it is curious that he had relatively little interest in identifying and glorifying the positive aspects of Castile and its history. On a more general level, however, he concurred with the other writers of his day in arguing that modern Spain's difficulties stemmed more from metaphysical and spiritual causes than from any other cause. And, like so many Spaniards from military and civilian circles, he betrayed the strong influence of Ángel Ganivet in his historical perceptions. Just as Burguete's writings on politics and the military revealed many similarities between his interests and ideas and those of Unamuno, Maeztu, and even Baroja, his vision of history and geography betrayed the influence of Ganivet. Paradoxically, Ganivet's popularity among early-twentieth-century conservative thinkers would reach its apex in national Catholic historical discourse of the 1930s—the same period in which Burguete publicly announced his allegiance to the principles of Spanish socialism.[4]

* * *

The spiritual basis of Burguete's vision of history is most evident in his *Dinamismo espiritualista* (Spiritualist dynamism), a rather peculiar book that explored the metaphysical forces behind humanity and nations. He based this work on the premise that the human spirit could be divided into forces of "ideas," "sentiments," and "sensations." He linked these three elements, respectively, to Plato's division of the body into cerebral, pectoral, and abdominal parts, which he in turn related to the "intellectual," "passionate," and "instinctive" types of the Pythagorean man. Employing diagrams to illustrate how the elements corresponded to one another, he argued that the ratio of the forces of intellect, passion, and instinct and the way in which they merged determined human character. A predominance of "abdominal spirit," for example, yielded the "instinctive type" of man.[5] Such analysis anticipated the similar approach employed nearly three decades later by the well-known writer Salvador de Madariaga, who shared the general preoccupation of many Spanish intellectuals of the period with defining the elements of Spain's national psychology.[6]

Burguete drew many of his ideas for this work from Edouard Schuré's *The Great Initiates,* a late-nineteenth-century attempt to trace the spiritual development of humanity and prove that Christ represented the spiritual unification of Rama, Krishna, Hermes, Pythagoras, and Plato.[7] Schuré also attracted the attention of many other contemporaries in the West, including J. F. C. Fuller. In fact, Fuller's first book, an interpretation of the works of the famous occultist Aleister Crowley that bore some resemblance to *Dinamismo* in spirit and tone, also made reference to Schuré.[8] Although Burguete did not make Schuré's argument the primary thesis of his own book, he appeared to have used many of Schuré's philosophical and historical explanations for his own purposes. Like Schuré, he argued that a universality linked concepts that had gone by different names among different peoples, but were essentially alike in nature. Burguete thus equated, for example, the Pythagorean idea of "spiritual substance [*substancia del alma*]" to the "Latin" concept of "*principio animador* [*anima*]."[9] He also renewed his attack on what he vulgarly termed *positivism,* lamenting that the guiding principles of science once associated with Bacon and Descartes had evolved, "on account of rational inquiry, from rationalism to materialism and positivism."[10]

The young Burguete's rejection of positivist science in favor of less tangible concepts of spirituality and religious syncretism, although somewhat odd from today's perspective, actually represented a common inclination on the part of many of his contemporaries. From the German emperor Wilhelm II to the visionary French artist Odilon Redon, before the First World War many Europeans shared Burguete's interest in parascientific studies in psychology, the occult, religion, and geography, sometimes even making selective use of the ideas of Taine, Hartmann, and even Schopenhauer. Along these lines, Schuré's *Great Initiates* made as strong an impression on Redon as on Burguete.[11] It seems, then, that Burguete's flirtation with telepathy, Far Eastern spirituality, and other such matters merely reflected his continuing efforts to explore a wide variety of the kind of ideas then popular in much of the Western world.[12]

The primary aim of Burguete in *Dinamismo espiritualista* was exploring the role of passion, intellect, and instinct in human history. But Burguete did not limit his discussion to the great historical figures, such as Hernán Cortés, whom he believed had embodied the ideal combination of the three primary forces. Instead he applied the same thinking to Spain as a whole, portraying its historical development as a reflection of the struggle for dominance among the three elements basic to human character. For him the greatness of medieval Spain thus stemmed from the role "sentiment" had played in shaping the national spirit, a belief he never abandoned. Even though he avoided explicit references to Pythagorean categories and diagrams of spiritual interplay in his later writings, the same basic emphasis on individual and national spirit that he had first revealed in *Zorrapastro* and developed to seemingly absurd lengths in *Dinamismo espiritualista* continued to underlie his ideas on history throughout his life.

The medieval union of Aragon and Catalonia served as the starting point for Burguete's discussion of the spiritual and metaphysical forces propelling Spanish history. According to Burguete, the Catalan principality, playing the "masculine" role, had joined with the "feminine" House of Aragon to produce offspring that reflected an ideal combination of vigor, exalted spirituality, and "cerebral culture."[13] As in *Zorrapastro,* Burguete referred to the legend of how the people of Aragon tricked their king into making love to his wife, whom he had married only for her inheritance, thereby producing a legitimate heir: the great King James the Conqueror. By taking such action, he argued, the Aragonese had forged their own will with that of their king, uniting the powerful religious sentiments that had propelled the reconquest of Catalonia and Aragon. The resulting mixture had represented the perfect combination of intellectual, instinctive, and passionate spirits.

The greatest human embodiment of the merging of these forces, Burguete believed, was the acclaimed Majorcan writer, mystic, scientist, and Christian philosopher Ramon Llull, a representative of the "spiritualist dynamism" inherent to his age. That Llull, who was and remains popular among theosophists, appealed to someone with Burguete's interest in history, mysticism, and the occult is not surprising. Drawing heavily upon Menéndez y Pelayo's hagiographic portrait, Burguete described Llull as the "knight-errant of deep thought" and the "origin and solidifier of that virile, exalted, and chivalrous Spain of immense Christian capacity, whose sparkle will forever shine." Differing markedly from the many military officers who lavished praise on Cervantes and his portrayal of Don Quixote, Burguete instead turned to Llull as the spiritual embodiment of what he saw as the true Quixote. Llull, who had argued that the Jews and Muslims could be converted by reason, was in certain respects an unusual man for a Spanish military officer to glorify. After all, as a founder of literary Catalan he was easily one of the most important intellectual figures in the history of Catalonia, and most of Burguete's colleagues had few positive things to say about the peripheral, non-Castilian areas of Spain. But Burguete contrasted Llull's faith, optimism, and vigor to the "disheartened pessimism of Spain" as revealed by Cervantes centuries later in his classic story of the pathetic knight-errant.[14] Here Burguete echoed the sentiments of the young Maeztu, who interpreted Cervantes's classic work as an apology for Spanish decadence that was unfit to serve as the spiritual guide for the many Spanish intellectuals who had adopted it as such.[15] In a sense Burguete's vision of the ideal Quixote—quite different from that of Cervantes and representative of the same medieval aristocratic values Zorrapastro had said would someday regenerate Spain—corresponded to the vision of the "third sally of Don Quixote" that Pedro Laín Entralgo claims was one of the most important myths created by the Generation of '98.[16]

In his portrayal of a strong and thriving Aragon, Burguete described the medieval kingdom as an "organism in which life flowed from inland to the coasts: from the heart to the outer surface. As in physiology, the blood received nutrition and life from its contact with the surface. It then would return in a richer and more vigorous state to the center, thereby replenishing the beating heart."[17] The first stage in the decline of Spain from the apex of the medieval period, Burguete wrote, was initiated by the "historical accident" of the union of Ferdinand's Aragon with Isabel's Castile in 1469. In marked contrast to his many contemporaries who glorified Castile and the marriage of the "Catholic Kings," he seemed truly to lament the creation of modern Spain. Describing the marriage as the "union of the two usurpers," he sardonically observed that "heaven was so pleased with their actions that they bore a mad daughter as their heiress." He strongly criticized Rome, charging that the papacy blessed "their crime of usurpation" just because it fit well with the Vatican's aspirations for strengthening Catholic centralism.[18] His negative appraisal of Ferdinand and Isabel coincided to a certain degree with that of Antonio Cánovas del Castillo, the architect of Restoration Spain whose politics and history writing Burguete criticized on other occasions. But whereas Cánovas identified the primary fault of the Catholic monarchs as their inability to unify Spain in a completely political and legal sense,[19] Burguete raised doubts about the actual desirability of a Castile-based centralization in the first place.

When Aragon had merged with Catalonia, Burguete wrote, the resulting "cerebral, passional, and bodily wills had formed a single harmony within the people, and its meaning in life thus faced a single direction: to the east."[20] But the union with Castile centuries later had forced Aragon to look to the west, thereby disturbing this harmony. And in turning its gaze westward, Burguete asserted, Aragon had thus resigned itself to decline. Burguete therefore chose not to adopt the argument embraced by many Spanish nationalist historians that the dominance Castile had historically enjoyed over the rest of the continent stemmed from its Atlantic orientation, which had brought more benefits than the Mediterranean expansion of the Aragonese-Catalan confederation. In fact, his praise for the confederation's "eastern" outlook seemed a clear reaction against the dominant historiographical trend. And his lament over Aragon's decline seemed to betray the long tradition of Aragonese regenerationism, which culminated in Costa, more than any of the Castile-centered ideas associated with the Generation of '98. Of course, he may have also been influenced by his own Aragonese origins.

In any case, Burguete was hardly alone in believing that after the Reconquest Spain's most vital forces had abandoned the heart of the peninsula in favor of expanding and cultivating the Spanish periphery and overseas empire. Like so many of his countrymen,[21] he viewed the growth of Spanish America with ambivalence, praising the conquistadors yet lamenting that their departure had left mainland Spain without the spiritual strength so characteristic of its medieval period. He also regretted that the emigration to the colonies had facilitated the replacement of the true Spanish religion as "formed by our spirit in the secular crusade of the Reconquest"[22] with doctrines dictated by Rome, a sentiment he reiterated in many of his works. Quite unlike Spain's traditionalist military and civilian writers, he often had trouble bringing himself to praise the institution of Roman Catholicism or its popes.

When the Bourbons took power at the advent of the eighteenth century, Burguete wrote, the condition of Spain only worsened. Not surprisingly in light of the influence of Marcelino Menéndez y Pelayo and the strong distaste for the "encyclopedists" that he had revealed in *Zorrapastro,* Burguete filled many of his later works with attacks on the age of the Bourbons and the Enlightenment. He strongly criticized the invasion of French intellectualism (a "*cerebralidad potente*"), which he said had penetrated Spain just as the country was struggling to come to terms with the "open and frank sensuality of the new era." Returning to metaphors of the Platonic division of the body, he described how after 1700 "cerebral" and "abdominal" spirits came to dominate in Spain. The role of the heart, or sentimentality, thus fell even more from the position of dominance it had held in the Middle Ages.[23] Moreover, with the focus of the eighteenth-century reformers centered squarely on the problems of the peninsula, the descendants of the conquistadors sensed that mainland Spain had abandoned them and began to entertain thoughts of independence. Reiterating a common argument, he thus placed much of the blame for the fall of the Spanish empire on the liberal policies of Spain's eighteenth-century rulers.[24]

In Burguete's view the opposing "instinctive" and "intellectual" spirits of the Bourbon era also harmed Spain by waging intense battles with one another to the detriment of the *patria.* Assuming the form of "clericals" and "anticlericals," he wrote, these conflicting spirits succeeded in weakening the forces of national sentiment without achieving a clear victory for either side.[25] His criticism of both sides of the controversy over the role of the church in Spanish society undoubtedly stemmed to a considerable degree from his objection to the political realm in which the fighting took place. Sharing the same disdain for "politics" characteristic of his many colleagues who had grown disenchanted with the Restoration, he wanted Spaniards to transcend such matters and strive collectively to achieve his vaguely defined vision of spiritual greatness.

According to Burguete, the profound imbalance in spiritual forces that had arisen from the union of Castile and Aragon had led to the rise of mysticism as a natural channel for the vital sentimental spirits that the union otherwise repressed. The often mystical form of modern anarchism (*mística ácrata*), he wrote, was merely a newer version of the Catholic mysticism of the sixteenth and seventeenth centuries.[26] He did not, however, devote so much attention to metaphysics in his analysis of more recent Spanish history. In contrast to the complete rejection of "progress" expressed in *Zorrapastro*, his later works revealed that he eventually came to terms with many aspects of the modern age. Once history had propelled humanity down the path of capitalism, industrialization, and mass politics, he came to believe, Spain had no choice but to learn to dominate the world by more modern methods. He continued to argue that Spain's salvation lay in its irrational and "sentimental" instincts, but he favored adapting these instincts to the current situation.

The notion that struggle inevitably yielded "moral vigor" remained a basic tenet of Burguete's thinking, and he continued to sprinkle many of his books with citations from Nietzsche, Spencer, Clausewitz, Carlyle, Taine, and others to support this view. But as the years passed his writing began to focus as much on *economic* warfare as on its other forms, a tendency that Maeztu had also revealed in his early writings. His reading of the works of Adam Smith, Malthus, Mahan, and even Theodore Roosevelt served to bolster his argument that although the gigantic and powerful states of the modern era did not wage religious wars in the manner of their counterparts of the past, the same "general laws of nature" still dictated their behavior. Hence states had to expand in order to satisfy the growing needs and desires of their peoples, and such expansion required the use of force. He considered the electoral success of Roosevelt and his imperialist platform a consequence of the "centripetal force" of massive industrial and commercial development within the United States, and he harshly criticized the noblemen of his own day for hesitating to serve in modern armies charged with defending mercantile interests.[27] Just as spirit had once served to further religious expansion, it was now a vital part of economic strength and growth. According to Burguete, "The moral vigor of a nation's people stems from economic struggle in the same manner as from armed struggle. In either case, it is necessary to invigorate the spirits before taking arms."[28] In the immediate aftermath of the Russo-Japanese War Burguete even attributed the Japanese victory in large part to the supposed emphasis of the country's leaders on economic rather than racial or religious objectives, going so far as to forecast the demise of pan-Germanism, pan-Slavism, and "Latinismo" as significant factors in international relations, describing them as mere "concepts of past aspirations with no link to reality."[29]

Burguete's praise of economic expansion and industrialism was, on the surface at least, at odds with the antimaterialist views he expressed so frequently elsewhere. On this matter he coincided less with Ganivet than with the young Maeztu, who expressed a strong faith in economic developments as the key to national regeneration, but also espoused radical Nietzschean precepts. The works of Maeztu and Burguete revealed a paradox in their promotion of capitalist growth but their criticism of both materialism and the effect of modern industry on the condition of the masses.[30]

But Burguete did not so much embrace capitalism as recognize the importance of the economic arena in which modern warfare now took place. He thus attacked tariffs as aggressive manifestations of a defensive posture detrimental to the national spirit, equating the adoption of protective trade policies to the behavior of dying organisms. After all, he reasoned, a nation had to fight to acquire and grow stronger, and tariffs produced more sloth than employment.[31] Expressing a classical liberal, laissez-faire viewpoint quite unlike the Catholic-corporatist mind-set of many of his fellow officers, he even charged that his country's protectionist stance had facilitated its military defeat of 1898. Spain's high trade barriers, he wrote, had contributed to the country's diplomatic isolation at the very moment when it most needed allies. Moreover, such a long-lasting tariff inevitably had profound effects on a nation, as it induced moral complacency and weakened the nation's healthy ability to fight. The specific aim of his criticism was the Spanish tariff of 1891, which he attributed to the influence exercised by the metallurgical industry of Vizcaya and the Barcelona-based associations for the protection of national industry.[32] Like many aspects of his thought, this disapproval of economic protectionism resembled the view of J. F. C. Fuller.[33]

* * *

Much like Mussolini years later, Burguete was especially impressed with countries in which the imperialist spirit transcended class lines, citing an article by his "much-admired friend [*mi admirado amigo*] Ramiro de Maeztu" that described the growing acceptance of colonialist policies by European socialist organizations. The open expression of imperialist sentiments by English workers earned Burguete's strong praise, and he argued that successful colonization in any country now required the support of the proletariat. If religion no longer sufficed to generate imperialist sentiment in workers, he wrote, they needed to be taught to find inspiration in "the desire to make new lives for themselves, with new ideals and new molds."[34] Of course, admiration for English jingoism was quite common among Burguete's contemporaries outside of Spain, and he also shared their tendency to base arguments for social imperialism on the Darwinist thinking that had been fostered by the writings of Spencer and popularized by such prominent figures as Roosevelt.[35] Moreover, the lack of popular support for Spain's imperialist ventures—typical of what one historian of Spanish Morocco characterizes as "second rate imperialism"[36]—reflected the more fundamental weakness of modern Spanish nationalism in general.

In addition to fostering social imperialism, Burguete wrote, Spain's government leaders had two crucial imperatives: exploiting the benefits of the Mediterranean's strategic and economic importance for other countries and expanding Spanish territory in northern Africa. The first task, he rather optimistically concluded, simply required Spanish leaders to demonstrate to their foreign counterparts the many advantages he believed Spain offered as a potential military ally. He argued that the same geographical attributes that made a neutral stance unthinkable for Spain also thrust the country into a position of potential global dominance. Tracing the role Iberia's Mediterranean and Atlantic coasts had played in the rise and fall of many of the great powers of world history, he described Spain as a "bastion which flanks all the great maritime routes linking Europe with the four major parts of the globe."[37] Burguete cited the lessons of the Russo-Japanese War and the writings of Mahan, Melville, and others on sea power, and he even advocated an alliance with England as the most practical way for Spain to achieve and maintain ideal commercial and military health.[38] He conveniently avoided discussing the many obstacles that stood in the way of any such alliance. But his reflections on history led him to discuss Spanish expansion in northern Africa, which he believed would help transform Spain into a more attractive military and commercial ally. Not surprisingly, beneath his wish to see Spain extend its reach into Africa lay less tangible motives as well. Largely adopting Ganivet's belief that the forces behind Castile's "natural tendency" to continue its historic struggle against Islam had been misdirected toward America, he betrayed the strong influence of *Idearium español* on virtually all aspects of his views on Morocco.[39]

On a more practical level, Burguete drew lessons from his understanding of the history of the French actions in Algeria and Morocco, assessing France's behavior as a colonial power considerably more critically than had many other Spanish officers. According to Burguete, the French conquest of Algeria had suffered profoundly from indifferent public opinion, faltering government policies, and the greed of the many businessmen who saw North Africa as nothing more than an opportunity to make money. He was especially critical of the latter, writing sardonically of the "infinite number of companies and firms founded to swindle the Moors, Jews, and Christians on an equal basis" in Algeria. Thanks to their efforts, the original and "romantic" idea of creating a protectorate "to bring the Moors the benefits of civilization and progress as compatible with their beliefs," which he associated with the supposedly more altruistic mind-set behind preindustrial European imperialism, had soon fallen by the wayside. Instead the French "had overthrown the power, tyranny, and depredation of the Turks just to replace them with other forms of depredation and tyranny." The Moors may have been a "covetous" people, he wrote, but this very characteristic probably explained their praiseworthy "attachment to independence and exalted individualism, which the Europeans have only stimulated further through their own covetous stupidity."[40] It seems clear, then, that even though Burguete may have come to accept mercantile interests and means as legitimate points of focus for the national governments of his day, "moral" and spiritual elements still underlay much of his weltanschauung. Of course, the views on imperialism of both Maeztu and Burguete also reflected the ostensible contradiction—discussed earlier—in their promotion of commercial expansion but antimaterialist outlooks.

Stressing the similarities he perceived between the early Algerian campaign and the current military situation in the Moroccan Rif, Burguete went into considerable detail in his analysis of the actions of the French general Pierre Berthezène in the Maghreb during the early 1830s. Berthezène's "disastrous operations" might have been avoided had he first studied the history of the Reconquest, Burguete suggested.[41] Arguing that El Cid's political feats deserved more praise than his actions as a *campeador,* he described the Reconquest as a long-lasting "war of peaceful repenetration [*guerra de repenetración pacífica*]" rather than a "war of extermination." He even attributed much of the success of the Christian forces to what he claimed was their policy of fostering the sympathy of the "more humble" elements of society, and he strongly criticized the French and Spanish governments of his day for ignoring the common people of Morocco and dealing almost exclusively with the few individuals whom they mistakenly believed to have power.[42]

Above all, Burguete's understanding of history compelled him to attack military plans that ignored the political, social, and cultural aspects of the enemy and occupied peoples, and he often expressed the Clausewitzian view of war as an extension of politics. Yet even if he was right to fault analyses of the Moroccan situation based solely on military factors, it soon became clear that neither he nor most of his colleagues were themselves particularly well qualified to offer appraisals of Morocco or its inhabitants. In fact, in some ways Burguete belonged in the same category as his many European contemporaries who simplistically perceived Morocco as little more than "a region without the supposed benefits of centralised government, an anarchic region without any strong political unity."[43] Burguete's arguments for a largely political and peaceful conquest of Morocco, which he supported with numerous references to the supposedly pacific nature of the *reconquista,* actually suggested the policy of "political penetration" adopted by the Spaniards after the Franco-Spanish protectorate had been imposed on Morocco in 1912. Of course, domestic political concerns were largely responsible for these policies; government leaders wanted to minimize public expenditures and outcry over the loss of Spanish lives in northern Africa.[44] In the end, however, Spain's endeavors proved a dismal failure, as the more than 10,000 Spanish deaths near the Moroccan village of Anual would make painfully clear in 1921.

But Burguete was not all wrong. In fact, to a certain degree the opinions on Morocco that he had expressed earlier—most extensively in his 1913 work *Teoría y práctica de la guerra*—proved reasonable, and after Anual he had the confidence to charge that a failure to heed his advice had helped make the debacle possible. He had advocated carrying out Spain's "civilizing mission" slowly and peacefully whenever possible, but he also believed in conducting "annihilating raids" if necessary "to teach a lesson" to any Moroccans who reacted violently to the overtures of the Spanish forces.[45] In general he had advocated "strategic occupation," which he characterized as offensive in nature, over defensive, tactical methods aiming only at establishing and holding points of fortification without removing the threat of further enemy actions.[46]

In typical fashion, however, Burguete did not limit his discussion of history's didactic potential to his perception of nineteenth-century Algeria's lessons for the Spanish protectorate. He also returned repeatedly to his perception of expansion into North Africa as an integral part of Spain's historical destiny, drawing from Ganivet and citing figures as disparate as Unamuno and the French socialist Jean Jaurès to criticize the dominant contemporary methods of conducting colonial ventures. He praised government officials in Paris for having sent Hubert Lyautey to North Africa in 1903 and then granting him so much more independence than his predecessors, stressing that even such a talented man could not succeed if he had to operate under restraints from the central government. And he reiterated his criticism of the French government for its impatience and its incomprehension of the situation in Morocco, even citing the charges made by Anatole France against the aims and means of French colonial policy in an article that had appeared in *Le Temps*. The French, Burguete repeatedly stressed, needed to pay more attention to the masses of North Africa and cease to overvalue their relations with Kaids and Sultans.[47] Here he again revealed his strong belief that ordinary people determine national character, a view that greatly influenced his notions of history.

History demonstrated that the interests of the North African peoples as a whole should underlie Spanish as well as French policies, Burguete wrote, and he noted that Jaurès had raised valid questions about the true intention of French colonization in a debate with French Foreign Minister Théofile Delcassé. According to Burguete, the socialist leader had rightly questioned how striking deals with the "dangerous and pernicious" sultan would help advance France's "humanitarian and civilizing endeavors" in Africa. Burguete compared the words of Jaurès to those of Spanish regenerationist Joaquín Costa in a well-known discourse delivered in late March 1884 at the Alhambra Theater in Madrid.[48] Costa had joined other leading figures in speaking at a public celebration organized in support of Spain's "historic rights" in northern Africa, an event that had revealed that the new imperialist sentiments growing elsewhere in Europe also had their Spanish counterparts.[49]

Burguete wrote of the "historic, geographic, and ethnic determinism" behind Spain's colonial aspirations with regard to Morocco, even suggesting that Spaniards had a "moral duty [*deberes de conciencia*]" to return and unite with the same people they had expelled from Iberia centuries earlier. After all, he reasoned, the Moors had brought a great civilization to medieval Spain, so it was only fitting that the favor be returned and that a "new Spain" rise in northern Africa to serve as "our brother."[50] He advocated joining together "the very hands which, because of historical fate, have remained separated by the straits for so many centuries," and he presented an idealized vision of a future world in which Spaniards and Moroccans would "return to fraternize with the same sentence consecrated so many times during the truces of the Reconquest and today used as a habitual greeting between Moors: *Es-Selam Alicum!* (May peace be with you!)"[51]

Burguete even suggested that Philip III had been wrong to expel the Moriscos in 1609, arguing that over time their descendants would have learned to embrace Christianity and eventually undergone "*españolización completa.*" During the Reconquest itself "archbishops, politicians, and leading intellectuals considered bringing Christian and Muslim religious ethics together into an ideal metaphysical union, which would have facilitated the fusion and amalgamation of the peoples." Only because of impatience—the same characteristic he blamed for more recent colonial debacles in Morocco—was this idea discarded during the final years of the Reconquest. But now Spaniards had to take advantage of the historical forces that propelled them southward, he wrote, for "anyone who feels exclusively European and fails to grasp that there's a wider line of division running through the Pyrenees than the straits of Gibraltar, or—as the much-admired teacher Unamuno puts it—does not feel proudly African, cannot get a feel for the political situation of Morocco or infuse it with ideality or spiritual exaltation."[52]

Burguete thus made his position clear in the ongoing debate over whether Spain's roots lay primarily in Europe or in Africa. The debate, which was especially vigorous during this period, influenced attempts to define Spanish national identity as well as the related search for regenerationist remedies. Burguete's fundamental distaste for rationalism, moreover, undoubtedly strengthened his enthusiasm for the "African" strains of Spanish identity even further. In fact, he acted in much the same fashion as European Romantics who had earlier turned to exotic cultures as they rejected western, scientific reason and materialism. Often renouncing the liberal establishment's faith in positivism and progress, they sought an "Orientalist" path to regeneration. As Edward W. Said has observed, the likes of Friedrich Schlegel and Novalis "urged upon their countrymen, and upon Europeans in general, a detailed study of India because, they said, it was Indian culture and religion that could defeat the materialism and mechanism (and republicanism) of Occidental culture."[53] Without question, behind at least some of Burguete's "Africanism" lay similar motives.

Several years after writing so prolifically on Spain's supposed historical destiny in northern Africa, Burguete managed to become a major player in his country's political and military activities in the region. As I will show, the record of his activities there offers an excellent opportunity to examine to what degree his actions actually reflected the ideas he had expressed earlier. Beginning in 1919, he sided with the juntas formed by junior officers stationed on the peninsula who feared that their corporate interests were threatened by the ability of officers serving in the Moroccan protectorate, the so-called africanistas, to earn promotions at an extremely rapid rate through combat merits.[54] This conflict within the army eventually played a significant role in weakening Spain's parliamentary government and paving the way for the military dictatorship of Primo de Rivera, and by pitting Burguete against other well-known military figures such as Franco and Millán-Astray it fostered the professional rivalries that clearly influenced the decisions of officers years later to support or oppose the military rebellion that sparked the Civil War.[55]

Burguete's participation in the political battles over the protectorate only increased after Spain's horrible defeat at Anual, when he joined another leading military figure, future dictator Miguel Primo de Rivera, in a well-publicized attack on Spain's high commissioner and commander in chief in Africa, General Dámaso Berenguer.[56] Burguete made ample use of the press and his position as a major contributor to the official inquiry into Anual, the so-called Picasso Report, to undermine Berenguer, whom he accused of having facilitated the "disaster" in part because of his basic preference for science over valor. In January 1922 Burguete requested, in the name of the juntas, that the Liberal politician Santiago Alba form a new government. The following July Alba, now foreign minister, repaid Burguete by nominating him to replace Berenguer as high commissioner. Therefore, after a considerable amount of the same kind of political maneuvering he had condemned so forcefully as a young officer, Burguete had attained Spain's top position in Africa.[57] As he discovered after assuming power, however, successfully pursuing in Africa the policies he had advocated in his writings was not so easy.

Initially the appointment of Burguete was received fairly positively in Madrid and by his colleagues in Morocco, and he quickly—and very publicly—recruited some very able assistants for the tasks that lay ahead. One, José Riquelme y López Bago, was a knowledgeable, Arabic-speaking infantry officer who had supervised some of Spain's educational programs for Moroccan children earlier in the century and had promoted various other methods of taking the "cultural approach" to colonization as well.[58] Having risen to the rank of colonel and earned the respect of Moroccan insurgent leaders as well as his own Spanish colleagues, Riquelme had previously been relieved of his Moroccan post for criticizing his superiors.[59] In another well-publicized move, Burguete enlisted the assistance of Juan Zugasti, a former Spanish minister at Tangier who had also held various other posts in Spanish Morocco. According to the U.S. military attaché in Spain, who was normally a fairly astute observer of Spanish military affairs, Zugasti had much praise for Burguete, which was duly reported by the Spanish press. The attaché described Zugasti as "regarded in Spain as especially well qualified" and as a man of "clear intelligence and of education" with a good knowledge of Moroccan dialects, culture, and "psychology." Initially, then, Burguete appears to have approached his strategic objectives in Morocco with what was by most accounts a practical combination of intelligent administrative decisions and the media savvy that is so often critical to military operations in the modern world, especially in foreign campaigns that face growing public opposition at home. In fact, the U.S. military attaché wryly noted that Burguete's initial promise to cooperate fully with the press was an indication that he had "learned one lesson at least from the fall of General Berenguer."[60]

At the same time, Burguete made it clear that his own powerful vision of Hispano-Arabic history would provide the cultural background to his more tangible military decisions. When he arrived in Tetuan on July 21 he reviewed the garrison and was then formally received by the zone's *jalifa,* or native Morrocan administrator. Then he delivered a speech with what the U. S. attaché called a "rather curious passage, " in the process betraying once again the high degree to which the popular regenerationist myth of Arab Spain colored his thinking. "I trust in your wisdom and in the intermixture of blood of these two peoples on the two sides of the straits," he stated to the *jalifa,* proclaiming that the Spaniards and Moroccans were both "originating from the same race and united by geographical and historical bonds to work together for the development of human progress."[61]

On a more concrete level, in the Jibala region to the west Burguete followed government instructions and his own arguments of years earlier by favoring political over military means to bring sharif Ahmed el Raisuni under control. Although Burguete's willingness to negotiate with native authorities and his policies of shared civil administration angered many Spanish military commentators, attacks on the Spanish positions in the Jibala declined markedly.[62] At the same time he took pains to make it known that he was working to return all draftees to the Iberian Peninsula as soon as possible, a move clearly meant to please the government in Madrid and the public in general.[63] In the Rif area to the east, however, Burguete's efforts to deal with the main force behind the Spanish "disaster" at Anual, Abd-el-Krim, met much stronger resistance than had opposed him in the Jibala. He began by proclaiming that Spain intended to restore order and rule through a native governor, but again echoed his writings of years earlier by warning that failure of such a "political" approach would lead to the use of force. Abd-el-Krim refused to accept any of Burguete's proposals, however, and the Spanish army's efforts to reoccupy the territory lost during the Anual debacle produced enough casualties to raise the ire of the Madrid government. In November the Spanish forces halted their advance and blockaded the Rif, because the strong military resistance from the Rifis left Burguete with no alternative but to cease the offensive and pursue a political approach. His efforts to foster discord among Moroccans in the area had only limited success, but he secured the release of the Spanish prisoners taken during the summer of 1921 by paying Abd-el-Krim a ransom of just over 4 million pesetas.[64]

In February 1923 Burguete was replaced by Luis Silvela, the first civilian high commissioner of the protectorate, and sent on an inspection tour of Poland, thus ending his tenure as leader of the Spanish forces in Morocco with far-from-ideal results.[65] As he had learned, the ostensibly clear lessons of history did not always facilitate immediate victory. Nevertheless, overall his stint as high commissioner cannot be judged a failure, and his active involvement in the Moroccan question had certainly brought him benefits. Under the dictatorship of Primo de Rivera, whom he had joined in attacking Berenguer so vociferously, he was appointed head of the Civil Guard, and in October 1927 he joined the king, queen, dictator, and leading military figures in a triumphant tour of the protectorate to mark the official end of the Rif rebellion.[66]

* * *

Despite Burguete's difficulties in putting historical knowledge to practical use, it is unlikely that his basic belief in Spain's "natural" destiny in Africa and the "African" qualities of Spaniards ever changed. Even in his 1915 work *Rectificaciones históricas,* a surprisingly well-thought-out and lucid discussion of several of the leading historiographical debates of his day, he had praised the spiritual consequences of the "racial fusion" fostered by the Reconquest. During the Middle Ages, he wrote, even kings and vassals never denied their mixed blood. In fact, he continued, the ethnic purity of other European peoples had actually contributed to their degeneration, since "improving the species" has always entailed "*renovación.*" On this matter his view contrasted sharply with the popular belief in fin-de-siècle Europe that a *lack* of racial purity contributed to degeneration. He referred to Ganivet's description of the "exalted fusion of mystic sensuality, or sensual mysticism," that characterized the Reconquest, and he cited the famous literary figure's assertion that the epoch gave birth to Spain's particularly "harsh and ascetic" form of religion: "*el senequismo cristiano.*" Burguete also wrote of "the Berber blood proudly circulating through our veins, which lent new life to the Iberian blood of our Celtiberian lineage." The blood of the Berbers had been "fortified by the African desert sun and invigorated in the heights of the Atlas Mountains," and it could therefore counteract the effects of the invasion of the barbarians, who had "morally and physically perverted Spain."[67] In 1921 José Ortega y Gasset's classic work *España invertebrada* would make essentially the same argument about the negative effects of the barbarian migrations on Iberia, portraying the Visigoths, who had settled south of the Pyrenees, as the weakest and most corrupt of all the Germanic peoples.

Interestingly, even with its passages of racial and metaphysical visions of Spanish history, *Rectificaciones históricas* actually fit the basic mold of the leading contemporary Spanish scholarship on medieval history. In fact, the entry on the medieval Asturian king Pelayo in the Espasa-Calpe encyclopedia referred readers interested in further information to Burguete's work, which had earned him membership in the prestigious Royal Academy of History.[68] The primary goal Burguete wished to accomplish through the book was to combat what he perceived as the overly analytical emphasis of contemporary historiography, and it focused on three topics then under the critical scrutiny of many medievalists in Spain: the battles of Guadalete and Covadonga and the first century of the Asturian reconquest. He argued against the contemporary scholarly criticism of many long-established historical beliefs—such as the traditional view that an important battle at Covadonga marked the beginning of the Reconquest—charging that the skeptics relied too heavily on the analysis of documents and "facts" without making good use of other sources or of the creative speculation and "synthetic reconstruction" of historians themselves.[69] And he attacked the inclination he sensed in modern scholarship to discount the extent of Muslim influence on Spanish history by "European or Europeanizing writers" who comprehended neither "*el genio árabe*" nor "*el genio español.*"[70] He also warned of the damage that a "noxious falsification of historical truths" could wreak on the soul of a nation, as it could "erase painful truths or sweeten bitter experiences."[71] In his eyes, for example, to deny the disaster of the Christian defeat at Guadalete was to rob Spain of a valuable lesson that could help prevent similar debacles in the future. Echoing the views of Rafael

Altamira, a famous educational reformer and regenerationist who undoubtedly influenced him at least indirectly, Burguete thus saw Spanish history as neither an uncritical glorification of the country and its people nor a demonstration of its inherent weaknesses. Although he did not share Altamira's unrelenting positivism, he agreed that history had the potential to serve as an important tool in Spain's regeneration, to be used with great caution but also with considerable effect.[72]

Burguete drew attention to two very different types of sources that he believed scholars often neglected: geography and oral accounts of historical events that were passed from generation to generation. His book relied heavily on his own geographical knowledge to reconstruct what he believed were the most probable itineraries of armies and the locations where battles had taken place. Often pointing out the failure of historians to consider "laws of terrain" in their accounts, he described military officers as especially well qualified to make use of geography in the writing of history.[73]

Burguete's criticism fell especially hard on the general history of Spain by the Royal Academy of History, which he faulted for ignoring the lessons of geography and more imaginative types of sources. The academy had published the relevant volume of its general history of Spain under the coordination of none other than Antonio Cánovas del Castillo—better known as the architect of Restoration Spain.[74] Burguete faulted the authors for relying too heavily on the works of the Spanish historian Eduardo Saavedra and the renowned Dutch Arabist Reinhardt Dozy, both of whom he praised, but at the same time faulted for placing too much emphasis on documentary evidence. In Burguete's mind the authors had been "lamentably influenced by the zeal of the Restoration, which introduced new political, economic, and historical values that were as flimsy as they were novel. And when these values were used in the attempt to create a new Spain, they yielded nothing more than an unstable renovation weakened by time and events."[75] Clearly implicit in Burguete's critique of the "scientific" reliance on documents of Cánovas and Dozy was a more fundamental disagreement with the latter's best-known scholarly argument: his debunking of the myth of El Cid as a glorious "nationalist" hero of medieval Spain. Like Ortega y Gasset, Burguete espoused a historical outlook that was strongly influenced by nationalist sentiment, conceding an important role in national regeneration to myth, but at the same time warning against ignoring the valuable lessons found in "the defects of our past."[76]

In spite of his criticism of Cánovas's scholarly as well as political accomplishments, however, Burguete saw hope in what he perceived as a growing reaction against the preponderance of overly analytical and detailed monographs. Now, he wrote, scholars were returning their attention to general trends in world history and making better use of "sources of oral tradition."[77] As Burguete was undoubtedly aware, Menéndez y Pelayo's student Ramón Menéndez Pidal was forcefully defending the validity of oral tradition as well as the traditional positive portrait of El Cid.[78]

Burguete's emphasis on the usefulness of oral folklore and chronicles for historians stemmed from his belief that the true history of a nation was to be found in its common people, a view he had already suggested in his arguments for aiming Spanish colonial policies more at the Moroccan majority than at the political leaders of North Africa. Of course, he held in common with many writers associated with the Institución Libre de Enseñanza and the Generation of '98 the conviction that ordinary men and women had determined Spain's historical character and fate, and a similar attachment to folklore had characterized many of the other nationalist movements that arose in nineteenth-century Europe. Unamuno's concept of "intrahistory," for instance, seems to have influenced Burguete's perceptions of Spanish history and its sources. Unamuno had described as superficial and without deep significance most historical events as recorded in such sources as newspapers, books, and official registers. Instead Unamuno focused on the "silent lives of the millions of people without history." For in them, he wrote, was to be found "the essence of progress and true, eternal tradition, not the deceitful tradition found buried in books, documents, monuments, and stones."[79] Burguete may have been influenced as well by Altamira's emphasis on the nonpolitical, "internal" history of Spain, which in some ways resembled Unamuno's historical vision. In calling for "*historia interna*" Altamira had advocated the writing of social and cultural history rather than the political and military—or "external"—history that most scholars pursued.[80]

Such a view of history, in fact, gained considerable ground in Spain during the first few decades of the twentieth century. The entry under "History" in the Espasa-Calpe encyclopedia, for example, echoed Burguete by paradoxically emphasizing the significance of "great men" who lead the masses—like the Nietzschean "*hombre inhábil*" of *Zorrapastro*—while at the same time stressing that "human history comprises the totality of what can be learned about Humanity's past" and that social groups in the form of "nations, races, institutions, and communities" play more important roles as historical agents than do individuals. But the encyclopedia lent considerably more credence than Burguete to documentary evidence, and it failed to duplicate his dismay at the current "widely shared opinion that the true history of a period, country, institution, etc., should be written on the basis of specialized monographs."[81] In fact, despite Burguete's belief in the value of "scientific" geographical study to historians, in general he swam against the strong historiographical current in Spain during the second half of the nineteenth century. For not only did he temper his praise of Castile, but he also resisted the movement that had emerged when, as Inman Fox writes, eighteenth-century "rationalism joined with positivism, leading to the exhumation of documents and an insistence on objectivity."[82]

* * *

Admittedly the ramifications of Burguete's perceptions of Spanish history on subsequent developments in Spain are difficult to identify with any sort of precision; many similarities but few explicit links tie his writings to the ideologies of Primo de Rivera's Unión Patriótica or the Nationalist "crusade." Although the cultural ideas and policies of the two dictatorships may have echoed aspects of his thought, Burguete clearly differed from the ideologues of the Primo de Rivera and Franco regimes most fundamentally in his far-from-glorious view of Castile and the union of Ferdinand and Isabel.

More important, however, was the way Burguete used history in the service of nationalist myth, which in turn formed a crucial part of the ideological foundation for his actions as a powerful military officer. And at the same time his historical views are significant because they demonstrate that the regenerationist thinking commonly associated with the members of the literary Generation of '98 actually had a powerful voice in a leading figure of what has traditionally been portrayed as one of the country's most inflexible and unintellectual institutions. Despite the impression left by the long-lasting Franco regime of the Spanish officer corps as a monolithic and traditionalist caste with scant interest in or knowledge of the cultural and intellectual pursuits of civil society, the army of Restoration Spain was clearly home to a disparate group of intellectual elites. Besides the political differences that divided both junior officers and their superiors—such as the conflict between the africanistas and their more domestically minded colleagues—philosophical and ideological variances on subjects as seemingly esoteric as the writing of history were great enough to foster intense debate by officers in both civil and military spheres. As the most important consequence of this debate, the historicist rhetoric employed by Burguete and its other participants would leave a cultural imprint well suited to the conservative nationalist ideals later imposed on Spanish society. Indeed, it was a much more traditionally minded colleague of Burguete, Antonio García Pérez, who served as the early-twentieth-century army's principal spokesman for this neo-Catholic, conservative-nationalist offensive.

Chapter Five

Fighting for God and King
Military Traditionalism

Despite Burguete's prolific writing and well-publicized political maneuvering, he never succeeded in winning over the great majority of Spanish officers to many aspects of his ideological program. Although he may have been the individual most responsible for introducing Spanish military culture to some of the modern philosophical notions that were gaining popularity elsewhere in fin-de-siècle Europe, his intellectual proselytizing had a formidable counterweight in the tracts of his colleagues who sought to bring about Spain's regeneration through programs based on a very traditional view of church and society. Rather than evoking Nietzschean and social Darwinist imagery in the manner of Burguete, these officers turned instead to "traditionalism," the antiliberal, counter-revolutionary, and fervently Catholic ideology of the extreme conservative right in Spain. Spanish traditionalism, which had come to characterize the Spanish Counterreformation and by the first part of the nineteenth century found expression in such works as Rafael Vélez's 1818 *Apología del altar y el trono*, became the principal ideological pillar of the Carlist movement that emerged in the 1830s.[1] Carlism had formed in support of a pretender to the Spanish crown, but its importance soon lay more in its relentless opposition to liberalism than in its dynastic politics.

Yet Carlism, which would play a prominent role in the breakdown of the Second Republic and the creation of Franco's long-lasting dictatorship, was hardly the only political force to embrace Spanish traditionalism in the twentieth century. Non-Carlist Spanish traditionalism also enjoyed notable popularity in conservative circles, and important contributors to Francoist ideology—such as the writers of *Acción Española*—made ample use of traditionalist doctrines. In fact, Catholic traditionalism came to dominate the twentieth-century officer corps and "official" Spain in general. Curiously enough, though, most scholars studying the ideological bases of the Primo de Rivera and Franco regimes have focused on traditionalist writers from outside the military community, even though the two dictators and most of the men they chose to help them run their governments came from the armed forces. Of course, the works of civilian writers—sometimes even those who were neither traditionalist nor "protofascist"—undeniably provided much of the intellectual material with which Primo de Rivera and Franco tried to justify their regimes. Joaquín Costa's observation that Spain needed an "iron surgeon," for example, was explicitly cited by Primo de Rivera when he seized power in 1923, and Ramiro de Maeztu's works provided important ideological support for Franco's dictatorship. But most Spanish officers did not share the intense passion for intellectual pursuits revealed by colleagues such as Burguete; their exposure to philosophical trends depended largely on the interpretations and explanations of the military writers, lecturers, and teachers who together helped shape the cultural world of the officer corps.

Antonio García Pérez, a longtime instructor at the Infantry Academy in Toledo and the author of more than seventy-five books and pamphlets and countless periodical articles, clearly belonged to the key group of ideologically influential officers.[2] He was, moreover, one of the most fervent supporters of Catholic traditionalism within the Restoration army, fueling the growth of the more conservative outlook that came to dominate the officer corps. Although the nineteenth-century Spanish army had exhibited strong anticlerical leanings, the period when García Pérez wrote saw the gradual transformation of much of the armed forces to a decidedly more conservative bent. The army's leading spokesman for traditionalism, he made a highly important contribution to the neo-Catholic, integrist offensive to restore the hegemony of Catholicism to Spanish social and cultural life. Although he parroted many earlier expressions of Spanish traditionalism, he also infused his rhetoric with unabashedly nationalist and militarist language, thus shaping the antiliberal, military mind-set that came to dominate official Spain's culture for much of the twentieth century. As Spain's most vigorous proponent of this new wave of Catholic conservatism, this hitherto overlooked figure played a crucial historical role. Traditionalist views of the sort espoused by García Pérez did not achieve absolute ideological hegemony in the army before or even after the Civil War, but during the Restoration period they played a role similar to that of Burguete's Nietzschean tracts—albeit from a radically different point of view—in undermining rationalist, "scientific" thinking within the Spanish officer corps.

Moreover, just as García Pérez's writings reveal much about the ideological world of an important segment of the Spanish officer corps, records of his career path and professional and political decisions can serve as useful means to increase our understanding of the environment in which he lived and worked. And a biographical approach to such an analysis can also add a human element to our understanding of the system that has had such a profound impact on Spanish society as a whole. Before exploring the content of his writings themselves, then, this chapter examines García Pérez's activities within the educational, intellectual, and publishing institutions in which he so expertly operated.

* * *

García Pérez was born in Puerto Principe, Cuba, in 1874. Although he then spent virtually all of his military career on the peninsula, beginning with his entrance to the Academia General Militar in 1891, he retained a lifelong affinity for the Americas that surfaced repeatedly in his writings. After three years of study at the Academia General he joined many fellow officer-cadets in choosing to spend an additional year at the Infantry Academy in Toledo. After completing his studies in July 1894 he became a second lieutenant, and the following March he was sent to Cuba. There he took part in various operations through the summer of 1896, when he began the six-year program at the general staff school, or Escuela Superior de Guerra. During this period, which included stints of duty in various regiments and military offices, he rose through seniority to the rank of captain. In 1902 he received the general staff school's diploma, and in 1905 he began teaching at the Infantry Academy. He taught courses on tactics, regulations, geography, Arabic, and a variety of other topics until his promotion to major in 1912. After a brief period as a historian and inspector of regimental educational programs, in July 1914 he was transferred to Morocco, where he saw combat and also continued his pedagogical endeavors as an instructor of recruits. In May 1916 he returned to Spain to spend the rest of his career engaging in a variety of administrative duties, military studies, and committee responsibilities.[3] Living in Madrid as a retired colonel when the Civil War broke out in 1936, he was briefly imprisoned for failing to act in defense of the Republic.[4] After the war's end he wrote several books and pamphlets praising the insurgents.

Above all, García Pérez's longtime association with Spanish military education defined his career. Even after the Civil War his professional identity was still linked primarily to his past as an educator; hence the title page of his postwar book *La Marina en la Cruzada* identified him simply as *"ex-profesor de la Academia de Infantería,"* noting neither his rank nor any of the civil or military awards he had received.[5] He had, after all, spent a significant portion of his life at the Infantry Academy in Toledo helping to shape the mind-set of a generation of officers who would play a key role in subsequent Spanish history. Francisco Franco, for example, entered the academy as a small, shy fourteen year old while García Pérez taught there, and the future Caudillo's experiences as a cadet during his most formative years clearly influenced his future actions. As Franco would acknowledge years later, the academy had infused him with a strong sense of military values, although he had also suffered considerable pain and humiliation as the victim of cruel pranks and initiation rites.[6]

García Pérez and his colleagues who spent long periods teaching in Toledo were not blind to the disagreeable elements of academy life, but they clearly preferred to emphasize its more positive attributes. Its very setting in the architectural splendor of Spain's imperial past had a strong impact on many who worked and studied there, undoubtedly influencing even Franco's subsequent vision of Spanish history.[7] García Pérez could implore entering cadets to make the most of their stay in Toledo and the centuries-old Alcázar, which housed the academy itself, by stressing the historical value of their new surroundings. He urged them:

> Enrapture your virile and serene spirit by contemplating this building and the vigor and courage of the happy age it embodies. . . . Forge your dreams in this mansion of Kings, bringing to your sentiments something beyond reason and inspiring in your will something that intelligence cannot elucidate.
>
> Infect yourself with the greatness of your dwelling, which to this day whispers of the courage of a people and the prolific abnegation of a race; think each day about what the barracks bordering the patio arches represent, about the bronze inscriptions that adorn the walls, about the past glory that sparkled in the same rooms in which you now walk; capture the spirit and let it take you through history, applauding and admiring those who in this very Alcázar earned the respect of the world. When tears drown your laughter and sorrow overcomes your joy, hold your head up and contemplate the stones of the Alcázar, for they lovingly enclosed other men who, before martyrdom of the flesh, betrayed the indecipherable smile of lips murmuring in faith.[8]

The mystical combination of military values, patriotism, and reverence for church and monarchy that García Pérez so closely linked to the Infantry Academy undoubtedly did much to strengthen his emotional attachment to the institution. But he also had significant ties of a more practical nature to the place. After all, his long-lasting position there made relatively few demands—critics complained that many instructors lacked sufficient knowledge to teach the subjects assigned to them—but it included many benefits.[9] Most notably, it allowed him to pursue the professionally advantageous and sometimes even profitable enterprise of writing for publication, which of course served only to fuel the criticism by Burguete and others of the business of education and the production of military textbooks.

The potential advantages to a military officer's career conferred by writing were nothing new to García Pérez's era. Even the great military historians of the previous century had always made sure that their literary endeavors received every possible official acknowledgment, because such efforts could actually lead to a rise in rank. For example, Modesto Navarro y García, whose love of history and writing was clearly genuine, regularly requested the recognition of his superiors for his published works.[10] During the period in which García

Pérez wrote, however, this practice seems to have increased in frequency. Whereas the works of military writers such as Navarro had often represented undeniably scholarly achievements, during the latter years of the Restoration the poor style and organization of many officers' works made it appear as though, in the words of one historian, their authors were "more interested in adding up pages than in expressing a new point of view."[11]

This harsh but often accurate appraisal applies to most of García Pérez's literary endeavors, which covered the full spectrum of forms of publication open to military writers. Of course, a small number of his books and essays merited attention in their own right. These works were often submitted to civilian writing contests, and García Pérez clearly hoped they would gain him recognition and respect in the Spanish intellectual world in general.[12] But regardless of his occasional noteworthy literary accomplishments, most of his writing served far more practical purposes. He benefited, moreover, from the need of many officers to use military publications when preparing the educational programs and speeches they were expected to provide for their men.

García Pérez's first written work, *Nomenclatura del fusil Maüser* [*sic*] *Español,* won him official acknowledgment in the form of a royal order that was duly noted in his personal service record.[13] As his career advanced, the motivation of such recognition as well as the financial incentive for much of his writing became increasingly obvious, and he often repeated portions of previously used texts in later works bearing different titles. The recycling of older works into new, often superfluous editions may have been common among the military writers and publishers of the day who sold their books and pamphlets to cadets and to pupils preparing for academy entrance examinations, but García Pérez seems to have made particularly good use of this practice; the most severe and perceptive critic of Spanish military education actually singled out the publication history of García Pérez's first pamphlet and its subsequent editions to exemplify the flaws in the system.[14] But García Pérez only repeated this method in many other pamphlets he wrote to aid cadets, officers, and sometimes even soldiers in learning basic facts and principles. In some instances he created essays and even books by simply copying the text from earlier works, such as in his 1907 article "Estudio político-social de la España del siglo XVI," whose text was identical to the main text of his book *Destellos de grandeza.*[15] In other cases he chose a format that would allow him to produce a work with little effort on his own part. For example, his short work on the Spanish possessions in Africa, designed for use during the 1909–10 academic year at the Infantry Academy, included nothing but brief bits of geographical and other factual information about the regions discussed.[16] Another style of publication popular with García Pérez and many other military writers of his day entailed collecting aphorisms, quotations, and historical anecdotes intended to convey basic patriotic, military, and sometimes even religious values to the reader. Virtually every military writer mentioned in this book—with the notable exception of Burguete—put together such a collection and tried to use it to help earn a promotion.[17]

Yet the popularity of this method clearly stemmed from more than the relative ease with which it could be used to create an officially recognized text. García Pérez, after all, wrote *La Marina en la Cruzada,* which consisted of nothing but brief quotations and descriptions of feats he attributed to various figures of the Spanish naval world from the fourteenth century onward, long after he had any interest in professional advancement. Indeed, publications of this or any other sort also could serve simply to feed an officer's vanity, gain him respect, and find an audience for his views, actions, or accomplishments. Hence the speeches officers delivered at the Ateneos of Madrid and elsewhere and at their own Centro del Ejército y de la Armada often found their way into print as pamphlets, chapters of books, or periodical articles, regardless of their subjects. Pamphlets were also published with the aid of sponsors such as the Stokes Gun Company[18] or at the behest of regiments[19] or municipal officials.[20] José Ibáñez Marín's publication of *Violación supuesta* (Supposed rape) stands out as perhaps the most incredible example of a Restoration officer's decision to publicize his views by means of a pamphlet. This work, which even appeared in a second edition including poetry and a new prologue, reproduced its author's eloquent but biased and sexist defense before a military court of a colleague accused of raping a Moroccan woman.[21]

Although it is, of course, difficult to gauge the reception among their intended audiences of the plethora of writings by military officers, there is no doubt that García Pérez's works reached a relatively large number of readers. This was partly because of the sheer number of his works, which saturated military libraries, and because of his position as an instructor of future officers at their most impressionable age. But his works were also popular because his style fit well the Spanish system of military education. The cadets, forced to endure a regime of sleep deprivation and pedagogical methods stressing rote memorization and recitation, had few chances to learn to digest sophisticated analyses or otherwise improve their intellectual skills. In such an atmosphere the rather simplistic exhortations of García Pérez on the values of patriotism, the sword, the church, and honor found particularly easy reception in the minds of the cadets, most of whom lacked the experience, time, and training to critically analyze what they were taught. As the teacher of nearly 700 cadets during his stay at the Infantry Academy,[22] García Pérez directly exposed a significant number of future officers to his views—including Francisco Franco—and even later his ideas continued to reach cadets through his writings.

* * *

Not surprisingly, García Pérez had a strong interest in the debate over pedagogy that raged within the military community of his day, although—as I show later—the educational theory he espoused did not always mirror his own practices or those of his colleagues at the Infantry Academy. In fact, his most articulate attempt to explain his pedagogical philosophy, an essay on primary education that won the first prize for its category in the literary competition of Seville's 1904 "Juegos Florales," espoused a relatively progressive outlook.

In this essay, which revealed much about his views on Spanish nationalism and neo-Catholic regeneration, García Pérez joined virtually all participants in the military debate over education in Spain in crediting Prussia's schoolteachers for their supposed role in creating the powerful nation that had emerged triumphantly from the Franco-Prussian War, and he profoundly lamented the teaching profession's lack of prestige in his own country. The administrators of Spanish education, he charged, failed to take into account the character and history of the people they served. Instead, "sometimes swept away by an enthusiasm for imitation and sometimes fueled by personal pride," the schools of his day suppressed "the individuality in each child and concealed the value of science and progress under an excess of useless studies."[23]

But despite his criticism of "enthusiasm for imitation," García Pérez was quite willing to look abroad in his search for an appropriate model for educational reform in Spain, even favoring English pedagogical methods over their German counterparts. Citing contemporary Germany's well-known critic of cultural "degeneration," Max Nordau, he argued that by "instructing" instead of "educating" the German educational method "sacrifices character and will for the sake of positivist knowledge" and "creates men who for lack of initiative never produce in relation to what they know." In contrast, English teachers struck the right balance by teaching "*in a Christian sense* of ethics and religion, and *in a positive sense* of physical and political sciences" and by cultivating physical strength and maturity through sports. He also quoted Taine's claim that English pupils finished school with no desire to rebel against the church, which they had learned to perceive as "quite reasonable," nor to oppose their country's already "quite liberal" constitution. In García Pérez's eyes even the schools of the United States merited praise, and he described them as functioning as "a natural part of a child's life [*para el niño una parte de su propia vida natural*]." These schools, he wrote, "cultivate enthusiasm and enjoyment instead of vanity and formulism, undoubtedly with the understanding that nothing hinders learning more than the habitual learning of definitions, than separation from nature, than the suppression of a child's initiative, and than the curtailing of intelligence by an overemphasis on memory."[24] Of course, the emphasis on formulas and memorization that he criticized here played dominant roles in Spanish military education, and many of the pamphlets and books he and his colleagues in Toledo penned were oriented toward such pedagogical methods. He failed, however, to address the contradictions between his theory and practice.

Yet García Pérez explicitly discussed extending to civilian primary schools a far more practical type of instruction that was common to the Spanish military world: the teaching of modern methods of farming. As he noted, in Spain soldiers learned during their military service new agricultural practices that they then took to their home communities when they returned to civilian life. In fact, the 1904 royal order calling for the teaching of farming as well as basic literacy skills to recruits had represented a significant victory for the many advocates of employing the army as a "school of the *patria*."[25] Teaching the same information to schoolchildren, he argued, would bring valuable benefits to Spain.

On a more esoteric level, García Pérez strongly advocated changing the way Spanish history was taught to schoolchildren. The current history curriculum, he claimed, resembled "a description of the national cemetery," filling pupils' heads with names and dates that they quickly forgot. Instead, he wrote, teachers needed to strive to teach "of the poetic History that exalts the struggles of progress; of the History of the martyr of labor fallen on the rough path of glory."[26]

* * *

In fact, many of García Pérez's publications demanded use of the same kind of mnemonic tasks in the teaching of cadets that he had condemned in the teaching of children. But he also wrote some works of history that were far more interpretive in nature, and his efforts earned him membership in the Royal Academy of History and the Royal Geographical Society.[27] One of his first books, a study of over 400 pages on Mexico during the 1860s, included far more than a mere recounting of names, dates, and events.[28] He also wrote other noteworthy works on the history of the American continent, an area that, he lamented, failed to receive the attention it deserved from his overwhelmingly Eurocentric colleagues.[29]

In general, however, García Pérez devoted his most passionate historical writings to Spain itself. Although his interest in the Americas stemmed in part from his Cuban origin, he also believed, as was stressed by virtually every Spaniard of his day who was writing on Latin America, that the inherently Spanish origins and qualities of Latin America had emerged in a "mature" state after their people had gained independence from Spain. He attributed the unique and often mystical characteristics of Spaniards themselves, which had left such a profound impression on America, to their deep roots in Iberia's past. Recognition of this very traditionalist vision of Spanish history, which influenced his writing, teaching, and even political decisions, is essential for understanding his conservative politics and nationalism.

Not surprisingly, García Pérez's vision of Spanish history rested largely on his perception of how Christianity had shaped Spain, although he credited medieval Islamic civilization with having revived the peninsula from its decadent and impoverished condition under the Goths. Only the Arabs, he believed, had been capable of "preventing the fall of the Gothic race and inflaming it with new ideas, propelling it toward new destinies, purifying it through war, exalting it through the arts." And when, years later, "Christian-Spanish civilization" took on its "Arab-Spanish" counterpart, the Arab spirit survived the conflict and fueled "the light that guided Columbus over the uncharted seas, the light that illuminated our soldiers in Flanders and Italy with the sparkles of glory, the light that formed the happy wake in the waters of Lepanto, the light that shone so brilliantly in Mühlberg and grew pale in Rocroi."[30]

García Pérez clearly shared, at least in part, his colleague Burguete's view of the inherently "Arab" characteristics of Spain and its inhabitants, and, as his emphasis on the "purifying" potential of military actions reveals, he believed war could play a key role in regenerating a nation. But he had a far more positive perception than did Burguete—and Ganivet—of the redirecting of peninsular interests toward the west and into the Americas, portraying the epoch initiated by Columbus's famous voyage as the apex of Spanish history. For him the "light" on Spain's glorious destiny had not dimmed until the seventeenth century, as he indicated in his reference to the 1643 defeat at Rocroi, which he thought marked the end of Spanish hegemony in Europe. Burguete had contemptuously branded Ferdinand and Isabel—who had sponsored Columbus's voyage and whose fortunes were so closely linked to the Catholic Church—as usurpers, pointing to the harm he believed their marriage and subsequent neglect of the country's interests in the Mediterranean had caused. García Pérez, on the other hand, had nothing but praise for the Catholic monarchs and their promotion of Spanish expansion westward. His views, although based on considerably more simplistic reasoning than those of Burguete, probably represented the historical outlook of a larger segment of the Spanish officer corps, as is demonstrated by the official histories later propagated by men he had educated.

García Pérez's paradoxical tendency to praise both Muslim Spain and the individuals most responsible for its demise surfaced most clearly in his praise for Isabel's confessor Francisco Jiménez de Cisneros, who, as the monarchy's most important collaborator, had pursued brutally intolerant policies toward Moors and Jews. García Pérez argued that Cisneros, the cardinal of Toledo, had not only saved Spain from the threat of the Reformation, but had also revealed remarkable toleration for many aspects of Muslim culture. After all, he reasoned, even when Cisneros had ordered the burning of 5,000 copies of the Koran he had spared the books of medicine, history, and science from destruction. García Pérez cited W. H. Prescott's 1837 classic *History of the Reign of Ferdinand and Isabella* to argue that Cisneros had been superior to the French cardinal Richelieu "from a moral perspective, and not at all inferior in his governing skills." He also gave Cisneros credit for creating the royal militia under Ferdinand and Isabel, which García Pérez described as "the true origin of permanent armies."[31]

Not surprisingly, García Pérez's writings on history often stressed its military aspects, and his admiration for the great Spanish monarchs of the sixteenth century stemmed largely from his perception of their reforms of the armed forces, which had in turn helped forge the Spanish nation. He lauded, for instance, the use by the Catholic monarchs of the Santa Hermandad, or peacekeeping brotherhood, as an instrument for strengthening royal power at the expense of the manorial armed retinues. Under the rule of Ferdinand and Isabel, he argued, the personal authority of the nobles declined as the national government made use of its standing armed forces "to form a collective, national mold." Moreover, in his eyes the national unity and loyalty fostered by the military reforms of the Catholic monarchs also promoted administrative and tactical unity within the Spanish armed forces themselves.[32]

García Pérez's praise for such centralizing and state-strengthening measures, which he later contradicted by extolling the independent guerrilla fighters who rose against Napoleon, emerged frequently in his articles, pamphlets, and books and undoubtedly influenced his faith in Castile-based Catholic corporatism as the best means to Spain's regeneration. He therefore described the Inquisition in terms of its efficacy both in consolidating state power and in defending the Catholic Church from the Protestant threat, even quoting Cánovas on the institution's crucial role in maintaining religious unity. Similarly, he rejected the condemnation by many contemporary historians of Philip II's Pragmatic Sanction prohibiting study at foreign universities, citing Menéndez Pelayo's apologetic description of the royal decision and praise for the king's cultural and intellectual achievements. In García Pérez's eyes Philip had merely continued the laudable tradition of the Spanish wars on Protestantism and the "Islamic threat," a struggle that itself proved Spain's status as "the nation of the perpetual Crusade, the sentry of Christian civilization."[33] Religiously defined "others," then, played an important oppositional role in the formation of his concept of Spanish identity.

To a certain degree the traditionalist views of Spanish history promoted by García Pérez and many of his fellow officers served as a bridge between the ideas propagated by Menéndez Pelayo during the nineteenth century and the historical interpretations promoted later by the writers of *Acción Española* and the ideologues of Spain's military dictators. Like Menéndez Pelayo and the rightist intellectuals who years later drew upon his ideas, García Pérez praised sixteenth-century Spain's accomplishments and resistance to Protestantism, and he believed profoundly in the country's inherently Catholic character and destiny.[34] Although Burguete had also made selective use of the writings of Menéndez Pelayo when convenient, he had departed significantly from the famed writer's traditionalist outlook on numerous occasions, often preferring to rely on more modern arguments associated with thinkers like Nietzsche. García Pérez, however, embraced a rather simplistic, traditional vision of Spain's uniquely "Catholic" history and historical destiny that, thanks to the hegemony over official culture later imposed by his intellectual successors from the ranks of the armed forces, would prevail for much of the twentieth century.

* * *

Of course, García Pérez's reverence for Catholicism extended well beyond the realm of history. He also believed that Catholic Christian values as he understood them should serve as foundations for virtually every aspect of life in Spain, including the country's educational, military, and social programs. His interpretation of these values was, moreover, quite traditional and conservative, although his proposals for restructuring society made ample use of Pope Leo XIII's famous 1891 encyclical *Rerum novarum,* which had rejected extreme manifestations of capitalism. In the eyes of García Pérez, the attraction of socialism to impoverished workers was misguided but understandable.

In 1906 García Pérez delivered a lecture at the Centro del Ejército y de la Armada on "the major forms of socialism," bringing together many of the ideas on modern society that underlay his writings and teaching throughout his life. A decade later he reiterated and expanded on his social views in his short story "Juan Soldado y Juan Obrero" (Soldier John and Worker John), which appeared in *Nuestro Tiempo.* The story, constructed around a rather absurd dialogue between the two characters of the title, began with the worker's argument for a society built around the principles of liberty, fraternity, and equality. Juan Soldado, however, eventually won over the worker by attacking equality as unnatural, fraternity as an "unattainable ideal," and true liberty as inherently incompatible with the first two concepts.[35]

García Pérez used his story of Soldier John's conversion of Worker John to military ideals to promote his fundamental belief in the army's potential for fostering individual as well as social improvement and national regeneration. Like Burguete in his early writings and the many other Spaniards who were appalled by the social ills stemming from rapid, large-scale industrialization, García Pérez sought to portray liberal economics and the principles associated with the Enlightenment and the French Revolution as inherently unjust and at odds with one another. He proposed curing the social problem and strengthening nationalist sentiment with what he called "militarism," which he insisted had much in common with socialist thinking. Although his conceptions of "socialism" and "militarism" always remained somewhat imprecise, it is possible to identify the basic ideas behind his use of the terms by reading his works carefully. In general he employed the term *militarism* as a reference to the common life and spirit of soldiers and officers, arguing that their institution offered the common man a unique opportunity to get ahead through hard work, bravery, honesty, and a profound dedication to his profession and his country. At times his understanding of the concept appeared relatively progressive; at one point he even stated that he defined *militarism* as not "the empire of the saber or the mastery of courage, but rather the supremacy of the force of reason or the combination of virtue and heroism."[36]

In his 1906 speech, however, García Pérez portrayed the bourgeoisie as the common enemy of both the military and the working classes, stressing middle-class fears of "militarism" and "socialism" alike and arguing that both movements shared a profound dedication to the "spirit of justice" and the "sentiment of abnegation." But despite his criticism of the bourgeoisie, in certain respects he seemed to advocate a sort of liberal meritocracy, and in later writings he would actually defend the middle classes and praise modern society's allowance for upward social mobility. These early, more anticapitalist tracts merely demonstrate that even as a young officer he could get caught up in at least some of the more radical regenerationist fervor that had so captivated the young Burguete. But García Pérez's belief that the best social model was an all-volunteer army, with soldiers who enjoyed equal rights and obligations and were judged by identical standards, differed from the more Nietzschean justifications Burguete employed in supporting small, professional forces. García Pérez believed that an equalitarian military system would "kill the caste of oppressors who live in the world of politics, industry, and commerce, planting in their place the sentiments of justice and social solidarity that today appear so weak." For even in an age characterized by

> useless bureaucracy, repulsive parliamentary government, and disastrous politics, there sleeps a military spirit confident of its power but unaware that it could function as the people's best social instrument, since the most altruistic ideas fit well in a world where virtue serves as capital and work entails limitless abnegation.
>
> Militarism lies at the heart of the social problem, for if the latter comes out of the organic life of all peoples, then the former is the just and moral distribution of the capital that finances work and of the energy that capital receives

> in return. For this reason, militarism is an integral function of socialism; and because the former brings the origins of its hopes to the aspirations of the latter, the latter takes in the former, just as the atmosphere returns to the earth giving it life and growth.[37]

Needless to say, García Pérez's rather muddled and obtuse attempt to explain his conception of the "militarist" alternative to orthodox Marxist economics could hardly have persuaded many socialists as easily as his character Soldier John had won over the worker. If anything, his use of terms such as *capital* and *work* revealed that he had limited knowledge of the economic processes he was trying to describe. Nevertheless, the underlying argument of the quoted passage that the military could serve as a viable model for the Spanish nation emerged clearly, and in the eyes of many readers García Pérez's ostensible knowledge of economic theory must have added credibility to his reasoning. Furthermore, his thinking undoubtedly appealed to many officers who were struggling to reconcile their genuine sympathy for the poor with their fear of the antimilitarism common to organized social movements and civilian politicians. When, for example, Franco's future propaganda chief José Millán-Astray founded the Spanish Foreign Legion years later, he portrayed the new organization's supposed ability to obliterate political, class, and racial differences as one of its most important attributes, and a similar vision of a harmonious, "organic" Spanish nation was unquestionably in the minds of the many officers who years later became disenchanted with the increasing turmoil of the Second Republic.[38]

García Pérez's ideas on "militarism" differed in many respects from those of Burguete, although both called for an all-volunteer army. Rather than evoking Nietzschean and social Darwinist imagery and arguments, García Pérez and his more traditionally minded colleagues showed far more enthusiasm for paternalistic, church-based programs of social reform. In addition to calling for restructuring society along "militarist" lines, García Pérez also advocated corporatist, social Catholic cures for poverty in Spain. He particularly admired the Catholic workers' organizations of Germany and Belgium, which he described as the most admirable of the "socialist"-inspired European mass movements.

The primary problem of secular, orthodox socialism, García Pérez believed, was its overemphasis on the value of labor and its failure to fully appreciate the essential role of capital for production. Despite his criticism of employers for exploiting human labor, he praised them for their willingness to take economic risks, for their "social value as patrons," and for their organizational and management skills. Social Catholicism (which he actually called "*socialismo católico,*" or "Catholic socialism") thus appealed to him for "legitimizing and advocating state intervention in the various elements of the social contract" without posing a significant threat to the status quo. He strongly praised Leo XIII's *De rerum novorum* and the Catholic *Volksverein* of Wilhelm Emmanuel Ketteler, who he said had built his party around the principles the pope had embraced in his famous encyclical. After all, García Pérez reasoned, Christianity—like the military—had an inherent appeal to and sympathy for the working man, since even "the son of God was a humble worker." Far too many members of contemporary Spain's aristocracy and bourgeoisie, he lamented in his 1906 speech, neither remembered the lessons of the Bible nor shared "the greatness of heart that could die for the *Patria* or endure the pain of hard labor"—the primary attributes of good soldiers and workers.[39]

In many ways García Pérez's social views resembled those of the Carlist writer Juan Vázquez de Mella, the period's leading exponent of traditionalist thought. Carlism, formed around the figure of an early-nineteenth-century pretender to the Spanish crown, would overcome its defeats in three earlier civil wars to enter the Second Republic in 1931 as what Martin Blinkhorn describes as "indisputably the oldest continuously existing popular movement of the extreme right in Europe," eventually playing a key role in the creation of Franco's dictatorship.[40] Like García Pérez, Mella embraced the ideas of Leo XIII and European social Catholic and corporatist writers, and he too justifiably blamed economic liberalism and modern industrial growth for many of his day's social ills. Moreover, both he and García Pérez lacked a clear vision of exactly how to realize their lofty proposals for restructuring society. Mella's explanations of corporatism retained their vague character throughout his life, a significant weakness that was seen also in the writings of García Pérez and shared by most other Catholic corporatist thinkers. In general terms their notion of corporatism implied the unification of all social elements into a natural, harmonious, and "organic" system of cooperation, a vision that was propagated by Mella, García Pérez, and many other Spanish conservatives for years to come and eventually found its way into aspects of the official ideologies espoused by Primo de Rivera and Franco.[41]

García Pérez also echoed Mella's criticism of basic Enlightenment concepts such as liberty, freedom, and democracy, as seen in the dialogue of the worker and the soldier. The famous Carlist thinker had written that no truly "liberal" freedom or system of government could exist outside the framework of a Catholic monarchy. García Pérez had merely extended this argument to the military world, which in his eyes offered the same potential as a monarchist, Catholic corporatist state for fostering authentic forms of "liberty" and "democracy."[42] Although he never embraced the dynastic element of the Carlist cause—as his repeated praise for the Alfonsist royal line attests—the writings of the movement's chief ideologue had clearly exercised a profound if indirect influence on his thinking. This was hardly surprising given the decisive role of

Mella's works in fostering increased respect for traditionalist ideas among Spanish conservatives. The praise for Mella voiced by such non-Carlists as Menéndez Pelayo, Antonio Maura, and Primo de Rivera illustrates this influence. Indeed, Mella's doctrinal foundations and political programs served as the basis for the non-Carlist Traditionalist Party that was established shortly after World War I.[43]

* * *

Yet García Pérez also embraced and propagated many tenets of Spanish traditionalism that predated Mella's efforts to bring greater ideological cohesiveness and respectability to the Carlist movement. Nineteenth-century Carlism, like earlier manifestations of Spanish traditionalism, frequently evoked a supposedly glorious tradition of violence and war. As part of his endeavors to "modernize" Carlism, Mella largely rejected such violent imagery. But the popular appeal of the legendary war exploits of the Carlists continued to thrive well into this century.[44] And García Pérez clearly had a similar fascination with the bellicose aspects of traditionalist religious views, frequently calling for an alliance of throne, sword, and altar to regenerate his country. His publications included countless references to what he presented as a consubstantial relationship between God, country, king, and army, and he frequently cited historical examples of Spaniards who had sacrificed their lives in the service of these ideals. In his eyes religion played a fundamental role in the life of every soldier, because "the disregard for his own life, the hardships he endures in war, and the abnegation he displays in peace all require a spirit of irrevocable faith and an invincible perseverance; only Religion can teach not to fear death and to view sacrifice as a sublime duty."[45]

Of course, a belief in the intimate relationship between war and religion was nothing new; the notion is as old as warfare itself, and it continues to be an integral part of some nationalist movements even today. Yet García Pérez's constant emphasis on such imagery reflected a significant rise in the popularity of such thinking within the Spanish officer corps. Although nineteenth-century Spain had certainly seen attempts to glorify the supposedly holy nature of war, most officers had displayed only moderate support for the church and its doctrines. Religious fervor was far more common among the Carlists, who during the nineteenth century had fought and lost against the Spanish army—and by implication against a modern conception of a centralized nation—in three bloody civil wars. In the years to come, however, religious imagery would find an increasingly prominent place in the writings and policies of many army officers, forming an inseparable component of the Spanish nation they sought to regenerate. In 1923, for instance, José Millán-Astray characterized the Foreign Legion he had founded three years earlier—which was itself a sort of microcosm of the kind of nation he advocated—as a "religion," and similar terminology fueled the Franco regime's subsequent "crusade" and "national-Catholic" propaganda.[46]

García Pérez's espousal of beliefs formerly associated primarily with Carlism thus mirrored a similar change in civil society, which saw conservatives becoming increasingly receptive to the traditionalist views typical of the rival dynasty's supporters—even if at the same time they paradoxically became more (Castilian) nationalist. On a more general level, García Pérez's emphasis on the religious character of warfare both exemplified and fostered a change within the Spanish officer corps that had an effect similar to that of the simultaneous attack by more "modern" thinkers such as Burguete on the scientific tradition of the nineteenth-century army and general staff. Employing a similar language of war in their criticism of materialist approaches to military affairs, both García Pérez and Burguete helped pave the way for the increasingly irrationalist, antiliberal mind-set of many officers. Similarly, García Pérez's invocation of tradition to discredit fundamental Enlightenment tenets had its counterpart in Burguete's writings, which often employed a radical and modern tone for the same purpose. Together, then, these two men from very different schools of thought contributed to the same end in Spain as elsewhere in Europe: the weakening of political liberalism. And, thanks to Franco's triumph in the Civil War, the Catholic traditionalist views proclaimed in the works of García Pérez have left an imprint on the Spanish armed forces that is still visible today. A recent issue of the military magazine *Ejército,* for example, echoed García Pérez's gushing praise of nearly a century ago for the Virgin Mary in her role as the patron saint of the Spanish Infantry.[47] The consequences of the neo-Catholic, conservative nationalist wave that García Pérez embodied thus remain with us today, even though traces of Spain's legacy of military liberalism—discussed in the next chapter—have survived as well.

Chapter Six

Enlightening the Soldiers
Military Liberalism

Despite the strong doses of mystical Catholicism, medieval warrior values, and traditionalist social thought administered to cadets by instructors like Antonio García Pérez, the Infantry Academy in Toledo was by no means devoid of rationalist and scientifically minded voices. After all, the largest component of the curriculum was devoted to ostensibly sober and nonideological subjects such as mathematics, tactics, geography, and languages, even if teachers and textbook authors like García Pérez injected their own views into the lessons.

In fact, a key figure in the world of Spanish military pedagogy, Enrique Ruiz-Fornells, was a self-proclaimed liberal who explicitly praised the eighteenth-century Enlightenment and condemned military interference in civilian rule. As the author of the text on "moral education" that was assigned to academy cadets for a quarter of a century, this highly influential officer espoused neither traditionalist doctrine nor the extreme vitalist rhetoric found in the works of Burguete. Although he, like Burguete and García Pérez, began his career at the Academia General Militar and became an important player in subsequent Spanish history, his ideas differed considerably from the views of those men. After serving on the general staff, at various educational institutions, as tutor to the young king Alfonso XIII, and as the commander of a battalion in Morocco, he ended his career as a military advisor to Republican war minister Manuel Azaña during the Second Republic's sweeping reforms of the armed forces. These reforms would prove one of the most divisive issues in the Spanish army before the 1936 military rebellion that sparked the Civil War.

In addition to making an impact by means of his professional accomplishments, Ruiz-Fornells also did so in a more general way as a highly influential advocate of reason, thereby representing a significant counterbalance to his antirationalist colleagues Burguete and García Pérez. For him, modern Spanish national identity was based on ideals of citizenship and liberal government, both of which were to be complemented by scientific progress. He enjoyed, moreover, the ability to spread his message to a large number of cadets and officers through his teaching, public lectures, and writing; relatively early in his career a prominent colleague described him as already "very well known" by many Spanish officers—especially the younger ones.[1]

Along with the archival trail left by Ruiz-Fornells' actions in Spain's politico-military world, his books, lectures, articles, and unpublished memoirs offer a valuable opportunity for analysis of the ideas and behavior of an unusually articulate spokesman for the liberal, rationalist segment of the Spanish military. His writings on history, education, science, the "moral" dimensions of humanity, and war itself not only shed light on his own ideological makeup, but also help us to contextualize the other schools of thought discussed earlier in this book. In particular, his vision of a democratic army of "citizen-soldiers" differed greatly from the programs espoused by Burguete and García Pérez. This vision was a component of his more general preoccupation with Spanish identity and the need for national regeneration, which was hardly uncommon for a military writer of his day. Unlike so many of his colleagues, however, he envisaged a national spirit that was liberal, democratic, scientifically advanced, and open to the influence of progressive forces from elsewhere in Europe.

Yet a full understanding of the place of Ruiz-Fornells in military culture requires analysis not only of his ideological program, but also of the way in which he expressed it and the underlying implications of his reasoning. For a careful reading of his works reveals that he actually shared with the antiliberal officers some fundamental philosophical assumptions about the nature of national character and the role of violence and warfare in Spanish historical destiny, even if on the surface he stood in obvious ideological opposition to Burguete and García Pérez. Ruiz-Fornells carried on the liberal and scientific tradition of so many nineteenth-century military officers, but not without revealing the subtle but significant influence of fin-de-siècle modernism embodied by the likes of Burguete.

Before examining his thought itself, however, I probe the professional and political decisions that shaped the life and career of Enrique Ruiz-Fornells. Although he has received virtually no attention from scholars, he was an important protagonist in modern Spanish history. Admittedly he did not assume his most outwardly noteworthy position—that of military advisor to Azaña—until long after the demise of Restoration Spain. But his career and actions both before and after Primo de Rivera's seizure of power, like those of Burguete and García Pérez, merit ample attention in their own right, because they shed light on how his ideas developed throughout his life as well as on the relationship between those ideas and his actions. An especially rich source—his unpublished memoirs—provides an unusually revealing look into the politics and professional outlook of this important army officer. Of course, the historian must remain cautious about using this sort of source, written years after the decisions and events they describe. But in the case of Ruiz-Fornells' autobiographical reflections substantial doubts seem unwarranted, since virtually all of the events he recounted can be confirmed by reference to his personal service record or other sources. Furthermore, the opinions he expressed in his memoirs remain consistent with the views found in the books, pamphlets, and articles he wrote throughout his life.

* * *

The son of a military musician of sparse economic resources, Ruiz-Fornells was born in Albacete during the excitement of Spain's "Glorious Revolution" of 1868. As a boy he had little opportunity to forge strong bonds to any particular place or its people, attending schools in his native city, Madrid, Valencia, Burgos, Santoña, and Santander before entering the Academia General Militar in August 1884. After three years of study there he was named a probationary second lieutenant (*alférez provisional*) in the infantry, an appointment that lost its provisional status the following year after he completed a course of study in gunnery and shooting. In July 1890 he returned to the Academia General as a teacher's assistant (*ayudante de profesor*), beginning work there during a period in which—as he later wrote—the army suffered from profound organizational deficiencies and from strategic and tactical doctrines so outdated that they failed to take into account the lessons of the Franco-Prussian War.[2]

It is clear that Ruiz-Fornells, regardless of whether he exaggerated somewhat when recalling the army's condition then, reacted with genuine outrage to the state of military affairs that he discovered after leaving the academy. His strong desire to transform the Spanish armed forces, which he rightly perceived as of vital interest to the condition of his country as a whole, remained his most intense passion for the rest of his life. He therefore regarded the attempted liberal revamping of the military during the 1880s by General Cassola very positively, writing that even though Cassola had failed to implement his plans completely, they had nevertheless served as the starting point for the long-overdue reforms that were realized more than four decades later under his guidance and that of Azaña.[3]

After the Academia General Militar was closed in the summer of 1893, Ruiz-Fornells was assigned to the newly established Infantry Academy, writing several instructional pamphlets and two major textbooks for use there. The first text, the product of a collaborative effort between him and a colleague, described the structure and organization of the Spanish army and several of its foreign counterparts. This work and the other book he wrote then, *La educación moral del soldado* (The moral education of the soldier), remained staples of academy life for years to come, appearing in a total of more than two dozen editions and earning their author some extra money.[4] This supplement to his army pay was not insignificant; like many officers, he spent a good portion of his career struggling to make ends meet, even working as a geometry teacher at various private schools while simultaneously carrying out his military duties.[5]

In January 1897 Ruiz-Fornells was sent to Cuba, where Spanish troops were struggling to suppress the independence movement's armed rising. He had scant opportunity to engage in combat, however, returning to the Iberian Peninsula only four months later after falling ill. Now a captain, he began work for the War Ministry, and the following year he was named a tutor (*ayudante de profesor*) to the young King Alfonso XIII. The king's strong interest in the armed forces, which became all too apparent after his mother relinquished her regency in 1902, did not, however, translate into a positive experience for Ruiz-Fornells. Although he had no significant personal conflicts with the king at the time and apparently carried out his assignment without hesitation, he later accused Alfonso of ingratitude and of foiling several of his chances for professional advancement.[6]

Such experiences undoubtedly served to reinforce Ruiz-Fornells' antimonarchist politics, even if his natural inclination toward liberal democratic government was already strong enough on its own. Although he never displayed any open opposition to the king's rule and—as long as Alfonso remained in power—he emphasized to cadets the importance of loyalty to the monarchy,[7] his writings betrayed a liberal disposition diametrically opposed to much of what the Spanish crown represented. As I show later, the vision of history he revealed early in his career had far more in common with the visions of leading Spanish antimonarchists than with those of colleagues such as García Pérez.

But there was clearly a personal element to Ruiz-Fornells' distaste for the monarchy. His ties with the king suffered from the same difficulty evident in so many of his other personal relationships: he often perceived himself as unappreciated and sometimes even as the target of conspiracy. Perhaps in part because of his ambulant childhood, he found it very difficult to forge close friendships for the rest of his life. Indeed, his memoirs include numerous references to attempts by colleagues and collaborators to damage his career. Besides the king, he asserted, other royal tutors, fellow officers, and even Manuel Azaña endeavored, often for selfish reasons, to thwart his professional ambitions and plans for improving the armed forces. He accused an infantry colonel, for example, of attempting to cut short his official trip to France in 1920 simply because the colonel had wanted the assignment for himself.[8] His later difficulties with Azaña, moreover, stemmed as much from the arrogant manner in which the Republican politician treated him as from professional disagreements.[9]

Ruiz-Fornells' attempts at reform and his harsh criticism of Spanish military affairs must have seemed iconoclastic to the many officers whose ideas and professional benefits he so harshly attacked, and it is likely that he engendered enough resentment to fuel some of the conspiratorial activities he perceived. After the king became old enough to assume power and Ruiz-Fornells returned to the Infantry Academy, his actions there as a cofounder of the infantry section of the Escuela Central de Tiro, or gunnery school, and later as a member of the general staff brought him into conflict with various powerful elements within the armed forces. He joined the renowned military writer Modesto Navarro, under whom he served on the peninsula and later in Morocco, in strongly opposing Burguete's proposed tactical program,[10] and disagreements with artillery officers characterized virtually every reform project he undertook.

Despite such conflicts, however, throughout his career many of his writings earned Ruiz-Fornells official endorsement and the praise of his superiors. For example, he penned the infantry's 1908 tactical manual, which even appeared in a French edition. He also received many choice assignments, including orders in 1905 to visit military training facilities in France, Italy, and Switzerland. During this trip he also traveled to Florence, Venice, Lucerne, Geneva, and other foreign cities, visits that, as he later wrote, allowed him to "grow culturally [*aumentar mi cultura*]."[11] Opportunities for such travel were quite rare for Spanish officers and civilians then, yet Ruiz-Fornells managed to return on official visits to Italy in 1924 and to France in 1923, 1924, and 1928. His distinctively "European" outlook was probably strengthened by these journeys, and—like many other Spaniards who rejected traditionalist proposals for national regeneration—his experiences abroad set him apart from a majority of his colleagues.

Ruiz-Fornells also spent time in Morocco, a far more common destination than France or Italy for Spanish officers. During the latter part of 1909 he served as aide-de-camp to Navarro, returning the next year to take a post on the general staff and rise to the rank of major. He returned to Africa as a lieutenant colonel in 1920, taking command of a battalion stationed in the Ceuta-Tetuán area. Although this assignment, as he subsequently wrote in his memoirs, proved to be one of the most satisfying of his career, he was disappointed to find that the officer corps in Africa still suffered from the same lack of tactical knowledge and basic military skills that he had observed in 1909. In strong contrast to many of his colleagues, he blamed the Spanish army's deficiencies largely on its *failure* to assimilate the lessons of European warfare. Officers who argued that continental military history had no relevance to northern Africa, he charged, really just wanted to avoid the serious study and reflection that understanding the European campaigns entailed.[12]

The 1921 Spanish "disaster" near Anual, Morocco, occurred during this period, although Ruiz-Fornells' battalion had no direct involvement in the debacle. Yet his relative distance from the actual event did not prevent him from subsequently identifying what he perceived as its principal causes. Using the same language as the antiliberal vitalists and traditionalists he normally opposed, he blamed in part "our inborn character, which causes us to disregard even the most elemental rules of security and defense." Ruiz-Fornells, it seems, had a historicist perception of national character, even if he failed to praise the insolent, passionate, and imprudent elements of that character that his antirationalist colleagues found so attractive. In particular, he criticized the impetuous general Manuel Fernández Silvestre for advancing too rapidly into enemy territory without the required means, materials, or "knowledge of the spirit and the means of the enemy"—by most accounts a reasonable assessment.[13] He also faulted the failure of the officers and their superiors to provide the soldiers with sufficient instruction, the lack of modern equipment and weaponry, the inability of any of the military commanders to exhibit the leadership qualities necessary to hold the soldiers together in the face of disaster, and finally the king's imprudent support of Silvestre's actions. In contrast, he maintained that High Commissioner for Africa Dámaso Berenguer deserved none of the criticism he received for Anual, because Silvestre had acted without the knowledge of Berenguer. In fact, Ruiz-Fornells lauded Berenguer for his subsequent leadership of the "reconquest" of the territory lost in the debacle[14]—praise that may have contributed to his subsequent appointment to a high post during Berenguer's brief stint as head of state in 1930.

In 1922 Ruiz-Fornells was promoted to colonel, returning to Spain for a brief posting at Teruel and then taking an assignment with the general staff. He also resumed work at the *Memorial de Infantería,* a journal he had founded ten years earlier while serving as head of the Infantry Section at the War Ministry. He had sought, as he later wrote, to replace the defunct *Estudios Militares* and *Revista Técnica de Infantería y Caballería* with a publication of a similar scientific and scholarly focus. One of his collaborators in these endeavors was León Fernández Fernández, a fellow officer, a psychologist, and a friend with whom he had taught at the Infantry Academy in Toledo. Fernández, who penned more than a dozen books and pamphlets, shared Ruiz-Fornells' strong interest in history, military education, and war studies in general, and his influence probably explains the inclusion of so much material on psychology in Ruiz-Fornells' textbooks.[15] Not surprisingly, then, the journal regularly published articles on such topics, which received relatively little attention from Spain's more politically oriented military dailies.

On the general staff Ruiz-Fornells devoted considerable efforts to reforming the army's educational programs and tactical doctrines, in the process provoking strong resistance from his more complacent colleagues, who, he charged, often protested his endeavors simply because of envy and their desire to avoid additional work.[16] He continued to display his passion for changing what he saw as outdated and ineffective policies when in 1925 he took over the infantry section of the Escuela Central de Tiro, an institution he had played an important role in creating years earlier. Needless to say, his lifelong willingness to attack the very institutions on which his livelihood depended set him far apart from García Pérez and the other officers who, like himself, spent most of their professional lives intimately involved with military education. He also differed from García Pérez in his mathematical and technical skills, which he displayed throughout his life in his writings and work at the Escuela Central.

Ruiz-Fornells strongly condemned General Miguel Primo de Rivera, who established his dictatorship in September 1923 in the wake of the political fallout over Anual and widespread social unrest. Primo de Rivera's seizure of power was in sharp conflict with Ruiz-Fornells' political views, and the dictator's military policies provided him with little satisfaction either. The army, he believed, continued to suffer from many organizational flaws, and the dictator's decisions in military matters clearly revealed "the pernicious influence of the king." Ruiz-Fornells came out strongly against Primo de Rivera's decision to reestablish the Academia General Militar, viewing it as a threat to the infantry's relative position within the armed forces, and he described the man chosen to run the new academy—Francisco Franco—as "*guerrillero e ignorante.*"[17] Unlike so many other Spaniards, Ruiz-Fornells employed the term *guerrillero*—closely identified with the rising of Spanish partisans against Napoleon—in a negative fashion, thereby rejecting a Spanish "national characteristic" that García Pérez and many others had praised. His sentiments about the new academy and its leader would manifest themselves very tangibly during the following decade, when the academy was dissolved as part of the reforms designed by Azaña and himself.

Ruiz-Fornells even condemned Primo's treatment of the artillery corps, whose members strongly resented the dictatorship's imposition of the system of merit promotion favored by the *africanistas*. Ruiz-Fornells had never regarded the artillery very warmly, nor did he support the system of merit promotions that so favored the officers who served in Morocco. He also charged that Primo's actions in fact facilitated the artillery's later "unfortunate resurrection [*resurrección con más empuje y más funesta*]" after the advent of the Republic. According to Ruiz-Fornells, the artillery corps, which became republican and antimonarchist in reaction to the dictator's policies, returned in the 1930s to "tyrannize" the rest of the army by shamelessly promoting its own selfish interests.[18]

In 1928 Ruiz-Fornells was named brigadier general, the position in which he would end his career. He blamed the king for blocking his promotion a year earlier, an action that had hurt him deeply and, as he painfully recalled, made it impossible for him to ascend to the rank of major general before being required because of his age to enter the reserves.[19] The thwarting of his professional ambitions did not, however, signify the end of his influence; during the brief regime of Dámaso Berenguer he served as undersecretary to General Manuel Goded,[20] and his subsequent assistance to Republican war minister Azaña was, of course, hardly a minor affair.[21]

* * *

Like Burguete and García Pérez, Ruiz-Fornells revealed his basic ideological outlook early in his career, and the first indications of his views emerged, as did those of the others, in his historical writings. Although he did not devote as much time to the study and writing of history as many military writers, he strongly believed in its didactic potential. Officers, he argued, should teach their men about the moral virtues and vices that drove important events and figures of the past, and they should teach their men history in order to help explain and inculcate military values.[22] His own interpretation of Spanish history and the development of Western civilization in general, moreover, revealed that he perceived an intimate connection between warfare and human progress. History also taught, he wrote, that the military should remain subordinate to civilian rule.

According to Ruiz-Fornells, history proved that violence was both necessary and natural and that its organized expression, war, stemmed from "a moral necessity, fostering the progress of nations and revealing in man and society the most admirable and sublime passion of sacrifice for the *Patria*." This characterization of war as a "moral" phenomenon closely resembled, of course, the sentiments of Burguete, García Pérez, and many other contemporaries both within and outside of Spain. But Ruiz-Fornells differed fundamentally from the great majority of war theorists of his day by stressing the "tranquillity, well-being, and dignity of the citizen" that he believed should serve as the ultimate goal of a soldier's sacrifices for his country. In other words, it was not some imprecise, mystical notion of a sublime fatherland that should inspire soldiers, but rather a clear conception of their rights and responsibilities as citizens. And, as in his emphasis on citizenship, he also betrayed a strong attachment to Enlightenment ideals in his praise for reason and science.[23]

The "ancient peoples," Ruiz-Fornells rather vaguely explained, had advanced the study of the "moral sciences" to a very high level, an achievement that explained the "great discipline, excellent spirit, and admirable moral forces" of their soldiers. Significantly, he not only lauded the technical prowess and mechanical skills he saw in the ancient world's great armies, but he also attributed their successes to the sentiment of duty and patriotism instilled in their soldiers. As his own endeavors as an army officer and teacher demonstrated, he felt that it was far better to educate soldiers to believe in what they were fighting for than to adopt the attitude of conservatives who perceived national armies of the masses as threats to the status quo and therefore demanded nothing but passive obedience from men in arms. Hence for him "military science [*la ciencia bélica*]" involved the use of "moral" and other human sciences as well as mathematics, physics, and other such tools.[24]

"The social state of all peoples and the state of military science have always marched together in perfect harmony," Ruiz-Fornells wrote, stressing the natural "correlation between how force is employed and the political and moral constitution of societies."[25] He also credited military science with sustaining all the legacies of ancient Greek and Roman civilization from which modern society benefited. In his eyes the fall of the Roman Empire corresponded to the simultaneous weakening of its military institutions and degeneration of its people, the latter stemming from the decline of Rome's formerly outstanding tradition of "scientific progress." He attributed the empire's past military strength solely to the way it had educated its soldiers, linking the decline of the Roman armed forces to attempts to substitute quantity for quality in the manning of its armies. At the same time that the empire had lost power, he wrote, the soldier had relinquished his role as a "citizen of the *Patria*" to become a mere "servant to a general." As I show later, Ruiz-Fornells' vision for the Spanish army of his own day would entail a fusion of quantity—in the form of the army of the masses—with the democratic notion of *every* soldier's rights and responsibilities as a citizen.[26]

After the fall of the Roman Empire, Ruiz-Fornells wrote, military domination by the barbarians and the subsequent rise of feudalism took place during a period characterized by "laxity and decay." In this epoch, which he placed between the fifth and eleventh centuries, neither arts nor sciences received significant attention from the people. Only the forces of what he vaguely referred to as "morals" could be sustained, he wrote, and they owed their flourishing state to constant religious strife. Military science mirrored society in general, entering "a real period of regression, accentuated because men abandoned themselves to softness and luxury, turning to defensive weapons and machinery to make up for what they lacked in valor, enthusiasm, and military education." Echoing the at least guarded admiration for the medieval Muslim world found in the works of virtually every Spanish military writer of his day, he characterized the war methods of the Arab peoples as better than those of the other peoples of the period, although he believed that they too exhibited signs of decline.[27]

According to Ruiz-Fornells, the period of the eleventh through the fourteenth century saw slight improvements, and the following 200 years marked a key period of transition in Western history. The forces of a "new civilization" arose to take on "the ancients," nations achieved some degree of political unity, and the "scientific state" of nations began to reflect their "social state." Feudalism no longer dominated during this period, "only intervening in the life of nations as a strong element of opposition." In general, Ruiz-Fornells wrote, feudal, communal, and ecclesiastical interests clashed without one type ever obtaining enough power to achieve complete supremacy over the others. He characterized these centuries as "an epoch of stalemate but not of peace, which nevertheless witnessed advances and progress and the growing importance of the middle classes."[28]

The arts, letters, and sciences flourished despite their constant conflict with "the ancient," Ruiz-Fornells wrote, citing the discovery of new mathematical applications and the invention of the compass, the printing press, and gunpowder. But science was still valued primarily for its ability "to satisfy human intelligence" instead of for its practical value, because "the beautiful and the true was of more interest than the useful," he lamented. Unlike Burguete, he clearly had little use for aesthetics. The failure to grasp the utility of scientific discoveries had a particularly adverse effect on the advancement of military art, he wrote, noting that the establishment of schools and universities for the study of medicine, law, and other sciences had no counterpart in the world of the armed forces, which still lacked educational institutions as well as factories and workshops for the production of arms. He claimed that even the growth of permanent armies of the masses failed to produce any true understanding of strategy, because the laws of war—"natural, eternal, and not created by man"—could be understood only with the aid of science.[29] In profound contrast to Burguete and so many of his contemporaries, who had rejected rationalist approaches to warfare, he clearly subscribed to a largely positivist interpretation of military history and development.

Ruiz-Fornells' vision of medieval history also revealed strong liberal strains in its portrayal of Spain's armed forces. Not only did Spanish feudalism differ fundamentally from its counterparts elsewhere in Europe because of medieval Spain's "democratic institutions and the struggle of the Reconquest," but in his view the Spanish armed forces also paved the way for the renaissance in the art of war that followed throughout Europe.[30] He wrote that the principal element of all armies, the infantry, arose first in Spain and that the Spanish military institutions together constituted the key link between the ancient and modern military arts. As I have shown, the praise of both Burguete and García Pérez for the military aspects of medieval Spain had focused largely on the essentially "moral" forces that had propelled its great caudillos, whether in the form of "passionate" sentiments or mystical, religious power. Ruiz-Fornells, in contrast, virtually ignored the religious and other less tangible elements of the Reconquest, emphasizing instead the roots of modern military science and democratic principles that he perceived in the period. In this way he made yet another contribution to the liberal-nationalist side of the regenerationist debates raging in Spain at the time.

The next historical phase, which Ruiz-Fornells placed between the mid-sixteenth and the early eighteenth centuries, saw the ultimate demise of the ideas, sentiments, and "individualism" that had characterized the medieval period. Popular interests became more important, he wrote, and people learned to use the results of scholarship and science to harness the power of nature. The increased opportunity for international exchange "awakened an intellectual movement," bringing with it notable progress in the study of languages, philosophy, and law. Curiously, he made no mention of Spain's extensive activities as a colonial power during this period. He wrote, however, in considerable depth on military developments during the period.[31]

Reiterating his thesis on the intimate link between military science and the general state of society as a whole, Ruiz-Fornells praised the early modern army for taking full advantage of the latest scholarly and scientific discoveries. War became a larger undertaking and far more scientific in its methods, he wrote, citing improvements in fortifications technology, the creation of doctrines and regulations, the publication of great works by military writers, and the establishment of military libraries and schools. Continuing his rather simplified exposition of Spanish history, he briefly explained that the period witnessed the consolidation of the permanent army into its own "compact society, with laws, rights, duties, and special virtues—no longer just an incoherent multitude."[32] Personal influence and hierarchical power no longer shaped the system of recruitment, he claimed, and regular instruction, discipline, and uniforms became staples of military life. Even the early modern officer corps, although drawn exclusively from the aristocracy, earned his praise for supposedly acting only within the boundaries of law. In general, then, Ruiz-Fornells could not resist the tendency of many military men to portray the army as a sort of microcosm of the *patria*. But for him principles such as rights and duties were as instrumental to the health of the army—and thus to Spain as a whole—as vital forces, sacrifice, and religiosity were for many other military nationalists.

In strong contrast to the many Spaniards who condemned the Enlightenment and Bourbon rule in Spain, Ruiz-Fornells portrayed the eighteenth century as the apogee of European and Spanish history. He praised the period's modernizing reforms for supposedly fostering administrative unity and commercial growth, completely ignoring the widespread signs of domestic and imperial decline in Spain that had largely awakened the "enlightened" leaders to the need for reform in the first place. He also failed to address the popular argument that the eighteenth-century attempts at modernization contributed directly to the demise of the Spanish Empire during the next century. Quite unlike García Pérez and so many other military and civilian writers of his day, Ruiz-Fornells expressed relatively little interest in Spain's colonial past, despite the attempts of many of his contemporaries to glorify it. Indeed, he played no part in contributing to the Spanish versions of the "new imperialist" sentiments seen all over Europe, which manifested themselves in Spain in the form of the loud outcry over the Spanish defeat of 1898 and the calls for expansion in northern Africa. Years later, in fact, he even made disparaging references to King Alfonso XIII's "imperialist" pretensions in Africa.[33] Thus in yet another way his vision of Spain's regenerationist needs could not have differed more from the conservative, national-Catholic vision.

Ruiz-Fornells directed his most fervent praise for eighteenth-century Europe toward its scientific discoveries and the spirit of the French Enlightenment in general, highlighting again his support for the liberal, nationalist program that would compete so violently with those of Spanish rightists. With sentiments in stark contrast to the antiliberal, reactionary sentiments of men such as Burguete, Menéndez Pelayo, and the many other fin-de-siècle writers who despised the intellectual legacy of the eighteenth century, Ruiz-Fornells characterized Diderot's *Encyclopedia* as "the great undertaking by which to measure the state of that society [*la grande empresa que puede servir de medida en cuanto al estado de la sociedad*]." He also stressed the benefits of the supposedly increased international and cultural exchange of that time, in the process revealing how much he believed that he himself had benefited from travel abroad and exposure to foreign ideas. And he argued that the period saw a decline in the regional "customs, ideas, sentiments, and forms" that had separated different peoples from each other. "Society underwent a transformation," he wrote, "and its agitated state was reflected in its laws, in its education, and in the works of its most renowned authors."[34]

Not surprisingly, Ruiz-Fornells also lauded the military developments of the eighteenth century, a period that in fact gave rise to considerable progress in the art and science of war. Most of the new ideas came from the pen of the Comte de Guibert, a French Academy laureate and drama critic who also happened to be Europe's most influential military writer. Although many of Guibert's ideas, which forecast mass conscript armies relying on the mobility, adaptability, and increased independence of regimental units and soldiers, remained unrealized until after the French Revolution, they left an imprint on eighteenth-century military thought that clearly appealed to Ruiz-Fornells.[35] Of course, he particularly liked the emergence of notions of universal military service and of professional advancement based on merit instead of blood, which eventually came closest to reality in the armies of the masses led by Napoleon Bonaparte—an artillery officer of relatively modest origins.

Ruiz-Fornells described Prussia as "the cradle of elementary and applied tactics," writing about how the country's instructional programs fostered the orderly deployment of weapons, formations, and wartime operations. But he did not extend this praise, which in fact could apply only to the period after Prussia's occupation by Napoleonic armies, to developments in strategy. Strategic thought, he argued, became "too scientific," relying disproportionately on quantifiable factors. Here his portrayal of military history betrayed his conviction that, despite the utility of positivist approaches to war, they too had their limits. He also criticized the severe discipline characteristic of the Prussian army, which he charged "went to the extreme of degrading men and converting the Army into an institution of servility."[36]

In general, though, Ruiz-Fornells believed that the historical developments of the preceding centuries brought with them scientific, military, and political advances that left the military leaders of his own day in an ideal position to mold the perfect army. He rather optimistically envisaged the contemporary armed forces as a reflection of humanity's progress in the fields of science, letters, and industry; in positivist and mercantilist thought; and in the growing reverence for the political principles of democracy, equality, and liberty. War itself had become far less frequent and of shorter duration, but its "scientific character" and other modern attributes demanded more skill and knowledge on the part of military commanders than ever before. The "military class" as a whole, he argued, served as an "instrument of society," composed of "citizens ennobled with the honorable mission of defending citizens—not fighting against the civilian class."[37]

Ruiz-Fornells' praise for the role of the citizen-soldier in history, with its obvious implications for his regeneratist views of how to build the Spanish nation, clashed sharply with the increasingly popular antiliberal works of writers such as Burguete and García Pérez. But his rationalist interpretation of Spanish military history rested on the more typical, very strong, liberal intellectual tradition of the officer corps. Indeed, the principal textbook on military history read by cadets during the latter part of the previous century, written by General Francisco Martín Arrúe, had expounded the same sort of arguments favored by Ruiz-Fornells. Both men, for example, praised the patriotic armies of the masses engendered by the French Revolution, arguing that they represented positive historical developments upon which the continuing improvements in military science of their own day depended.[38]

* * *

Of course, Ruiz-Fornells was well aware that even if such a military organization as a successful army of the masses represented the natural culmination of historical progress, the Spanish army could never hope to assume this form without drastic changes of the kind he himself promoted. In particular, he advocated a sweeping overhaul in the systems for the recruitment, education, and deployment of Spain's men in arms, basing his proposed reforms on well-developed arguments that went far beyond his often cursory explanations of military history and Spanish history.

Above all, Ruiz-Fornells' ideas regarding the role education played in shaping an army's social, military, and "moral" effectiveness profoundly influenced his thoughts and actions, as did his strong belief in the pedagogical potential of military service itself. Even as a young officer he demonstrated an understanding of educational theories that rivaled that of many of his most forward-looking and progressive contemporaries in Spain. In addition, he was one of the first military figures in all of Europe to grasp the potential for the use of modern educational methods by officers and to develop that potential into tangible, institutionalized measures. His *Educación moral del soldado* appeared in 1894 and immediately found a permanent place in the Infantry Academy's curriculum. Although this work has received little notice from scholars of Spanish history and absolutely no attention from European military historians, it in fact represented a much more comprehensive and pragmatic articulation of many of the same ideas found in the better-remembered article "The Social Role of the Officer," by French officer Hubert Lyautey, which had been published three years earlier in the prestigious *Revue des Deux Mondes*. And it almost surely had a more significant impact than Lyautey's article, which succeeded in little more than upsetting the French high command and earning its author the "punishment" of assignment to Hanoi.[39] Ruiz-Fornells, in fact, never even cited Lyautey, but instead drew explicitly on the studies of Carlo Corsi and Paul Simon on the educational and social mission of military service.[40]

As its title suggests, Ruiz-Fornells' book reflected its author's conviction that officers should actively promote the education of their men. It informed infantry cadets of the reasons behind the pedagogical duties they would someday assume, of various methods they could employ as teachers, and of the subject matter around which they were to plan the educational programs for their units. Although a good portion of the book was significantly restructured, altered, and expanded as new editions appeared, its fundamental message remained the same: that an officer's activities as a teacher, role model, and shaper of "moral" values was of crucial importance to the state of the army and of the country as a whole.[41] And the values that cadets were told to emphasize, such as patriotism, valor, subordination, honor, and respect for civil government, remained constant as well.

Of course, most of these values espoused by Ruiz-Fornells have served for centuries as the basic precepts for armies all over the world. Others, however, stood in stark contrast to what many academy instructors undoubtedly emphasized, regardless of the subject matter they taught. The national-Catholic ideas that permeated García Pérez's thought, for example, were nowhere to be found in the textbook by Ruiz-Fornells. Although the latter referred to the utility of strong religious feelings in battle, it did so in a highly scholarly and theoretical fashion, not even mentioning Christianity or the Catholic Church.[42] And the belief of Ruiz-Fornells that the proper attitude and actions of soldiers were best fostered through rational instruction had little in common with the pedagogical methods of José Millán-Astray, who later claimed that he had evoked the more emotional tenets of the Japanese warrior philosophy of Bushido in the lessons on "morals" he presented to infantry cadets during the 1911–12 academic year.[43]

Most strikingly, Ruiz-Fornells' text strongly emphasized his faith—discussed earlier in this chapter—in democratic values, respect for civilian government, and the concept of the "citizen-soldier." As early as 1894 the book's prologue, by the renowned military writer Pedro A. Berenguer, argued that the growing "democratic spirit" of the age meant that "military authority cannot prevent the soldier from freely examining his conscience." Rather than attempting to prevent the dissemination of subversive ideas within the barracks by banning periodicals, Berenguer had argued, military authorities should instead strive for "the gradual and patient conquest of our soldier's spirit." Citing Tocqueville, he wrote that although the obedience stemming from such an approach may not be as "exact" as that produced by harsh discipline and other authoritarian measures, it will be "more forceful and intelligent, since its roots will lie in free will supported not just by instinct but by reason as well."[44]

Twenty-four years later Ruiz-Fornells, in his prologue to the textbook's eighth edition, was still praising Berenguer for the wisdom of his observations. By striving to educate soldiers in the fashion Berenguer had advocated, officers helped to "prepare their men to sacrifice themselves spontaneously for the *patria,* inculcating in them the proper ideals and fortifying their aptitudes and energies so that they pass their qualities on to their descendants." Most important, Ruiz-Fornells wrote, the officers' endeavors would yield "citizens capable of elevating and glorifying" their country.[45] In his 1902 speech to fellow officers he demonstrated that his textbook's stated goal of molding soldiers into "good citizens" was more than just a lofty ideal intended to inspire cadets. The "officer-citizen" himself, he exclaimed, served as "priest to a divinity: the *Patria*!"[46]

Ruiz-Fornells' case for universal military service depended to a considerable degree on his insistence that soldiers and officers identify themselves primarily as citizens. The notion of the intimate relationship between soldiery and national citizenship itself rested on a view of history that, as we have seen, had its roots in Enlightenment-era military thought. Mere mercenaries, after all, had no stake in the wars in which they fought, so they could hardly be trusted to operate with the autonomy that the new tactical programs presupposed. Only after the French Revolution and subsequent Napoleonic rule engendered mass nationalism, Ruiz-Fornells had argued, did "citizen-armies" come to predominate in Europe. This belief in the patriotic and military power of such "nations in arms" was common among his contemporaries and characterized a view of history that has prevailed to this day, as does the notion that military service itself can play a key role in the formation of modern national identities.[47]

Ruiz-Fornells' arguments for universal military service, like those rejected by Burguete and García Pérez but lauded by many other officers and even such progressive entities as the Institución Libre de Enseñanza, thus represented the logical culmination of an idea that had existed for centuries and had first found a strong voice in Spain in the liberal rhetoric of the Napoleonic period.[48] But for Ruiz-Fornells the recruitment of the masses into large armies that practiced patriotic indoctrination was not enough; nothing less than service by *all* levels of male society would do. And the goal of indoctrinating soldiers was not loyalty to the monarchy or some other authoritarian representative of the state, but rather the instilling of democratic notions of rights and responsibilities. Conversely, "the citizen's most transcendental and important" responsibility was to offer military service in times both of war and of peace.[49] In the appendix to the 1918 edition of his textbook Ruiz-Fornells even included a sample speech, based on French captain Charles Jacob's "Discours d'un capitaine à ses soldats," on the importance of obligatory service. The speech, he believed, served as a good model for Spanish officers designing educational programs for their men.[50]

Ruiz-Fornells' campaign for truly universal military service, from which neither personal connections nor wealth could be used to obtain an exemption, echoed many of the ideas found in French socialist Jean Jaurès's *L'Armée nouvelle*. This book, which had made a strong impact across Europe, had stressed the social potential of a truly national army based on obligatory military service. Ruiz-Fornells by no means embraced every argument made by Jaurès, but his strong support for creating a Spanish "nation in arms" seemed to put him in agreement with the French socialist thinker on a key issue. And his passion for the idea undoubtedly explained part of his initial willingness to collaborate years later with Azaña, who greatly admired the spirit behind the military ideas of Jaurès even when doubting their practicality.[51] Conversely, Ruiz-Fornells' vigorous promotion of ideas associated with Jaurès's military program may well have helped attract Azaña to him when he undertook his reforms of the armed forces.

Ruiz-Fornells' relatively progressive political views did not, however, translate into much sympathy for the rapidly expanding workers' movements in Spain. But he eschewed the point-blank, morally based rejection of socialism and anarchism typical of many Spanish traditionalists, as the discussion of the two movements that he added to the 1918 edition of his *Educación moral del soldado* made clear. In it he avoided the conservative tendency to ascribe the rise of socialism and anarchism in Spain to the intrusion of foreign, "godless" forces, instead recognizing why socialism could appeal to many workers and attempting to analyze it rationally. After discussing socialism and anarchism in surprising depth, he concluded by characterizing some socialist precepts as "just, viable, and rational" but the others as hopelessly unrealistic. For, as the failure of social experiments such as those pursued by Robert Owen in New Harmony, Indiana, had demonstrated, the pretext of economic equality "implies a political-civil organization based on unrealistic and impractical conditions which do not fit within the molds of human nature."[52] Therefore, although he may not have understood socialist and anarchist thought completely, he at least attempted to grasp its essentials and explain them to cadets in rational terms.

But Ruiz-Fornells was considerably less generous in his appraisal of socialist leaders, whom he dismissed as "clever exploiters who, without working themselves, thrive upon the money and savings of poor workers and who will become the most horrible despots and tyrants should we ever have the misfortune to see socialism triumph completely."[53] He also attacked their efforts to engender antimilitarism and "antipatriotism," insisting rather unconvincingly that the military posed no threat to civil society. This argument, which seemed even less tenable in light of the need he felt to include admonitions in his textbooks to respect civilian rule, foreshadowed the later writings on Spanish antimilitarism of General Emilio Mola. Mola, who would plan the military rebellion that sparked the Spanish Civil War, rather curiously concluded that although antimilitarist movements normally surfaced only in militarist societies, in Spain they had somehow appeared without the requisite precondition.[54]

In the 1918 edition of his textbook Ruiz-Fornells also felt it necessary to warn cadets that as officers they would have to learn to cope with insults directed at them and at the army as a whole in periodicals, books, and socialist organizations, and he forecast that subversive ideas might very well surface within their own barracks. An officer's duties, then, included educating his men to understand "the prejudices and false concepts behind the argument that the military deprives a man of his will and dignity."[55] After all, he reasoned, the demands of military service do not merely serve the whims of one person, but instead allow the army to perform most effectively its "elevated mission" for the *patria*. Moreover, he continued, it was truly most "debilitating for an individual's will and human dignity to submit oneself to a committee and blindly and without knowledge of its motives obey its orders to go on strike, despite the clear prejudice of this action to one's own interests and to the material needs of one's family."[56] Thus, his response to attacks by socialists against the army was simply to turn one of their most potent accusations—against the "enslavement" of military service—on its head.

Ruiz-Fornells' slightly more positive appraisal of German and Italian socialists, which echoed that of Burguete, stemmed from his perception that many of the leaders of those countries—"above all those who follow the inspiration of Hervé"—understood the power of nationalist sentiments.[57] Along the same lines, he condemned the supporters of contemporary European pacifist movements as hopelessly deluded. Echoing the reasoning of Burguete and García Pérez—and virtually all of his other colleagues at the time—he perceived war as an unavoidable product of human nature.

* * *

Ruiz-Fornells' conception of human nature itself rested largely on his own fervent faith in the power of science. Just as scientific study provided ample proof of the absurdity of pacifist contentions, he maintained, it also had much to offer the military world. Accordingly, his textbook provided cadets with a strong dose of science—especially in its biological and social forms—which he believed would aid them greatly when they became officers.

In his prologue to the 1918 edition of *Educación moral* Ruiz-Fornells happily reported that even in Spain the "constant evolution" of human progress had finally brought with it more modern educational methods and an extension of scholarly focus from "speculative sciences" to "positive sciences, where one finds the most solid foundations."[58] As he had revealed in his historical writings and continued to demonstrate throughout his career, he perceived that the value of science lay primarily in its practical applications. Therefore, his calls for a complete modernization of military education in Spain did not imply so much instruction in the latest scientific knowledge as the imparting of its *practical* utility. When he first began teaching at the Infantry Academy, for example, he was dismayed to discover a program of studies that he felt focused on fostering an understanding of science that was of little real use to cadets.[59] His own positivist inclinations, however, prevented him from reacting against the scientific slant of the day's army in such an extreme fashion as did colleagues such as Burguete. In his 1902 speech he therefore emphasized at length the need to properly balance the theoretical and practical aspects of military science and education. He advocated an approach that emphasized applications of a "rational" nature and were supported by theory of practical, positive utility.[60]

Interestingly Ruiz-Fornells applied his belief in the utility of scientific methods and knowledge not so much to purely military subjects as to human nature and behavior in general, revealing the same paradoxical tendency seen in many of the period's avowed enemies of reason to use biology, sociology, psychology, and even geography to better understand the inherently nonquantifiable, "moral" nature of humans and their world. The first part of the later editions of his *Educación moral,* for example, included a long discussion of the physiological, psychological, and spiritual forces in humans and in life in general that in many respects echoed Burguete's *Dinamismo espiritual* and, of course, the writings of his many contemporaries of similar views.[61]

In a discussion that was rather remarkable for a military academy textbook, Ruiz-Fornells pushed his positivism to extremes, dividing everything on earth into the categories of "inert bodies" and "living bodies," carefully describing each and then subdividing the latter into "vegetable" and "animal." He then examined the different qualities of animals, distinguishing those characterized by a state of "sensitivity [*sensibilidad*]," as manifested by their purely instinctive actions, from their "rational" human counterparts. Humans are superior to all other animals, he wrote, because they generally act according to "conscience, reason, and free will." His description of humans in general corresponded largely to Burguete's description of the "intellectual" man, who differed from those dominated by the forces of "passion" or of "instinct." Most unlike Burguete, however, Ruiz-Fornells devoted practically no analysis whatsoever to the subject of passion, even though the two men agreed to a certain extent about the "moral" character of the forces shaping humanity. Yet Ruiz-Fornells did not neglect the concept of "spirit [*alma*]" entirely, defining it as "the vital principle in man" that represents "the spirit united to the body, which makes it possible to live, move, feel, think, and want."[62]

The knowledge of this sort imparted to cadets did not stop there. In fact, readers of Ruiz-Fornells' textbook learned about cells, tissues, organs, senses, memory, imagination, and other such topics through analytical descriptions, and they were also taught to apply the methods of natural sciences such as biology and chemistry to their examinations of psychology, sociology, and even willpower and morale. Like Burguete and so many other writers of his day, Ruiz-Fornells revealed the influence of Hippolyte Taine in his writings, and his book referred explicitly to the famous French thinker.[63]

At first glance the inclusion of so much of this sort of material in a textbook for infantry cadets seems rather odd, especially in light of its author's stated opposition to instruction in pure "theory." But, unlike Burguete, Ruiz-Fornells focused above all on Taine's positivist methods and attitudes toward knowledge. In this sense, at least, his reasoning was more consistent than that of many antirationalists of his day, who paradoxically used the intellectual tools of science to attack its basic validity. Hence, in his mind it made perfect sense to teach these topics to future officers, whose positions would require the fullest possible understanding of the army's "principal element and indispensable and irreplaceable basis": man.[64] Moreover, scientific knowledge of mass psychology and sociology could serve an officer for other reasons as well. The army, Ruiz-Fornells argued, "is nothing but its own society within a broader society or nation, and in consequence its rules and laws grow out of the nation's sociological rules and laws and the psychological traits characteristic of its inhabitants."[65] Besides justifying the study by military officials of sociological principles, this argument also fit well with his belief that the Spanish army—as the supreme institution of the Spanish nation as a whole—should reflect the rise of modern democratic values. In addition, his patronage of the social sciences put him on the same ground as many officers with whom he otherwise had little in common, such as Burguete, as well as with his friend and colleague at the academy León Fernández. And, on the most basic level, it again revealed his tendency, common to many of his colleagues, to view the army as a sort of model for the Spanish *patria* in general.

The scientific slant of Ruiz-Fornells' textbook also extended to its discussion of human morality and the moral qualities supposedly inherent to warfare. Again revealing the influence of the Enlightenment's optimistic vision of humanity and progress, he deemed it necessary to define the "good" as "all that is desirable because it is directed toward the *human purpose* and is useful or profitable to all men." He defined its counterpart, the "bad," in an equally simplistic manner, writing that it stood "in opposition to that purpose, and is in consequence prejudicial or harmful to all men." Significantly, these definitions underlay his attempt to scientifically define "happiness" as a concept. Cadets learned that happiness, which he described as the feeling of satisfaction stemming from "good," served as the motive of all human conduct. To attain happiness, he wrote, "we must adjust our conduct to a series of principles dictated by science." Understanding those principles requires the use of "moral science," he wrote, defining it as "the science which contains the laws by which man should act in order to obtain his own happiness and that of his peers."[66] His emphasis on proper behavior toward one's "fellow men [*semejantes*]" contrasted sharply with the attitude of Burguete. Whereas Ruiz-Fornells believed that the "duties" informing proper conduct toward one's neighbors stem from the Golden Rule, Burguete had echoed Nietzsche's condemnation of moral systems built around the precept of love for one's neighbor.[67]

In Ruiz-Fornells' mind, matters of morals and duty were intimately related to pedagogy. To educate, he wrote, is to foster the linking of "moral ideas" with "sentiments." Like Burguete and García Pérez, he stressed the distinction between education and instruction. According to Ruiz-Fornells' textbook, "moral instruction" involved defining and explaining "moral laws, rules, and precepts," whereas "moral education" entailed exploring the relationship between those laws and human sentiment.[68] As the basic foundation for the book itself, his notion of moral education underlay every aspect of his portrayal to cadets of an officer's proper comportment before his men, and throughout his life it played a substantial role in shaping his identity as an officer. In his prologue to the Spanish edition of J. F. C. Fuller's *Training Soldiers for War,* for example, he would reiterate these views on moral education, citizen-soldiers, and the "social mission" of officers.[69]

On a more specific and practical level, Ruiz-Fornells' conception of education manifested itself in his suggestions that officers employ the latest scientific methods in order to shape their soldiers morally. He even discussed the use of music, art, and ceremony to foster a sentiment of duty and a willingness to sacrifice oneself for the *patria,* although he especially favored daily readings and lectures organized by officers for their men. His lessons to cadets included a discussion of the power of suggestion (*"medios de sugerir la emoción"*) and mass psychology—subjects that Burguete had urged the academies to make a part of their curricula.[70] He also argued that modern pedagogical science cast serious doubt on the efficacy of using punishment to obtain discipline, maintaining that officers should resort to harsh measures only as a last resort. This view corresponded to his basic belief that the best soldiers were those who had been both morally prepared and convinced through reason to remain loyal to their officers and to fight and die for the *patria* when necessary. "The true roots of discipline," he wrote, "lie in the sentiments of affection, confidence, and respect for one's superior."[71] Companies and squadrons should function more as families and schools than as institutions of coercion, he instructed cadets.[72]

Despite his tendency to portray the education of soldiers as a sort of scientific endeavor best approached through clearly defined principles, Ruiz-Fornells also realized that attaining the confidence and respect of soldiers often required tailoring one's methods to unique situations. In particular, he stressed the need for officers to consider the differing geographical and cultural characteristics of enlisted men, noting that within different regions as well as countries "ancestry, climate, customs, and religion can change one's character and inclinations."[73] Revealing the influence of Taine's geographical determinism that is also found in fin-de-siècle works by writers such as Burguete and Ángel Ganivet, he emphasized the importance of employing educational methods in harmony with the "character" of the pupils. Spaniards in general, he wrote, had little in common with the *"carácter vivo del francés, la calma y tenacidad germanas y la flema inglesa,"* but they enjoyed an ability to thrive in various regions as well as an aptitude for foreign wars and "long and adventurous expeditions." He also asserted that the Spanish character was "sober [*sobrio*]" and "long-suffering [*sufrido*]," thereby reiterating a common theme of Spanish intellectuals—witness Ganivet's praise for "the natural and human stoicism of Seneca"—that also flourished within the ranks of the country's armed forces.[74] Like so many of his compatriots, Ruiz-Fornells believed that the peninsula's history had left its people with pronounced "Arab" and "Gothic" traits, and he described the typical Spaniard as "serious, intelligent, imaginative, impressionable, lazy, and arrogant." To this combination of adjectives he added traces of

"Arab fanaticism," which he claimed remained a part of the Spanish character. The latter trait, he wrote, explained how a Spaniard could remain indifferent to discomfort and to a certain point forsake the pleasures of life unattainable without work. This indifference, however, had its limits, for "at a given moment we can become empowered with a fury that makes us capable of the greatest feats."[75]

Not surprisingly, Ruiz-Fornells emphasized the meaning for the military man of all these qualities, some of which he cast in a positive light. In battle Spanish soldiers have traditionally exhibited valor, resistance, tenacity, steadiness, enthusiasm, and a tendency toward exaltation, he claimed. Officers must act with full knowledge of the wide variety of traits found in their soldiers, which he believed to stem from "the ethnic diversity that shapes our character and the physical contrasts found in the country's climates and landscapes. The great spiritual endeavors that were sustained for so long [such as the Reconquest] can be explained by the succession of forces, the repetition of emotions, actions, and continuous reactions—short and violent—all within periods of time long enough for energy to be consumed and then arise again; in other words, there exists an exquisite *impressionability* which makes it possible for the spirit to experience a new sensation after barely recovering from its last exaltation."[76] He also repeated the widely held belief in the proclivity of Spaniards for guerrilla warfare, and he stressed the need for officers to combat the "Arab" characteristics of pride, arrogance, and indolence they would encounter in their soldiers.[77] For Ruiz-Fornells the "Arab" elements in the Spanish character—which meant in essence the "anti-European" elements—were far from praiseworthy; they stood for the negative aspects of that character. Although he may have concurred with the traditionalist and antirationalist writers in recognizing the presence of this supposed national characteristic, he condemned it rather than seeing it as a possible source of strength.

In Ruiz-Fornells' view the ethnic and geographical differences within Spain had also contributed to the strong feelings of regionalism that colored Spanish history. Although he maintained that a common national character served as a fundamental link between all Spaniards, he also acknowledged the need for officers to reckon with the "great differences between the prudent and deliberate Galicians, the dignified Castilians, the forthright Aragonese and Navarrese, the serious Catalans, the festive Valencians, the clever Andalusians, and the Basques, who still dream of special privileges and speak a language completely different from Castilian."[78]

* * *

Finally, Ruiz-Fornells held a vision of war itself that—like his views on human sciences and education—paradoxically reflected both the liberal positivist heritage of the nineteenth-century officer corps and the growing influence of vitalist reverence for the power of "moral" forces. As he demonstrated in a series of speeches on the infantry's use of firepower, he was capable of conducting sophisticated analytical and mathematical studies of military tactics, and he put these skills to good use in his work at the Escuela Central de Tiro.[79] But a less materialist perception of war itself, not entirely unlike that of his more vitalist and mystical colleagues, lay behind some of his attempts to analyze warfare scientifically. War, he argued, was "a necessity of moral origin," and he echoed Burguete's conviction that an army's "moral force" had more value than its "material" counterpart.[80] Moral force in general was inherently superior to the intellectual and physical, he wrote, thereby explaining why he deemed moral education so much more important than instruction aimed at improving the theoretical abilities or physical skills of soldiers.[81]

Although Ruiz-Fornells' perception of the moral character of warfare by no means surfaced as often or prominently in his writings as in many other vitalist works of the day, it remained a part of his thinking even after World War I led many believers in the primacy of war's spiritual dimensions to revise their views. In a speech he delivered in the 1930s on the Great War's effect on subsequent tactical thought, he noted that the previously popular belief in "offensive war at all costs" had lost much of its appeal. Of course, he himself had resisted joining the prewar enthusiasm for the offensive, as his criticism of Burguete's tactical program had made clear. But even after the war he warned against completely discounting the moral elements of combat associated with offensive doctrine; he had never, after all, entirely dismissed such elements himself. Although the bloody stalemate on the western front had demonstrated the failure of military thinkers to understand the consequences of the growth in firepower, he wrote, they had not erred completely in focusing on the moral qualities of warfare. Moral force without tangible, material support may not do the job alone, he maintained in his speech, but it was nevertheless of crucial importance, and without it the troops on the western front could never have advanced after more than three years in the trenches.[82]

* * *

Despite this assertion, however, for most of his life Ruiz-Fornells' belief in the moral qualities of warfare occupied a relatively minor position in his overall *Weltanschauung;* his works leave the reader with a far more powerful impression of his reverence for science, human progress, and reason. His discussions of morale in warfare represented above all an admission that purely quantitative approaches to military affairs were not sufficient to deal with *every* possible variable, even if they were of great utility in preparing for and waging war. Indeed, he employed the term *moral* most frequently in conjunction with education, which for him had far more to do with the rationalist humanism he associated with the Enlightenment than with the vitalist rhetoric that was popular among his colleagues who favored offensive doctrine at all costs. And the changes he made to subsequent versions of his textbook indicate that, if anything, as time passed he distanced himself further still from excessively emotional, romantic, and intolerant militarist rhetoric. In the first editions, for instance, he had instructed cadets that "what should be most worthy and beautiful for a Spaniard is to die for the good of Spain. He who acts against the *Patria* deserves unanimous condemnation; he is a depraved person [*malvado*] who commits a crime and a horrible act of treason for which even the most terrible punishments cannot do justice."[83] After 1900, however, he excised these words from his textbooks.

Yet this is not to say that this kind of patriotic sentiment disappeared entirely from the writings of Ruiz-Fornells; he was, after all, a career army officer who very much believed in the need to make soldiers willing to give their lives in combat if necessary. But terms such as *citizen, democratic spirit, rights,* and *civil society* had a permanent place in his nationalist language, even if—like the civilian liberal regenerationists—he would never go so far as to deny that "*love for the Patria* is something better felt than explained."[84] He may have joined Burguete, García Pérez, and other nationalists of both modernist and traditionalist bents in acknowledging that nonquantifiable elements were important to war, armies, and the health of a country overall. But, like Sigmund Freud in his attempt to understand feelings, sentiment, and other intangibles of human psychology, Ruiz-Fornells took a very rationalist approach in his analysis of the irrational. He also advocated strengthening nationalism, discipline, and even moral strength in soldiers through reason. He therefore did his best to define terms and concepts that he knew to be inherently ambiguous, warning cadets that they might be difficult for their soldiers to grasp. True to his positivist inclinations, he even provided future officers with a fairly detailed illustration of the place of patriotism in a general definitional scheme of "the soldier's moral duties"(see Appendix 4). And he warned readers of the need to avoid using terms such as *patriotism, military spirit,* and *bandera* ("regiment" or "flag") without first explaining their precise meanings to soldiers.[85]

Yet it was simply not possible to remove the inherent emotional and mystical connotations from such terms entirely. Ruiz-Fornells could never, then, succeed entirely in his attempts to reconcile the logical contradiction between his liberal, positivist views and the innately irrational character of unavoidable terms such as *military morale* and *patriotism*. He may have been a powerful spokesman for the liberal, scientifically minded officers who carried on the tradition of their nineteenth-century predecessors, but his interpretations and arguments also betrayed the degree to which that tradition had failed to maintain its position in the face of the turn-of-the-century climate of rising military nationalism. As the next chapter demonstrates, a more dynamic, conservative, and vitalist military leader could use the inherently ambiguous and emotional nature of concepts such as national identity, moral forces, and the *bandera* in the molding of more effective, albeit primitive, ideological weaponry.

Chapter Seven

"Long Live Death!"
José Millán-Astray and the Intellectual Roots of the Nationalist Crusade

Even today, few Spaniards have not heard of the 1936 encounter between Miguel de Unamuno and José Millán-Astray Terreros, the founder of the Spanish Foreign Legion whose battle wounds and bodily amputations had earned him the epithet "El Glorioso Mutilado." Although the details of the incident are debatable, an unforgettable, dramatic public confrontation of some sort clearly took place between the distinguished elderly writer and the one-eyed, one-armed Millán-Astray.

The incident occurred on October 12, the "Día de la Raza" honoring Columbus's journey to the New World and the subsequent growth of the Spanish Empire, during a ceremony at the University of Salamanca, where Unamuno was rector. After a speaker's violent, sweeping condemnation of Basques, Catalans, and defenders of the Republic, Unamuno rose to speak in protest. He condemned the rebels' glorification of the civil war they were waging in Spain and their fierce repression of all possible dissent in the territories they controlled, arguing that they would need to learn to convince ("*convencer*") as well as conquer ("*vencer*"). His assertion triggered an uproar, with someone in the audience injecting the Spanish Foreign Legion's battle cry, "Long live death!" and Millán-Astray losing his temper and shouting, "Death to the intelligentsia!" It also brought about the poet's dismissal as rector. Two months later, ostracized by the Nationalist status quo he had initially supported, Unamuno died.

After the war Francoist writers attempted to discount the philosophical and political differences that separated the two Spaniards and to place them together under the "Nationalist" banner, but even such partisan observers could not deny that the incident of October 12 had taken place.[1] As the exiled Spaniard Arturo Barea later wrote, "Regardless of the exact details of the discourses and shouts, the essential truth remains that in that large lecture hall in Salamanca the old, fanatical general represented brute force and death, and Don Miguel de Unamuno free intellect and life."[2]

Besides its undeniable appeal as a colorful story and as a symbol in the eyes of Franco's opponents of his regime's brutal response to reason and intellect, the event has remained a part of public consciousness in Spain simply because of the continued fame of its principal players. Not only is Unamuno considered one of Spanish literature's most important figures, but the exploits of Millán-Astray, who through combat injuries in Morocco lost an arm in 1924 and an eye in 1926,[3] still provoke much the same fascination and horror as when he was alive. To this day references to him surface periodically in the press and other forms of popular culture, and books on the period almost always include a description of the colorful general.[4] Indeed, his actions and proclamations during the war have left a more prominent mark on history than any other aspect of his life. In particular, the encounter with Unamuno, who at first lent his support to the 1936 military rebellion that sparked the Civil War, has largely defined his historical significance in the eyes of most scholars.

Yet Millán-Astray's ideas and their influence over the officer corps, especially during the period preceding the Second Republic, have received surprisingly little attention from serious scholars.[5] This scholarly neglect is unfortunate, because he so evidently represented an ideological bridge between military culture during the latter years of the Restoration and the national-Catholic cultural offensive of the Civil War. Although he hardly belongs in the same category as someone like Unamuno, a careful analysis of his thoughts and actions reveals that his infamous cry "Death to the intelligentsia!" actually stood in stark contrast to his reverence for ideas and their role in human history. The brother of a well-known intellectual in her own right, the playwright Pilar Millán-Astray, he echoed many of the views found in works by leading civilian as well as military writers. He shared, for example, the fascination of Burguete and Maeztu with certain aspects of Japanese philosophy, even claiming to employ Bushido tenets when creating and running the Spanish Foreign Legion. And as a teacher at the Infantry Academy in Toledo he also revealed the same interest in the field of education and in the discipline of history that so many of his contemporaries shared. His activities much later as Franco's propaganda chief during the first year of the Civil War—to which I return in the epilogue—were colorful and telling, and he provided noteworthy political support for Franco's dramatic rise to power. This chapter, however, focuses on his more significant but previously ignored earlier actions and ideas, many of which eventually merged into the Franco regime's peculiar union of vitalist and traditionalist propaganda. It also explores some possible links between his mystical, vitalist nationalism and the conduct of battle of the men he led, including the future Caudillo.

* * *

A Galician like his colleague Franco, Millán-Astray was born in 1879 in La Coruña. His father first brought public recognition to the name Millán-Astray by serving in various prominent positions, including that of head of most of the penal colonies in Spain and in Havana, superintendent of the "model" prison of Madrid, secretary-general for the civil governor of western Cuba, chief of police of Madrid and Barcelona, editor of *El Día,* and author of a two-volume autobiography.[6] The latter position, however, represented at least in part a late attempt to restore the family name after he was implicated in a well-publicized murder case during the late 1880s. His son's subsequent quest for military fame, in fact, may have stemmed from his desire to make up for his father's disgrace.[7] In any case, in late August 1894 the younger Millán-Astray, having just turned fifteen, began his military career in an abbreviated course of study at the Infantry Academy. After graduating in February 1896, the sixteen-year-old newly commissioned second lieutenant was assigned to the King's First Regiment, but six months later he gained entrance to the Escuela Superior de Guerra. The Philippine insurrection soon intervened, however, and while serving there from 1896 to 1897 he earned several decorations for his performance in combat, including what was then Spain's highest award for bravery, the Cross of María Cristina. He then returned to the peninsula to study at the Escuela Superior. At the completion of his studies he chose to become a *diplomado,* thereby joining a privileged group within the Spanish military establishment. At that time graduates of the Escuela Superior could choose to return to their corps of origin as *diplomados* or enter the staff corps. Faced with a conflict of ambition versus corps loyalty, Millán-Astray apparently viewed becoming a *diplomado* as the most attractive option, as did many fellow graduates of the Escuela Superior. After a yearlong stint as an instructor at the Infantry Academy he saw action in Africa, arriving in Melilla in 1912.[8] With the creation of the Spanish Foreign Legion eight years later, Millán-Astray would become one of twentieth-century Spain's most important military figures.

* * *

On May 14, 1920, Millán-Astray, having advanced to the rank of lieutenant colonel, presented the results of a study of the French Foreign Legion that he had undertaken in Algeria on behalf of the Spanish armed forces. The text of his presentation indicated that he would follow the French example as he perceived it quite closely when leading the Tercio. Although he focused on the technical and organizational aspects of the French Foreign Legion, he also stressed the legion's function as a melting pot in which various elements from different societies came together to form an effective fighting machine. He viewed the organization as "a mixture of men of distinct races who all contribute their virtues and vices, some of which are immense, at the hour of heroic fulfillment of duty." He spoke of the legion's "primary position among all the regiments of the allied armies" during the First World War, and he noted that its ranks included many Spaniards.[9] In the French Foreign Legion loyalty to the legion itself superseded all other obligations and affections, he claimed. This notion of the legion as a unifying force that eliminated differences between men and served as the object of their deepest affection would come to play a fundamental role in Millán-Astray's thinking, and it represented a model for the vision of the more homogenous kind of Spanish nation—lacking the democratic pluralism and diversity many liberals embraced—that many military nationalists hoped to build.

Millán-Astray's report on the French Foreign Legion apparently made a favorable impression on his superiors, and recruitment for its Spanish counterpart began three months later. The general staff had previously concluded a study on the formation of a fighting force based on the French model, and on January 28, 1920, the king had issued a royal order creating the "Tercio de Extranjeros," or Spanish Foreign Legion. But recruitment had been delayed by opposition from General Manuel Fernández-Silvestre in Melilla and by the protests of the Juntas de Defensa. The members of the Juntas, syndicates formed by junior officers on the peninsula to oppose merit promotions, feared the creation of "elite" units, and for a while the strong animosity between them and Millán-Astray became a prominent feature of the Spanish political scene. Silvestre based his opposition on the belief that Spain ought to use Spanish conscripts in its war efforts. His reluctance to use non-Spanish soldiers made little sense. Other European countries had learned by the late nineteenth century the benefits of using only volunteers in their colonial armies, and the *Regulares,* shock troops composed in part of North Africans, had served Spain in Morocco since 1911.[10] Opponents of the Tercio also feared the possible "revolutionary nature" of the recruits, warning that the creation of the Legion might prove "equivalent to the introduction of Bolshevik germs, officially and at the cost of the state," and they noted that budgetary and legal constraints posed serious obstacles.[11] But on August 31, 1920, after Millán-Astray had delivered his presentation, War Minister Viscount Eza finally authorized recruitment for the Tercio.

At least in part because of Silvestre's continued opposition to the Legion, it was not deployed in the Melilla area, which meant that it played no direct role in the mass slaughter of Spanish troops near Anual in July 1921. Conveniently, Millán-Astray thereby found himself detached from the ensuing conflict regarding "responsibilities" for the debacle. Thereafter, however, the Legion's successes in combat would begin to accumulate, and through its combat skills and successful operations it was instrumental in the restoration of Spanish control of much of the protectorate during the following years.[12]

The Legion's military successes increased its founder's popularity in Spain, but his political activities also helped him become a well-known figure. In March 1922 the Juntas, now exercising considerable political power, reaffirmed the principles of compulsory unionization and opposition to all merit promotions. They enforced their will by insisting on the renunciation of all merit promotions awarded after April 30, 1921; those who refused to act accordingly would have to leave the corps. Not surprisingly, this declaration was followed by the collective resignation of a large group of "*africanistas,*" a term used in military discourse to identify those officers who favored the vigorous military presence in Morocco that facilitated their rapid rise in rank. Millán-Astray and Franco announced their decisions to resign in letters marked by a strongly self-righteous and morally indignant tone, which were widely reprinted in the Spanish press. The government felt the ensuing public pressure, and on July 20, 1922, a bill was passed restoring merit promotions.[13]

The public debate surrounding the issue of merit promotions failed to disappear, however, and Millán-Astray continued to play a part in it. When King Alfonso XIII demonstrated his support for the africanistas in October 1922 by sponsoring a ceremony on their behalf in Seville, Millán-Astray attracted attention by collecting money from his men in order to buy the queen a jewel. In November he publicly resigned again, issuing a dramatic manifesto. He sent copies of the manifesto, including reproductions of his correspondence with Sánchez Guerra and leading *junteros,* to Spain's civilian and military newspapers. In one of the letters to Sánchez Guerra, dated September 15, 1922, he claimed to be acting only in accordance with "the ideals that dictate my military life: love for discipline, loyalty to the Throne, and faith to the higher designs of the *Patria.*" His actions yielded a massive outpouring of public support. *El Heraldo de Madrid,* which normally covered its front page with four or more separate articles, greeted its readers on November 10 with a banner headline announcing Millán-Astray's decision and devoted the entire page to the news. The following day the paper described him as a soldier "of manly vigor, gallantry, indomitable will, courage, and the force that brings victory on the battlefield," words of the sort that Millán-Astray would later use to describe himself and his men.[14]

In Madrid, Barcelona, and elsewhere in Spain, right-wing students reacted to the news of the resignation by demonstrating in support of Millán-Astray and against the *junteros.* On November 11 a reported 3,000 students gathered in front of his Madrid residence in a show of support for the legionnaire, and three days later security forces shot and severely wounded several student demonstrators.[15] Four days later, however, Prime Minister Sánchez Guerra reasserted his authority by introducing a bill dissolving the Juntas. The bill's popularity ensured its swift passage, and Sánchez simultaneously acted to demonstrate the primacy of civilian government over military interests by dismissing Millán-Astray as head of the Spanish Foreign Legion. The legionnaire would not be reinstated until after Primo de Rivera established his dictatorship in September 1923.

Yet Spain would continue to feel the ramifications of the controversy that had led to Millán-Astray's dismissal. He had generated, of course, a considerable amount of support for the *africanistas* on a political level. But, more important, he had promoted the ideal of the patriotic and unselfish Spanish soldier who sacrificed everything for his *patria*. Millán-Astray now saw himself as both a martyr and a crusader, and he had already endeavored to promote his outlook. Moreover, Franco, who would assume command of the Legion in June 1923, soon began to absorb some of the organization's brand of mystical and religious military nationalism.

After his dismissal Millán-Astray found the time to write *La Legión,* which he completed in March 1923.[16] Although publishing may have served as an accepted instrument for earning promotions for officers, in the case of Millán-Astray the writing of the book had a far more general aim. He penned *La Legión* in part to generate positive publicity for his accomplishments as founder and commander of the Tercio, but he might never have completed such a work had his dismissal not afforded him more free time and the political motive to generate more positive publicity for himself. For the rest of his life—even when he served Franco as propaganda chief—he produced few significant written records of his thinking. *La Legión,* written in the form of a handbook, thus provides us with a unique opportunity to analyze his thoughts on politics and war during a key period in his career.

* * *

An especially morbid and apocalyptic tone characterized Millán-Astray's portrayal of war, and he presented life and death in similar terms. The prominent role death played in his thinking stands out as perhaps the most striking aspect of *La Legión;* its author clearly believed he could create the most effective fighting force by using an exalted vision of death as a spiritual pillar. "To die in combat is the highest honor," the "Legionnaire's Creed" proclaimed. "You only die once. Death comes without pain, and to die is not as horrible as it appears. More horrible is to live as a coward." The Tercio's motto, Millán-Astray wrote, consisted of the words "Legionnaires, to fight; Legionnaires, to die," which the men cried out to the sound of a bugle. When officers called out, "Volunteers to die," their men customarily responded by shouting, "Everyone!" in unison. Millán-Astray also referred to the Tercio's most popular hymn as "the wedding march of the soldier who betroths death," and the soldiers called themselves "the bridegrooms of death."[17]

Under Millán-Astray, moreover, this rhetoric of "glorious" violence and death in combat—which was already beginning to saturate military culture thanks to the efforts of Burguete, García Pérez, and others—came to manifest itself in a very real fashion through the growing acceptance of brutality and inhumanity on the battlefield. One legionnaire, for example, subsequently described how his colleagues tore the entrails out of their fallen enemies and cut off their victims' ears and heads, placing the latter on their bayonets and carrying them along.[18]

Of course, the legionnaires were hardly the first soldiers in Spain or elsewhere to mutilate the bodies of their enemies and commit other such atrocities. In Millán-Astray's organization, however, the dehumanization reached an extremely high level thanks to the sanction—if not explicit encouragement—of such actions by the officers. In 1922, for example, a group of legionnaires felt it appropriate to express their gratitude to the Duquesa de la Victoria, who had organized a team of volunteer nurses, by offering a tribute that included a basket of roses surrounding two severed North African heads. And such acts were tolerated by the leading figures of the Spanish Foreign Legion, including future dictator Franco.[19]

Millán-Astray's development of an ideology of death corresponded well to the acts of his soldiers he encouraged, even though he was certainly not the first military figure to promote such thinking. Elsewhere in Europe regiments had called themselves "Hussars of Death," and Spain had hosted the cavalry order Hunters of Lusitania, which had featured a skull and bones on its shield and had taken the name "Dragoons of Death" during the eighteenth century. Moreover, the Spanish Infantry Academy's hymn, composed in 1909, included the following stanza: "And in order to see you feared and honored / Your sons happily go to their deaths."[20] Franco, whose book on the Spanish Foreign Legion appeared in 1922, shared at least partially this vision of a soldier's intimate relationship with death. As commander of the Legion's first battalion (*bandera*) he worked closely with Millán-Astray. And despite the considerable differences in form between the two *africanistas'* works—Franco's book is comprised primarily of narrative accounts of battles to which he added a dose of anti-Junta sentiment—both highlighted the notion of "glorious" death in battle.[21] The more prolific military writers of the period, moreover, also stressed the "moral" value of mortal sacrifice in battle, as the previous chapters on Burguete and García Pérez have demonstrated. Although these writers may not have elevated the concept of death itself to the level promoted by Millán-Astray, their visions of the glories of mortal combat helped pave the way for the extreme views of the Spanish Foreign Legion's founder.

Gabriel Cardona writes that many of the *africanistas* experienced what he calls a "mythification of the feeling of death [*mitificación del sentido de la muerte*]," and Carlos Blanco Escolá has demonstrated how the system of values and mind-set fostered in northern Africa came to dominate the Academia General after it was reestablished under Franco's leadership in 1928. According to Cardona, "The mentality of these officers was shaped during this very long colonial war, which lasted from 1909 until 1927." It was "war without great maneuvers and spectacular advances, with great hardship and cruelty. With the anguish of thirst, heat, and the guerrilla tactics of the enemy. With the cruel characteristics of war in the Rif: torture, murder, the castration of prisoners. . . ."[22]

Yet Millán-Astray's vision of death advanced beyond even that of his colleagues in northern Africa. The hardships in Morocco that Cardona so aptly describes indeed created a shared mentality and common feeling of martyrdom, as Franco's book demonstrated. But the mythical conception of death in war did not merely culminate with the founding of the Legion. Instead it was with the founding of the Legion that Millán-Astray began to add a new dimension to the vision. For Franco and most of his colleagues death in battle may have represented the supreme sacrifice and war a most noble cause, but in the eyes of Millán-Astray these concepts were already attaining more transcendental overtones. Millán-Astray even referred to the Legion as a "religion" in itself, and he viewed death in battle as "holy sacrifice" and one of his faith's foundations.[23] War was a personal and spiritual matter, and a soldier's intimate relationship with a mystical vision of death superseded all other concerns. *La Legión* made virtually no references to the more tangible, human elements in Morocco against which the Spanish troops had to fight; even when Millán-Astray finally used the term *enemy* to refer to the opposing soldiers, the word clearly described something of secondary importance. As usual, he focused on a soldier's greater concern: death.[24] Neither the defeat of the enemy nor any other possible justification for war even entered the picture.

The obsession with death in war would find its way into right-wing military conceptions of national identity shared by other prominent *africanistas* as well. Sacrifice and death served as prominent motifs in Franco's early writings on North Africa, in which he frequently cited cases of soldiers who died "gloriously for the *Patria*." Franco clearly believed that the most morally superior form of patriotism was sacrificing oneself in battle. In his eyes "those who make the *Patria*" were none other than the soldiers who died in its name.[25] For him no other displays of patriotic sentiment—from constitutional loyalty to earnest attempts to strengthen the *patria* through social, economic, and governmental reform—came close in their nationalist value. Millán-Astray's Legion thus provided the setting in which the future Spanish dictator could develop the ideals of militarist nationalism that he would subsequently try to impose on Spain as a whole.

Explicit references to religion sometimes accompanied the exaltation of death in war, and in many cases patriotic and "Christian" sacrifice blended together in the minds of men of the military right. In *La Legión* notions of spirituality surfaced that would eventually become—like the ideal of sacrifice—an integral part of the Francoist "crusade." "The Legion is a religion," Millán-Astray wrote, and its "tenets [*comprendidas*]" embraced ideals such as "suffering, hardening in the face of fatigue, fellowship under fire, and the cardinal virtues: Discipline, Combat, Death, and Love for the Battalion [*Bandera*]."[26] In his writing service in the Legion, like war itself, signified an overwhelmingly spiritual affair in which death played the leading role.

In a related fashion, the unification of Spain's diverse elements and peoples was also an obsession of Millán-Astray from early in his career. The same lack of unity that Loyola had opposed later threatened pre-Franco Spain, Millán-Astray would later assert. "Separatism was a matter that worried us enormously," he wrote.[27] Of course, the lack of harmony among the country's different elements had long troubled many Spaniards, and Millán-Astray had greatly admired the sense of unity he perceived in the French Foreign Legion. He portrayed the Spanish Foreign Legion as an organization in which differences in class, race, nationality, and political outlook disappeared. The initial recruits, he wrote, included 200 Catalans, "an 'undesirable' Belgian," and a "gigantic black man from New York," each of whom had come for different reasons. "They are life's fighters, adventurers, dreamers, the hopeful and the desperate," he continued, citing financial woes, women, "the desire to die," the law, alcohol, patriotism, a yearning for excitement, and the hope of a successful military career as common reasons for enlisting.[28] The Legion continued, moreover, to attract this sort of recruit, as a German who joined up three years later subsequently wrote. Largely rejecting Millán-Astray's more romantic, positive characterization of his men as an adventurous lot, the German flatly described his comrades-in-arms as "a bunch of unhappy men." The new legionnaires from Spain, he wrote, betrayed their criminal past by arriving in North Africa in shackles. "It is not such a bad idea of the Spanish after all," he wryly observed, for they "cleanse their own country of a pest, of the men who have run afoul of the law so many times; incorrigible, but in Morocco they become useful in some way. Thus the Spanish have a shock-brigade for the frontline of attack against the Rifian in the Rif."[29]

British, Americans, and other non-Spaniards who enlisted in the Legion had similar ill feelings about the organization. They complained not only that they failed to receive the wages that had been promised them, but also that they suffered "cruel disciplinary measures." According to a report from the U.S. consulate general in Madrid, these measures included being "burdened with rocks" and forced to go into action tied to one another.[30] Hence in 1922 eighty Americans, many of whom were U.S. army or navy veterans, joined British subjects serving in the Legion in requesting help from their respective governments for their repatriation.[31]

Yet, in a patently false claim, Millán-Astray argued that in spite of the various nationalities of its recruits, the Legion acted as the "loving mother of all who come, obliterating racial differences and hatred between nations." Political differences ceased to play a role for the soldiers, he wrote. "In the Legion there have been men of all ideas and all leanings: syndicalists and antisyndicalists from Catalonia and other areas; anarchists, nationalists, and foreign Bolsheviks"—but all left their political ideas "at the door." Actually, even among Spaniards his perception of an apolitical Foreign Legion represented at least in part wishful thinking; the 1936 revolt saw the creation of the "Committee of the Rising," which was charged with breaking up a communist cell operating within the Tercio.[32]

Nevertheless, in an atmosphere characterized by the widespread aversion of military officers to civilian politics, Millán-Astray's claim to have created a truly apolitical body in the form of the Spanish Foreign Legion must have had considerable appeal. In fact, as the writings of Unamuno and other civilians demonstrated, many Spaniards from all walks of life yearned for the sense of unity ostensibly felt by the members of an organization like the Foreign Legion. In the minds of soldiers such as Millán-Astray and Franco, the Legion could thus become a sort of paradigm for the kind of Spanish nation they hoped to forge when they rose against the Republic in July 1936.

* * *

Interestingly, beneath Millán-Astray's conception of a unified Legion lay aspects of traditional Japanese military thought, to which he would publicly devote a considerable amount of attention during the final years of his life. As early as 1922 he referred to a "Japanese statute" as the model for the sense of unity and fellowship he tried to foster in the Legion. The statute proclaimed, he wrote, that in "a regiment the Colonel must be the father and the highest-ranking major the mother, and in the company the captain will be the father and the commissioned subofficer the mother." He also revealed that his perception of Japanese military thought may have helped shape his notion of death in war. As a result of the excellent care given in a certain modern and well-equipped Moroccan hospital, he wrote, any soldier who entered would surely live. This meant that "combat death was reduced to glorious death on the battlefield[—]'To be taken on the green hill staring at heaven,' as the Japanese samurai warrior requests."[33]

Millán-Astray later wrote that Bushido, a code of unquestioning obedience and loyalty that bound samurai warriors to their lords, strongly influenced his actions as founder and commander of the Tercio. "I am profoundly convinced that Bushido is, as a path, way, or rule of conduct for gentlemen, a perfect creed," he wrote. Moreover, "Bushido inspired a large portion of my lessons in morals for the infantry cadets at the Alcázar of Toledo, when I had the honor of teaching them during the years 1911–1912. Bushido also abetted the Legion's creed, with its legionary spirit of combat and death, of discipline and fellowship, of friendship, of suffering and resolve, of facing fire. The Spanish legionnaire is also a samurai and practices the Bushido essentials: Honor, Valor, Loyalty, Generosity, and Spirit of sacrifice. The Spanish legionnaire loves danger and despises material wealth."[34] The Bushido "vows" of death, fidelity, dignity, and prudence and the opposing "plagues" of "*sueño,*" squander, sensuality, and avarice all applied to the legionnaire as to the samurai, he wrote, associating the same traits Ganivet had associated with Seneca with the Far East instead. Eventually these principles would become key elements of Nationalist military ideology. The Franco regime would even use the disavowal of material wealth to justify the dismal salaries paid in its army. Until the Caudillo's death in 1975 the government exalted the figure of the soldier, but it paid army officers so little that they often had to seek outside work. Army salaries were especially low during the 1940s[35]—the same period in which Millán-Astray embraced Bushido thinking most openly and enthusiastically.

On a national level Millán-Astray would focus on the similarity he perceived between Japan's debilitated condition in 1855 and that of his country after the Civil War, arguing that adherence to Bushido principles could transform Spain into a great power of Japan's status. "Japan is a high and dazzling example for a people who possessed in their souls the most pure qualities of the Christian religion, of chivalry and valor, but fell to vilification after forgetting these virtues," he wrote. He even found a way to justify the incorporation of Eastern spirituality into Catholicism, asserting that the "Principles of Christian morality are not in conflict with, nor much different from, Bushido, which is older than Jesus Christ." After all, he reasoned, "Bushido infuses into the mind the purest morality and in practice applies to all men—as does Christianity." He also wrote of "the sublime spirit of sacrifice, which is grounded in the norms of our Christian morality and in Bushido." And finally, he was quick to assure his readers that the author of his primary source on Bushido, Inazo Nitobe, was a Christian.[36]

Yet Millán-Astray conveniently failed to mention that the famous Japanese writer had explicitly rejected the type of dogma that constituted the Nationalist "crusade" and characterized Spanish national Catholicism. "I have little sympathy for ecclesiastical methods and forms that obscure the teachings of Christ," Nitobe had written. "Moreover, I believe that God has made an alliance, which could be called 'ancient,' with every people and nation, whether Gentile or Jewish, Christian or pagan." Millán-Astray apparently chose to ignore these words, which appeared in the preface to the 1909 Castilian edition of Nitobe's work. And after the Civil War the Franco government, presumably at Millán-Astray's urging, believed enough in the book's didactic potential to subsidize its distribution to Spanish youth.[37]

Ironically, it was probably through the writings of Ricardo Burguete, a committed Republican during the Civil War, that Millán-Astray first grew interested in the Bushido tenets he would later work to incorporate into Francoist ideology. Although interest in Japan had grown markedly in Spain and elsewhere after Russia's military defeat in 1905, within the Spanish officer corps Burguete had disseminated an interpretation of the war that stressed Bushido philosophy in particular as an explanation of the Japanese success. In the cultural world of the officers he thus had played a role similar to the one his friend and source of inspiration Ramiro de Maeztu had played in introducing the Spanish general public to the principles of Bushido. And thanks to its later promotion by Millán-Astray, the "Bushido spirit" continued to influence Spanish military thinking even after the Civil War and World War II.[38]

* * *

Finally, Millán-Astray also developed a view of history that, like his intertwined conceptions of war, religion, and death, reflected the mind-set of the *africanistas* who rose with Franco in 1936. Not surprisingly, what originally united the dedicated officers in Morocco was their fear that Spain might abandon its African protectorate. Millán-Astray, like many Spaniards, based his argument for Spain's presence in Morocco on a flawed view of Spain's historical mission as a colonial power. Although he could convincingly employ historical examples in order to advocate reasonable responses to specific problems, he came up with a very weak justification to answer the broader question of why Spanish troops were there in the first place. Interestingly, in certain respects his views resembled the interpretations of major military and civilian writers, including Ángel Ganivet. The renowned cultural critic, who also influenced Burguete so profoundly, had written of "excessive vitality" and a strong spirit of independence as Spain's most important gifts to the peoples it subjugated in America. Both qualities, Ganivet wrote, were necessary for the growth of "true social progress."[39] Millán-Astray, however, unhesitatingly applied the same sort of thinking to northern Africa in a manner that even Ganivet resisted.

In a speech he made after his active duties in Morocco had ended, Millán-

Astray attempted to justify his actions there as well as Spanish imperialism in general. Spain's mission, he said, was "to bring civilization and culture to Humanity, adding to the golden list of twenty flowering nations—her children, today free and independent—the name of the zone of her Protectorate of Morocco, where she came in her secular mission to calm, civilize, and extol." Referring to Spain's colonial past, he echoed García Pérez in maintaining that due to "Spanish generosity" Spain "conquers first, gives culture and wealth, and then leaves her protégés free and independent in order to enjoy happily the gifts she has given them at the cost of her blood and her treasury." As a result, he concluded, "Spain can render her noble account before the Supreme Tribunal of God and before Humanity."[40]

Quite clearly, Millán-Astray viewed Spain's fall from the position of world dominance she had enjoyed in the sixteenth century through rosy but seriously distorted lenses. Moreover, his description of the former Spanish colonies as "flowering" was hardly apt. Ganivet himself viewed the conditions of these countries as anything but ideal, although he believed that their "Spanishness" might eventually enable the young nations to become great powers. And although scholars are hardly in agreement over how to interpret many aspects of Ganivet's writings, it is clear that the cultural critic did not simply transfer his vision of America to Morocco in the primitive manner of Millán-Astray or even the slightly more sophisticated fashion of García Pérez.[41] Thus, although Millán-Astray undoubtedly shared some of the basic notions espoused by contemporary Spanish literary figures, by equating Africa with America he demonstrated that his perceptions were even more simplistic than those of other military writers.

Furthermore, it was by no means clear, not even to many Spaniards, that Spain had any business "civilizing" other peoples anyway. Arturo Barea, who had served as a soldier in the Spanish protectorate, illuminated the Spanish hypocrisy in an oft-cited passage. Soldiers sent to the protectorate, he wrote, could not help but ask themselves: "Why do we have to fight against the Moors? Why must we 'civilize' them if they don't want to be civilized? Civilize them—we? We from Castile, from Andalucia, from the mountains of Gerona, who cannot read or write? Nonsense. Who is going to civilize us? Our village has no school, its houses are of clay, we sleep in our clothes on a pallet in the stable beside the mules, to keep warm. We eat an onion and a scrap of bread in the morning and then go work on the fields from sunrise to sunset."[42] And this view was by no means foreign to the officer corps. Even Primo de Rivera expressed serious reservations about the utility of Spain's efforts in Morocco before buckling under the pressure of colleagues such as Millán-Astray and Franco.

Unfortunately, Millán-Astray left few clues as to the specific beliefs that lay behind his faith in Spain's historic mission to conquer and civilize. Yet although written records do not reveal that he had as great an interest in history as many other military writers, the evidence that I have found indicates that he too interpreted the conditions around him largely through his historical perceptions. For example, in the prologue to a book on Aben Humeya and the 1568 Morisco rebellion he asserted that Spanish soldiers could learn a considerable amount by studying the uprising's history. Referring specifically to the 1921 debacle at Anual and its causes, he linked the methods with which Cardinal Cisneros and his predecessors had treated the Moriscos with the policies of the recent high commissioners in Morocco. Such comparisons are necessary, he wrote, because historical events "repeat themselves isochronally in broad outlines."[43]

* * *

Woven together into a single fabric, the historical, vitalist, religious, and conservative threads in Millán-Astray's nationalist outlook formed the ideological backdrop to his actions and those of the Legion on the battlefield. Admittedly, it is impossible to prove the existence of a direct relationship between such cultural intangibles and tactical, operational, and strategic behavior. And it is usually easy to find a sound, purely practical rationale for military policies and methods. At the same time, however, one should not dismiss out of hand the ways intangible and undefinable influences can color otherwise "objective" and rational judgments. Just as cultural myth and imagination may partially explain differences in the conduct of battle between U.S. forces in the Pacific and their counterparts in Europe during World War II, the combat culture and propaganda that surrounded Millán-Astray's Legion probably informed its actions at least somewhat in the bloody war of counterinsurgency and "pacification" it waged against Moroccan rebels.[44] In any case, the basic operational style that the Legion successfully employed in Morocco in the 1920s undoubtedly had an impact on the subsequent actions of Franco's Nationalist forces in the Spanish Civil War.

The extreme brutalization of military life and the dehumanization of the enemy that characterized the Spanish Foreign Legion under Millán-Astray and Franco conformed to a more general belief in the possibility of redemption of the soldier through sacrifice for the *patria*. The Moroccan experience was, moreover, that of waging war against a religiously defined "other." Even if a paradoxical reverence for "Arab" fanaticism and fighting abilities was displayed by many Spanish *africanistas,* their writings also highlighted the importance of the Christian "Reconquest" of medieval Spain in their conception of Spain's historical identity. Further, a mystical, spiritual vision of war that repeatedly stressed sacrifice was hardly incompatible with the tactics of frontal attack and the morally charged offensive spirit that the legionnaires—as the shock troops of Spain's colonial army—often used. In a similar fashion, their pride in their ability to hold out for long periods of time when attacked by a numerically superior enemy can be related to the religious, sometimes apocalyptic, notion of sacrifice for the *bandera* seen in the Legion's mythology. Although an idealization of military sacrifice is common to many fighting forces, in the Spanish Foreign Legion it was especially strong. Viewing the Legion as the military savior of Spanish Morocco after the "sacrifice" of Anual, its officers therefore found it easy to regard those who cast doubts on Spain's mission in Africa as traitors. Much like some Americans who after World War II opposed returning to Japan territory that had been conquered at great human cost, the likes of Franco and Millán-Astray interpreted the possible abandonment of Spain's Moroccan project as a betrayal of the many Spaniards who had lost their lives there. Years later, one of the most important symbols of the Francoist mythology of the Civil War also rested on the principle of sacrifice: the death of Colonel José Moscardó's son at the hands of "godless" Republicans during the famous siege of the Alcázar.

The very term *bandera* was, moreover, an inherently ambiguous and romantic notion, not unlike the idea of the *patria*. The word, which literally means "standard," "flag," or "colors," did not refer just to the Legion's basic organizational building block, its equivalent to a battalion. It also referred to a more abstract object of profound loyalty, as Franco's mystical account of his days in the Legion, *Diario de una bandera,* demonstrates. Not surprisingly, then, the liberal positivist Ruiz-Fornells had explicitly warned against using this word—or the closely related term *patria*—without first supplying a precise definition. But, as I have shown, this was an unrealistic expectation. In addition, the inherent ambiguity of the word *bandera* went well beyond its two usual meanings. After all, both of the things to which it usually referred—a flag and a military unit—could in themselves be made into powerful symbols of collective identity, and Millán-Astray and Franco, like Burguete, García Pérez, and Ruiz-Fornells, tended to view military organizations as models of the nation.

On the more concrete, operational level of war, Millán-Astray's Legion had a profound, lasting effect on the military thinking of men such as Franco who served as its officers. Understandably, the horrors of Anual deeply affected their ideas on the conduct of war, even though the Legion itself was not in the area at the time. To the misfortune of the Spanish troops who were present when the Moroccans launched their counterattack, General Silvestre had laid the path to the disaster by rushing to take enemy territory through the piece-by-piece accumulation of tactical victories. Without a sound operational plan in place, the sum of these small geographical conquests had not added up to sustainable strategic superiority. As a result, the Spanish troops had soon crumbled in the face of a strong surprise Moroccan attack. The Legion, on the other hand, had then employed what most military analysts today would consider sound operational methods in light of its limited resources, methodically retaking and establishing solid control of each piece of territory before advancing farther. In addition to setting up strong defenses against possible counterattacks and paying sufficient attention to logistics, this entailed eliminating all possible resistance while moving forward. The Legion employed brutal methods to this end, including the torching of homes and requesting deadly attacks from the air on insurgent-held areas.[45] Franco's firsthand experience in this kind of fighting, then, helps explain the extremely cautious way in which he acted as Nationalist commander-in-chief in the Civil War. Not only did it play a role in his failure to act quickly to exploit tactical victories to their full strategic potential in his struggle against the Spanish Republic, but it probably also contributed to his willingness to erase all possible sources of resistance without mercy or remorse whenever he conquered an area.

* * *

Both warrior and Christian mystic, in some ways Millán-Astray truly was a modern incarnation of his exemplar Loyola, whom he held to be a savior of Catholic civilization. Fallacies in his view of Spanish history made little difference in the end; the popularity of his ideas demonstrated that flawed or incomplete ideology can prove effective, especially when propelled by the powerful alliance of nationalism, emotion, and mysticism. Moreover, the combination of strength and social harmony that the Legion represented seemed ideal in a country that largely lacked such attributes. Even Miguel de Unamuno, who in his encounter with Millán-Astray would demonstrate his preference for reason over irrational violence, had initially found the rebels' promise of a harmonious society too attractive to resist. Yet the ideal of a united Spain composed only part of the Nationalist vision. The rebels' belief in the righteousness of their cause and their conception of sacrificial death in battle as inherently glorious played more important roles: they shaped an extreme rightist conception of national identity, and they facilitated the interpretation of the rebels' struggle as a holy war. Millán-Astray, more than any other individual, had brought together various ideological strands from Restoration military thought in a way that would prove to be most useful for the later propagators of the "Nationalist Crusade."

Epilogue

Like Millán-Astray and most of their other colleagues, Burguete, García Pérez, and Ruiz-Fornells apparently viewed the establishment of Primo de Rivera's dictatorship in September 1923 as scant cause for alarm. After all, the final collapse of an increasingly weak and ineffective system of government hardly came as a surprise, and the military community itself had played a noteworthy role in its demise. Indeed, during the previous years Burguete and Millán-Astray had personally contributed to the weakening of Spain's parliamentary monarchy in several ways. Above all, their well-publicized participation in the controversies over the Juntas de Defensa and the military debacle at Anual, although intended in no small part to bring them personal political gain, had also contributed to the weakening of the parliamentary system in general. As Carolyn P. Boyd has demonstrated, this process helped create a climate particularly friendly to Primo de Rivera's *pronunciamiento.*[1]

As the dictator remained in power, however, support for him began to wane among important segments of the officer corps. Burguete, García Pérez, Ruiz-Fornells, and Millán-Astray, now at the apogees of their careers, reacted differently to the evolution of the regime and the short-lived dictatorships of General Dámaso Berenguer and Admiral Juan Bautista Aznar that followed. Burguete and Ruiz-Fornells came to object strongly to Primo's authoritarian rule, although only the former—as I show later—acted publicly to undermine the principle of military dictatorship and thus helped pave the way for the Second Republic. Millán-Astray and García Pérez, although undoubtedly dismayed at Primo's initial desire to withdraw Spanish troops from Morocco, displayed notably more support for authoritarian rule as an alternative to liberal parliamentary politics.

Yet, like most other officers of their generation, the four officers found their dominant positions within the army gradually superseded by their younger colleagues as the dictatorship lingered on. Of course, Burguete, Ruiz-Fornells, and Millán-Astray continued to play highly visible roles in their professions long after 1923. Burguete's actions in 1931 as head of the military's high court, for example, dealt a severe blow to monarchical-military rule in Spain, and Ruiz-Fornells took a high position in Berenguer's short-lived government and then assisted Republican leader Manuel Azaña in implementing the program of military reforms that angered so many officers. Even Millán-Astray, who helped propel Franco to power and became a key symbol in his own right of the Francoist "crusade," probably did not wield on his own the political power he had enjoyed during the early years of the Spanish Foreign Legion. Although he had no qualms about serving as a propaganda tool for the Franco regime, his influence on high-level policy decisions paled in comparison to that of the new, younger leaders.

On a less tangible level, the influence of the four officers on Spanish history after 1923 was probably more significant, as many of the widely varied imprints they left on military culture retained their form for years to come. Of course, it is impossible to determine with certainty their ultimate responsibility in shaping the subsequent behavior and beliefs of the officer corps as a whole or of leading military figures in particular. Nevertheless, the many ideological continuities extending beyond the period of the Restoration warrant our attention. As becomes clear, personal and professional concerns could strongly influence the ideological and political positions they adopted.

* * *

In the case of Ricardo Burguete the division between personal concerns and political ideology was especially blurred. Still a very powerful figure in Spain throughout the 1920s, he assumed the leadership of Spain's notorious Civil Guard in 1925. In 1928 Primo de Rivera, with whom he had clashed in the past, made him head of the military's high court, the Consejo Supremo de Guerra y Marina, in hopes of drawing him into his camp. But Burguete failed to act as the dictator had hoped, and the following year he even may have joined his sons in their active involvement in conspiracies against the regime. In any case, his republican views expressed themselves in their most extreme fashion in March 1931, when the members of the antimonarchist, revolutionary committee behind the failed December rising at Jaca stood trial before him. Among the defendants were such important public figures as Niceto Alcalá Zamora, Francisco Largo Caballero, Miguel Maura, and Fernando de los Ríos. As head of the court, Burguete not only allowed the trial to become a large, public demonstration against the authority of the king—who had supported the recent military rulers—but he also made significant contributions to the rising tide of republicanism himself. The court sentenced the accused to the minimum possible penalty: imprisonment for six months and a day. Burguete then held a press conference in which he championed the virtues of popular sovereignty and civil authority, announcing that he had voted for absolution. In typical fashion, he included in his rather convoluted rhetoric quotations he attributed to Napoleon and Ortega y Gasset as well as plenty of thinly veiled praise for himself and the supposedly legally and constitutionally minded character of his profession. As a result of his insubordination he was sentenced to a two-month prison term in the castle of Santa Catalina, although the new Republic would soon release him and briefly return him to his post.[2]

Burguete's actions had a significant political impact, weakening the authority of both Alfonso XIII and Admiral Aznar. The motives fueling his behavior, however, are less clear. Besides his well-known antagonism toward many of the military figures to whom the king had recently lent his support—most notably Berenguer—Burguete had an even more personal stake in the proceedings: implicated in the Jaca conspiracy was his son Ricardo, an aviator who shared the strongly republican sentiments of his better-known friend and colleague Ramón Franco. In fact, the son's name surfaced on various occasions during the trial over which the father presided. Burguete's other two sons, Luis and Manuel, were also known to be opponents of the monarchy. But perhaps even more important than these familial ties was his resentment of the king for not having heeded his advice in December to appoint a new government made up of men he recommended, which undoubtedly strengthened his republicanism. Furthermore, as Emilio Mola would later argue, Burguete may have favored the fall of the monarchy because he thought a change of regime would foster his own professional advancement.[3]

Nevertheless, it is probably unfair to attribute Burguete's republicanism solely to personal concerns. Like many other military figures who turned against dictatorial and monarchical rule, he had an ample number of selfish, professional reasons to reject the monarchy and the dictatorship. But he and the rest of his family would remain strongly republican even long after large segments of the army had given up on the young Spanish democracy. Most likely his political outlook evolved from a mixture of personal animosities, professional interests, and a genuine belief that a leftist form of government was the only hope for Spain after so many disappointing years of right-wing, military rule.

Burguete's leftist sentiments manifested themselves most spectacularly shortly after the declaration of the Republic, when he announced with great fanfare his intention to join the Spanish Socialist Party. In a front-page article in *El Socialista* on his impending new affiliation he revealed that he had already traveled to Madrid to pay visits to such prominent Socialist leaders in the new Republic as Indalecio Prieto, Fernando de los Ríos, and Francisco Largo Caballero, and he claimed that he had been a "platonic pacifist" ever since serving in Cuba and the Philippines. Not surprisingly, though, the ideas behind his political actions remained paradoxical as ever, and to explain his decision he cited the likes of Georges Sorel and Georges Valois—both of whom espoused vitalist messages that appealed to European radicals associated with the extreme right as well as the left. He was, however, far more moderate now than in his days as a young officer, and he portrayed the violent message of Sorel as "philosophical," criticizing those who embraced the calls to violence in Sorel's book while ignoring the French author's accompanying "reflections." And in what must have pleased mainstream Socialist Party members, he derided Spanish anarcho-syndicalism as "savagery," although he also said he could imagine a future world of "perfect harmony between reflective syndicalists and socialists, who already share a common goal." Although in the end the Socialist Party rejected Burguete's application for membership—probably because of bitter memories of his role in the Asturian repression of 1917—his later activities in peace movements, as head of the Spanish Red Cross, and as an open supporter of the Popular Front indicate that his leftist republicanism and devotion to socialist ideals as he understood them were genuine.[4]

In the autumn of 1931 Burguete was a guest speaker at a peace conference and several rallies in northern Germany, where he was scheduled to share the stage with former French president Edouard Herriot and retired major general Paul Freiherr von Schoenaich, who now headed the Deutsche Friedensgesellschaft, or German Peace Society.[5] Although Burguete would later refer to this trip to Germany in typically self-esteeming rhetoric, the rally in Hamburg was actually a rather tumultuous affair at which he received by no means universal acclaim. Herriot had to cancel his participation at the last moment because of illness, but the turnout for the event was nonetheless large. Burguete's speech, which he delivered in Spanish, was interrupted by numerous catcalls and insults that Burguete himself clearly could not understand, although many other listeners apparently received him warmly. The troublemakers included several hundred Nazis who tried to break up the event by shouting down the speakers and singing the "Deutschlandlied," but after about an hour the police finally succeeded in ending the disturbance by expelling the unwanted listeners. The response of the crowd to Burguete was especially positive when he spoke of the prominent role he believed Spanish students played in the republican pacifism.[6]

After returning to Spain Burguete continued to espouse pacifist rhetoric as head of the Spanish Red Cross, writing articles and delivering speeches in which he criticized capitalism and its role in fostering war. He explicitly drew upon the works of Georges Valois and the German pacifist Otto Lehmann-Russbüldt in attacking the relationships between war and banking, industry, business, and trusts.[7] At the same time, however, he did not go so far as to deny the necessity of armies in modern states, and he reacted angrily to those who regarded socialism as inherently antimilitarist and unpatriotic. But, unlike his protagonist Zorrapastro of three decades earlier, he called for the Spanish army to adopt a purely defensive posture, because war—"like homicide"—could now be justified only as an act of self-defense. The impact of the Great Depression on Europe and the rise to power of Hitler only strengthened his opposition to war and the economic system he believed fostered it. By the end of 1933 he was speaking sadly of the disappearance of the "pacifist Germany of Kant and Heine," of the members of the German peace movement now held in concentration camps, and of the disappearance or exile of such great Germans as Einstein.[8] In late 1934 he wrote a public letter to his counterpart at the German Red Cross protesting the internment of publisher Fritz Küster in a concentration camp.[9]

It seems, then, that Burguete's activities as president of the Spanish Red Cross, from his protests on behalf of a prisoner in a Nazi concentration camp to his condemnations of the horrors of war in general, did not reflect what Azaña's memoirs unfairly portray as merely the attempts of a vain man to find a position of importance in the face of professional disappointment. His wife had long been very active in the Spanish Red Cross, and documents pertaining to administration and internal disputes within the organization during the 1930s indicate that Burguete took his position very seriously and had an active interest in its day-to-day affairs.[10] Admittedly, as Azaña noted disparagingly in his diary, Burguete probably resented his failure to receive a promotion given to someone he deemed less qualified. And the praise he continued for the rest of his life to give himself for his earlier actions and books seemed to betray a combination of conceit, insecurity, and a desire for the rank and appreciation of which he—like so many of his colleagues—felt he had been cheated. Burguete's inflated sense of self-worth was undeniable; years earlier the U. S. military attaché had even commented on Burguete's strikingly unabashed praise for himself. But the attaché had also noted that "such a naïve statement of honest admiration for one's own work accomplished and of confident promises for the future would be unusual in perhaps any other country but Spain."[11] Azaña, however, had no understanding of or patience for this aspect of military culture. He was a very hardworking, intelligent Republican who devoted tremendous efforts to trying to make Spanish democracy succeed, and in a sense his lack of tolerance for military vanity and the incompetence that reigned in segments of the officer corps is understandable. But by refusing to see anything good in a strongly republican officer and vociferous antiwar speaker like Burguete he tragically displayed another form of the same arrogant shortsightedness that he categorically identified with military professionals.[12]

With the outbreak of the Civil War, Burguete and his family would suffer dearly for the same leftist politics that Azaña could not bring himself to appreciate or employ to the Republic's advantage. In Burguete's last known written work, an open letter published as a pamphlet during the early part of the Civil War, the personal consequences of his family's politics were made painfully clear. In it he viciously attacked the rebel general Gonzalo Queipo de Llano, who is best remembered for his nightly, infamous radio diatribes against the Republic and its supporters during the Civil War. Laden with intense despair and hatred, the pamphlet revealed how the recent deaths of his three sons had left the Nietzschean general a broken man.[13]

Not long after Burguete's son Ricardo had finally succumbed to injuries he had suffered as a pilot in the Spanish air force, the Civil War had taken the lives of his other two sons. During the first days of the war Luis had died at the hands of Nationalists in an act, Burguete believed, for which Queipo de Llano bore responsibility. Luis, a Communist Party member and the most radical of the three brothers, had been serving as commander of an air squadron in Morocco when he had received news of the military rebellion. He then had flown to Seville to help in the efforts to suppress the uprising. Unbeknownst to him, however, in the meantime the city had fallen to the rebels—thanks in large part to the actions of Queipo. After landing in Seville and then making an unsuccessful attempt to escape, Luis had been killed by the Nationalists.[14] Burguete's third son, Manuel, who had fought in Morocco and had also served in the Civil Guard, had been retired during the early part of the Republic. But with the outbreak of the Civil War he had taken up arms again, leading a Republican militia at the Granada front. Captured in 1937, he had been executed by the Nationalists.

The elder Burguete believed that the real motive behind the killing of his sons Manuel and Luis was Queipo de Llano's long-standing hatred of the Burguete family. In his open letter Burguete charged that Queipo had never forgiven him, in his former role as head of the high military court during Primo de Rivera's dictatorship, for ruling that Queipo had failed to perform his duties in a battle in Morocco.[15] Moreover, Queipo was well aware that it was one of Burguete's sons, Luis, "bleeding from his wounds and carried down the mountains in the arms of his loyal Moorish soldiers," who had personally witnessed Queipo's cowardly behavior. According to Burguete, after the Civil War broke out Queipo therefore made sure that the two Burguete sons did not survive their capture by the Nationalists.[16]

In his letter Burguete also described Queipo's allegedly long history of cowardice, hypocrisy, and treason both on and off the battlefield. Returning to his longtime source of inspiration, he cited Nietzsche's *Así hablaba Zarathustra* on the virtue of bravery. "But what do you know about this, you miserable traitor?" he asked Queipo in the letter, threatening to strangle him with his bare hands—"like a rabid dog."[17] After Burguete passed away shortly thereafter, his widow wrote a letter to the Socialist intellectual Luis Araquistain attributing his death to sadness over the loss of his sons. The triumph of the Republic, she wrote, had been her husband's "most ardent desire."[18]

Yet by employing such vitalist, Nietzschean rhetoric throughout his life Burguete himself had undermined military liberalism and thus tragically helped set the stage, albeit unintentionally, for the war that took the lives of his sons. For by this time his greatest influence on Spanish military culture overall took the form of ideological residue from his days as a young officer. During the

1930s he may have publicly proclaimed himself a republican at every opportunity, but the fact remained that years before he had vigorously promoted and disseminated the same kind of nationalist rhetoric now employed most frequently and effectively by right-wing, antidemocratic officers.

Even well before the outbreak of the Civil War, Burguete's impact on Spanish military thinking manifested itself most obviously in the *Colección Bibliográfica Militar,* a series of books published monthly from September 1928 until the outbreak of the Civil War in July 1936. Founded and edited by Emilio Alamán Ortega and Vicente Rojo Lluch, the latter of whom would lead the Republican army after the war broke out, the *Colección* strove to educate its readers on a wide variety of military affairs. In its premier issue its founders justified their endeavors by claiming that, "from a scientific point of view, the military officer is a slave to the other sciences, undergoing perpetual evolution." In their eyes "the militia, like other professions and like all aspects of the life of a citizen, is subjected to the inescapable law of renewal and progress."[19] Attempting to keep their readers informed of the latest developments in military sciences, they often published Spanish translations of important works from outside of Spain, such as J. F. C. Fuller's early treatise on armored warfare.[20]

Like Burguete, however, these editors added strong doses of antimaterialism and historicism to an ostensibly internationally and scientifically minded outlook, and their *Colección* assumed a markedly national orientation and a spiritualist tone on occasion. The December 1929 volume, for example, consisted entirely of selections from the works of such famous Spanish writers as Cervantes, the Infante Don Juan Manuel, Villamartín, Galdós, and Ganivet. In the introduction to this compilation Rojo explained that the "true crux of our intellectual independence and our military efficiency" lay in the ability to think and work "in Spanish," and he said he hoped the texts that followed would help serve that purpose.[21] And in another volume the *Colección* included a review of Ernst Jünger's *In Stahlgewittern* (The storm of steel), a celebration of the dangers, vitalist excitement, and quixotic heroism the author had experienced in World War I.[22] Officers thus continued to be exposed not only to new ideas in military technology, strategy, and tactics, but also to the works of some of Europe's leading antimaterialists from the intellectual vanguard.

Juan García Gómez-Caminero's *De la guerra* (On war) represented by far the most notable post-1923 successor to the vitalist works Burguete had penned at the beginning of the century.[23] Liberally sprinkling his book's 476 pages of text with numerous quotations from Nietzsche, Bernhardi, Clausewitz, Villamartín, and Ganivet, the career military man Gómez-Caminero wrote extensively on the philosophical, historical, social, political, technical, and spiritual dimensions of war.[24] Like Burguete, he cited Nietzsche's attacks on science and ostensible praise for men in arms.[25] He also made ample use of Darwinian terms and imagery, describing armed struggle as "a biological necessity, a security valve for the race, a regulating element in the life of peoples."[26] He demonstrated, moreover, the profound effect that Ganivet's *Idearium español* continued to have on military thinkers—as had been so apparent in the works of Burguete—by including an extensive discussion of the late-nineteenth-century writer's ideas on the influence of geography on national character and history.[27] Gómez-Caminero's work so impressed the War Ministry that it awarded him the Villamartín Prize along with the professionally advantageous official recognition so often granted books by his colleagues.[28]

Interestingly, even the political and professional path of Gómez-Caminero resembled that of Burguete, revealing the same paradoxical mixture of elitist philosophical tendencies and leftist politics. An open opponent of Primo de Rivera, a socialist candidate for the Cortes, and a member of the Unión Militar Republicana Antifascista, he lent important support to the Republic in the Civil War before retiring because of poor health and then dying in December 1937.[29] Like Burguete, he never seemed to grasp that social Darwinist and vitalist rhetoric praising Nietzschean *Übermensch* and war was fundamentally incompatible with the liberal principles upon which the Second Republic had been founded. However unwittingly, he thus joined Burguete in undermining democratic values in military culture.

* * *

For Antonio García Pérez the period after 1923 failed to bring with it the personal fame or power that Burguete would enjoy, but the overall political situation eventually evolved in a way far more to his liking. As always, he devoted much of his professional life to writing. But his literary endeavors yielded even less of intellectual value than during his days as a young officer, when he had managed to compose at least some thoughtful essays on subjects such as militarism, socialism, history, and religion. During the later years of his life his dozens of books and pamphlets consisted entirely of compilations of quotations and brief descriptions of military heroism in Spanish history, including—with increasing frequency after 1923—feats attributed to Primo de Rivera and his ancestors. Consistently recorded in his personal service record, they chiefly served to enhance his own professional gain. Although he spent some time in a Republican prison during the Civil War, he survived the conflict to pen more pamphlets championing the same traditionalist, militarist values he had always favored.[30]

* * *

A military writer and teacher of radically different views and a much more successful career than García Pérez, Enrique Ruiz-Fornells attracted nearly as much public attention after 1923 as his vitalist colleague Burguete. Ruiz-Fornells had, of course, ended his active duty as a brigadier general, blaming the king for preventing him from reaching the rank of major general before being forced by his age to enter the reserves. But with the establishment of the Second Republic in 1931 his active role in military affairs actually reached its peak, albeit as advisor to a civilian—the new minister of war, Manuel Azaña. Although a full analysis of Ruiz-Fornells' role in the Second Republic's military reforms, which could easily make up a lengthy study of its own, falls outside the primary scope of this book, it is worth commenting on several of his subsequent remarks about his work with Azaña.[31]

Ruiz-Fornells claimed to have taken on his position in the War Ministry expecting to lend his expertise to the technical aspects of the proposed reforms. His decision did not, he wrote, reflect a desire to "become republican." In fact, he had never considered himself "political" enough to be either republican or monarchist, he asserted, although "my temperament and my liberal ideas always left me more inclined toward a republic than a monarchy." But despite his assertion that he had wanted nothing more than to provide apolitical, technical assistance and "desired only to serve the Army and Spain," his long-standing antagonism toward certain elements within the military, such as artillery officers, clearly colored his judgments as advisor to Azaña.[32]

This is not to say, however, that Ruiz-Fornells did not believe that his actions were for the good of the armed forces or for the country as a whole. In his eyes even his eventual falling-out with Azaña on a personal level did not detract from the merits of the war minister's professional intentions. He lauded, for example, Azaña's attempts to shrink the officer corps and change the system of merit promotions that had so benefited the *africanistas* and angered the *junteros,* whom he had strongly opposed despite his agreement with them on this issue. And he confessed that "only Azaña had the guts" to tackle the controversial issue of military reform adequately. "Did Azaña have a secret desire to destroy the Army?" he subsequently wondered, no doubt referring to the war minister's alleged statement that he intended to "crush [*triturar*]" the army. "Who knows; maybe he did," Ruiz-Fornells reflected. "But there is no doubt that he resolved a problem that all previous Ministers had failed to overcome."[33] Ruiz-Fornells, although in the end very bitter toward Azaña, clearly had strong enough political convictions to put personal animosity aside and support the Republic in its attempt to reform the armed forces. After ending his work as assistant to Azaña, he withdrew from public life, retiring to Jaén and dying in the summer of 1938 of natural causes.[34]

* * *

José Millán-Astray, on the other hand, remained a prominent figure in Spain far longer than virtually any other military officer of his generation, in large part because of the important role he came to play in the Franco regime's propaganda front. In the eyes of his supporters as well as his enemies, he remains the symbol par excellence of the antirationalist, mystical, and traditionalist components of ultrarightist Spanish nationalism. For not only did Millán-Astray consciously base his writings and actions on a strong belief in the more irrational forces of human nature, but his admirers have joined his detractors in continuing to propagate such an image of him as well. The authors of the 1970 official history of the Spanish Foreign Legion, for example, introduced their two-volume work with the amazing statement that they had not tried to write an "exact and accurate biography, with precise dates, numbers and facts, since history and fiction as well as truth and legend come together in an admirable fashion in the figure of the FOUNDER."[35]

Without a doubt, these words would have pleased Millán-Astray had he lived to read them. He shared, after all, Burguete's vitalist views and his distaste for overly scientific and materialist approaches to history and war. But instead of turning to Nietzsche and his supporters elsewhere in Europe for ideological support, Millán-Astray instead relied overwhelmingly on the same Catholic traditionalist tenets and mysticism that appealed so strongly to more conservative nationalists such as García Pérez. Even Millán-Astray's interest in Far Eastern warrior philosophy, which appears at first glance to lack any ties whatsoever to Spanish tradition, actually stemmed from his belief that Bushido represented a modern equivalent of Spanish medieval Christian war values.

After the collapse of the final government of the Restoration, religious imagery surfaced repeatedly in Millán-Astray's speeches and essays. But after 1931 he began to focus his attention increasingly on everything he disliked about the newly established Republic. The object of his ire shifted from civilian politicians and the bureaucratic *junteros* of the Spanish army to the democratic government and its supporters, and at the same time his attacks began to take on the moral and religious tone that he had previously reserved for his abstract conception of war. Eventually, then, his vision of war and death in battle would become an integral part of the "Nationalist crusade" envisaged by the rebels.

Millán-Astray employed a notable amount of religious imagery in a speech he delivered to the Spanish community in Italy in 1926. He had stopped in Rome on the way back from Germany, where he had gone to get an artificial eye. His hosts in the Italian capital received the "*mutilado de Africa*" enthusiastically, greeting him as "the great soldier, the true example of the valiant and enduring Spanish soldier." While in Rome he was also decorated by Pope Pius XI,[36] and he met Mussolini, with whom he said he conversed "honestly and cordially regarding Spain, the Monarchs, and President Primo de Rivera." In his speech he referred to "the absolution in *articulo mortis*" he had first received as a young second lieutenant in the Philippines, and he offered his listeners his "mutilations as sacrifice [*holocausto*]." He also emphasized the similarities he perceived between soldiers and members of religious orders. Speaking to the clergy in the audience, he said that they "endure for the faith the same hardships that we endure for the *Patria*."[37] Such a strongly sympathetic view of the church was not widespread within the Spanish officer corps in 1926; the writings of Ruiz-Fornells and even Burguete had demonstrated a clear reluctance to embrace many tenets of traditional Spanish Catholicism, Franco himself was not yet particularly religious, and in 1936 General Mola would plan the July uprising with the intention of maintaining the Republic's separation of church and state. But officers such as García Pérez revealed few of the liberal, anticlerical sentiments of their nineteenth-century predecessors, and Millán-Astray joined them in perceiving Catholicism as an intrinsic part of Spanish nationalism. By the outbreak of the Civil War, moreover, Franco had come to perceive Catholicism in similar terms. As Stanley G. Payne writes, Franco now believed that "the Catholic faith and Spanish nationalism were inseparable, fully subscribing to the traditional Spanish ideology that stressed a special national relationship to Catholicism and a unique religious mission for Spain."[38]

Highlighting the ostensible relationship between spirituality and death in war and then pushing it to even further extremes than other writers, Millán-Astray thus played a key role in popularizing an outlook that would prove crucial in shaping Spain's future. These ideological influences combined with his more concrete role in promoting Franco's rise to *Generalísimo* of the Nationalist side in the Civil War.[39] Although political beliefs undoubtedly explained many rebelling soldiers' actions in 1936 and thereafter, another set of fundamental values and beliefs—based on the perceived apocalyptic and purifying nature of war—helped motivate the rebels to continue the struggle in spite of the magnitude of their initial failures.

After all, although the rebels of 1936 had expected that they might fail in Madrid, they were hardly prepared to see their efforts meet defeat in three-fifths of the country. In order to generate support for the long, difficult struggle, Franco and his colleagues turned to the Falangist movement, which they had previously ignored. The Falange helped form the ideological and political basis they needed to generate broad appeal, and as the war dragged on it became increasingly apparent that they would need to recruit militia from political groups such as the Falange and the Carlist Comunión Tradicionalista.[40] The rebel leaders—and most likely a good portion of the rest of the orthodox right—needed "a *mystique* adequate to sustain a civil war."[41]

In fact, for many of the rebels the concepts of war, death, and nationalism as developed in Spanish Morocco undoubtedly served as the starting point for the creation of such a mystique, whose origins could be traced to their days at the military academies under the tutelage of men such as García Pérez and Millán-Astray and which drew most of its ideological material from the church. Hence arose the interpretation of the uphill struggle as a "reconquest" and "crusade," and Millán-Astray, as Franco's first propaganda chief, occupied an ideal position from which to foster the vision of the "holy war."[42]

When Millán-Astray's religious ideal culminated in the "crusade" of the Civil War, the rebels portrayed their endeavors as a struggle against godless Marxism and freemasonry. In a speech Millán-Astray delivered to cadets at the rebel military academy in Valladolid during the third year of the war he extolled the virtues of "service" and "sacrifice," and he employed an especially threatening tone in demanding both from his listeners. He also advised the cadets to remember their "moral mission: to establish the spiritual perfection of command." In the prologue to a Tercio chaplain's biography that was probably published during the final days of the war he once again emphasized the similarities he perceived between the Spanish Foreign Legion and the Society of Jesus. "Jesuits and Legionnaires grounded their souls and their bodies in a single block when danger threatened the Religion of Christ and the *Patria*," he wrote. "Hence the Jesuits are Legionnaires and the Legionnaires are Jesuits at the sublime hour of sacrificial death before the altar of God and the *Patria*: Spain."[43]

Other ways in which the Nationalists made use of "crusade" imagery are already well known and too numerous to be treated here. Yet a book of poetry to which Millán-Astray contributed the prologue merits attention, because it best exemplifies to what absurd lengths the religious metaphors were pushed in the service of Franco's cause. The title page featured a full-color illustration of a gallant Saint James riding a white horse and clutching a spear, which was pointed at a place below the surface of the earth. There a group of devilish creatures, several of whom sported communist red stars, tore apart religious relics, and in the background several churches were aflame. The book's following pages bore similar illustrations and lots of bad poems devoted to the "holy war" and to the figures of Franco, Millán-Astray, and other key rebels.[44]

Long after Franco's victory in 1939 the "crusade" myth persisted; the Caudillo relied heavily on such ideals to legitimize his dictatorship. As Paul Preston writes, for more than two decades the Franco regime propagated its "more or less racist vision which linked the Civil War to the crusading spirit of the wars between Christians and Moors and to the evangelical imperialism of the conquest of America." This ideological offensive continued, albeit with decreasing efficacy, even into the late 1960s, when "the maintenance of an idealized notion of the Civil War as a medieval religious crusade was even more anachronistic."[45] Not surprisingly, the ideas of Millán-Astray made important contributions to this propaganda front. Moreover, until his death in 1954 he continued to view war as a spiritual and morally cleansing affair. He could therefore speak of the "ex-combatants of the War of the Holy Crusade, who have passed through its purifying crucible, where man's virtues are exalted and his defects, vices, and egoisms surface." In his eyes a soldier's defense of his country was "the most glorious of all enterprises" and soldiery a "temple of Duty."[46]

In the prologue to a Jesuit's biography of Loyola that appeared shortly after the war Millán-Astray once again emphasized the solidarity with the religious order that he felt as a legionnaire. According to the Tercio's founder, the injuries Loyola suffered defending Pamplona against the French made him "a Mutilated Knight of War for the Fatherland. And when the Virgin inundated him with faith and transformed the Mutilated Legionnaire into a mystical saint, She did so without removing his military and legionary qualities and created the founder of the Society of Jesus, in which mixed consubstantially and inseparably Religion and Soldiery, charity and work, austerity and energy, intelligence and modesty, the most pure faith and the exact appreciation of reality, the immaculate honor; heroic, sublime, and magnificent valor."[47] Similar assertions regarding "the legionary-Jesuit Honor" and "the victorious battalions of Christ in the ruins of the atheistic enemy's redoubts" followed, and Millán-Astray characterized the activities of a Christian warrior as "wrapped in the unsoiled cloak of ascetic virtue." He concluded by saying that "Saint Ignatius was first a Mutilated Legionnaire and then the Most High Founder of the Society of Jesus."[48]

Although Millán-Astray stepped down from his position as head of the Francoist press and propaganda office on January 23, 1937, he clearly continued to play an important role in the Nationalist ideological offensive. Throughout the war he gave patriotic speeches, including several discourses that he delivered under Franco's orders on the Madrid front in 1938 and 1939. In 1937 he also became head of the newly formed Distinguished Body of Disabled Veterans of the War for the Fatherland *(Benemérito Cuerpo de Mutilados de Guerra por la Patria)*, a position that he held until his death in 1954. The organization promoted the same values that he had developed in Morocco and that had become so important for the Franco regime's ideology: love for the *patria* and glorious redemption through sacrifice in the "holy war."[49]

One historian has written that the Tercio "ceased to have a discernible influence on Spanish political and cultural life after the victory of the Nationalists in 1939,"[50] but in fact Millán-Astray and his ideas had a lasting effect on the long-lived Franco regime. His ideas permeated even the school textbooks of postwar Spain, which portrayed Loyola as an exemplary member of a race "of mystics and knights, captains and conquistadors, saints and ascetics."[51] Millán-Astray's spiritual vision of war culminated during the period immediately following the Civil War, when, in Raymond Carr's words, the world "saw ambulant missions to reconvert Spain to a harsh brand of Tridentine Catholicism." The 1940s were "the *blütezeit* of what was called 'National Catholicism,' the modern edition of the old alliance of throne and altar."[52] Millán-Astray had both exemplified and promoted the transformation of an abstract concept of glorious death in battle into the apocalyptic vision of the "crusade." And the former self-styled anti-intellectual who was still best remembered for attacking Miguel de Unamuno with cries of "Death to the Intelligentsia!" even began to play the role of a sort of official, state-sponsored cultural spokesman: between the war's end and his death he joined José María Pemán, Joaquin de Entrambasaguas, Manuel García Morente, and other leading authors and academic figures of the far right in the service of the state-sponsored Asociación Cultural Hispano-Americana and the Consejo de la Hispanidad.[53]

* * *

In general, however, Franco's military victory meant that the ideological vision adopted by official Spain had far more in common with the conservative, Catholic traditionalist views of García Pérez than with the vitalist rhetoric of Burguete or even—in its most extreme rightist form—of Millán-Astray. Payne observes that "when Franco emphasized that Spanish 'totalitarianism' would be derived from the monarchism and cultural policy of the Catholic Kings, he was not merely coining a symbolic phrase. The Franquist regime was embarked on the most traditionalist, indeed reactionary, cultural policy of any twentieth-century Western state, bar none. It was an enterprise virtually without parallel."[54]

Yet even Burguete, by attacking the values of the Enlightenment and the French Revolution with the same fervor as the more traditionally minded García Pérez and the writers of *Acción Española,* helped set the stage for the mystical, medieval image of Spain's national identity that was expressed so dramatically in the mural described at the beginning of this book. In fact, Burguete's fascination with foreign ideas such as Bushido and with the apocalyptic and vitalist aspects of warfare found a prominent place in the "crusade" ideology and nationalist vision promoted by the likes of Millán-Astray. Hard-core Falangists would therefore view Japan's successful attack on Pearl Harbor much as Burguete and Millán-Astray had interpreted the Russo-Japanese War: as a positive example of material triumph through spiritual regeneration and cultural traditionalism.[55] Of all the approaches to regeneration that had been discussed in

Spanish military circles, only the Enlightenment-inspired approach, exemplified by Ruiz-Fornells' markedly liberal and "European" arguments for military, social, and political modernization, had no real place in early Francoist ideology. The Spanish officer corps, once one of Spain's most progressive bodies, had become more typical of military institutions in general: it was now a bastion of cultural conservatism.

Appendix One

Acquisitions of the Library of the Centro del Ejército y de la Armada in 1918

Subject Classification	Works	Volumes
Military (*Milicia*)	133	151
Mathematical, physicochemical, natural, and medical sciences	61	97
Metaphysical, moral, and political sciences	128	172
Arts	6	6
History	47	53
Geographical sciences	28	34
Literature	221	224
Philology and linguistics	9	9
Fencing and duels. Gymnastics and physical exercises. Games (*El juego*)	4	4
Encyclopedias and bibliographies	—	—
Nonmilitary periodicals	45	101
TOTAL	682	851

Source: Manual Antolín Becerro, *Centro del Ejército y de la Armada Biblioteca: Memoria correspondiente al año 1918 y suplemento al catálogo general de 1917* (Madrid, 1919), iii.

Appendix Two

Materials Ordered by Patrons of the Library of the Centro del Ejército y de la Armada in 1918

Subject Matter	Number of Materials
Military (*Milicia*)	10,767
Mathematical, physical, chemical, and medical	10,225
Metaphysical, moral, and political sciences	4,577
Arts	440
History	3,942
Geographical sciences	3,771
Literature[a]	4,747
Philology and linguistics	3,540
Fencing, dueling, games	2,428
Encyclopedias, bibliographies, magazines	4,110
TOTAL	48,547

Source: Antolín Becerro, *Centro,* v.
[a]Excluding novels (*novelas*).

Appendix Three

Partial Bibliography of Works by Antonio García Pérez

The following list, intended to demonstrate the abundance of García Pérez's writings and the breadth of his subject matter, includes only works for which I found substantial evidence of publication. It does not include all titles listed in the bibliographies of his books and pamphlets, because they sometimes included works still in progress, manuscripts that never saw publication, and incorrect or slightly different titles for the same works listed elsewhere.

Each work is placed within a category defined by García Pérez's rank at the time, which was often listed on a title page that lacked the year and place of publication. A year or place in brackets indicates that although the title page lacks this information, the approximate year or place of publication could be ascertained from the printer's notes, García Pérez's personal service record,[1] other references, library records, or a date given in the introduction, prologue, or dedication. In cases where I have listed only later editions, such as the third and seventh editions of *Patria,* it is probably safe to assume that earlier versions indeed saw print, even though I was unable to locate them or reliable references to them.

1896–1899—LIEUTENANT (*Primer Teniente*)

La Guerra de Africa de 1859 a 1860: Lecciones que explicó en el Curso de Estudios Superiores del Ateneo de Madrid el Coronel de Infantería Francisco Martin Arrúe. Extracadas por D. Antonio García Pérez. Madrid, 1898. García Pérez's summary of a series of lectures Francisco Martin Arrúe delivered at the Ateneo of Madrid.

Nomenclatura del fusil mauser español, modelo 1893. N.p., 1896.

1899–1912—CAPTAIN (*Capitán*)

Añoranzas americanas: Conferencia pronunciada en la noche del miércoles 21 de diciembre de 1904. Madrid, 1905.

Antecedentes político-diplomáticos de la expedición española á México (1836–62). Madrid, 1904.

Árabe vulgar y cultura arábigo. N.p., [1908].

Catolicismo y libertad. Badajoz, 1909.

Consejos á los caballeros alumnos de la Academia de Infantería. Toledo, [1910]. At least two editions were published.

La cuenca del muluya. Madrid, [1910].

La cuestión del norte de Marruecos. Barcelona, 1908.

Deberes morales del soldado. Toledo, 1905.

Derecho internacional público. With Manuel García Alvarez. Toledo, 1909.

Diario de las operaciones realizadas en Melilla á partir del día 9 de julio de 1909. With Manuel García Alvarez. Toledo, 1909.

Don Vicente Moreno y las Cortes españolas. Madrid, 1910.

Estudio político-militar de la campaña de Méjico, 1861–1867. Prologue by Antonio Díaz Benzo. Madrid, 1900.

Fortea: Conferencia pronunciada en el Centro del Ejército y de la Armada de Madrid. Madrid, 1910. García Pérez's personal service record also mentions an edition in 1921.

Geografía militar de Marruecos y posesiones españolas en Africa. Prologue by José Garrido de Or. Barcelona, 1910. Other editions may have appeared in 1911 and 1916.

Glorias de María Inmaculada en los hechos de armas más salientes del ejército español. Prologue by José Ibáñez Marín. Madrid, 1905.

Guerra de secesión: El General Pope. Madrid, 1901. A version of this ran as a series in *Revista Técnica de Infantería y Caballería* (1901).

Influencia en el arma de Infantería de su patrona la Purísima Concepción. N.p., 1905.

Inmolación del Capitán Don Vicente Moreno. Toledo, [1910].

Isla del Peregil y Santacruz de Mar-Pequeña. Madrid, 1908.

Javier Mina y la independencia mexicana. Madrid, 1909.

Leyes de la guerra. Madrid, [1910].

Manual de la guerra de noche. Barcelona, 1912.

Melilla, después de la campaña de 1902. Madrid, n.d.

Militarismo y socialismo: Conferencia pronunciada en la noche del sábado 27 de enero de 1906. Madrid, 1906.

Muerto por su Patria y por su Rey el 27 de Julio de 1909 (Melilla): Braulio de la Portilla y Sanchos. Toledo, 1911.

Ocho días en Melilla. Barcelona, 1909.

Organización militar de América: República de Brasil. Madrid, 1902.

Organización militar de América: República de Ecuador. Madrid, 1902.

Organización militar de México. Madrid, 1902.

Posesiones españoles en África. Toledo, 1909.

Posesiones españoles en el África occidental. Barcelona, 1907.

Un programa para la enseñanza primaria en España. Madrid, 1905.

Reflejos militares de América. Madrid, 1902.

Religión y la Guerra. Madrid, 1912.

Reseña histórico-militar de la campaña del Paraguay (1864 á 1870). With Rafael Howard y Arrien. Burgos, 1900.

S. M. El Rey Don Alfonso XIII en la Academia de Infantería. N.p., 1911.

El Sacerdote Pinto Palacios y el Capitán D. Vicente Moreno. Madrid, 1909.

El Sagentino Romeu. Toledo, 1912.
El Soldado. Toledo, 1911.
Tánger. Madrid, 1910.
Vocabulario militar hispano-magrebino. Melilla, 1907.

1912–1918—MAJOR (*Comandante*)

El Cadete D. Juan Vázquez Afán de Ribera. Toledo, n.d.
La Casa solariega de la Infantería Española. Toledo, n.d.
Compendio histórico del Regimiento de Córdova. Malaga, 1917.
Destellos de grandeza. Madrid, n.d.
Egregio historial de la 2.a Academia de Infantería. N.p., 1915.
Estudio geográfico militar de las posesiones españolas en Marruecos. N.p., [1916].
Historial de guerra del Regimiento de Borbon 17. de Infantería. Malaga, [1915, 1921].
Ifni y el sáhara español. Toledo, [1916].
Juan Soldado y Juan Obrero. Madrid, 1916. Originally published in *Nuestro Tiempo,* Dec. 1915.
Siete años de mi vida (1905–12). Madrid, [1912]. Originally published in 1912 in *Estudios Militares.*
Zona española del norte de Marruecos. Toledo, [1913].

1918–1931—LIEUTENANT COLONEL (*Teniente Coronel*), COLONEL (*Coronel*)[2]

Campo florido. Toledo, n.d.
Cervantes, soldado de la Española Infantería. N.p., [1921].
Compendio de moral. N.p., [1927].
Conceptos españoles de moral militar. [Toledo], n.d.
Ejemplos de moral militar. N.p., [1928].
Fe y patriotismo en los campos de batalla. Toledo, n.d.
Florilegio bélico. Toledo, 1928.
Heroicos artilleros. N.p., [1928].
Heroicos infantes en Marruecos. [Madrid], [1926]. Several editions of this work were published, including one that served as an "Obsequio de la 'Stokes Gun Company á la Oficialidad de la española infantería.'"
Heroicas ofrendas. Prologue by Salvador Rueda. Epilogue by Antonio Rey Soto. Madrid, 1920.
Historial del Regimiento Infantería de Tarragona n. 78. Prologue by José Díaz Fernández. Gijon, 1920.
Máximas de mando y obediencia. Toledo, n.d.
Patria. 3rd ed. Toledo, 1923. This title was first noted in García Pérez's personal service record in 1922. A seventh edition appeared in 1925.

Patria y bandera. Toledo, n.d.
El Patronato de la Inmaculada. Prologue by Ricardo León. Gijon, 1919.
Plumas y espadas. Toledo, [1924].
La Realeza. Madrid, n.d.
Reyes y soldados en los campos de batalla. Toledo, n.d.

PUBLISHED AFTER THE CIVIL WAR

¡Arriba España! [Larache], 1943.
Banderas de España. Ceuta, [1944].
Cabos y soldados de la Española Infantería. N.p., n.d.
Grandezas artilleras. N.p., [1944].
Héroes de España en campos de Rusia, 1941–42. Madrid, 1942.
Historial del Grupo de F.R.I. de Infantería Alhucemas Núm. 6. Cordova, [1944].
El Infante de Loyola. N.p., n.d.
Jardines de España. Tánger, 1941.
La Marina en la Cruzada. Canarias, n.d.
Simancas glorioso. Ceuta, 1944.

PROLOGUES BY ANTONIO GARCÍA PÉREZ

Alhucemas. By Adolfo Aragones de la Encarnación. Toledo, [1910].
Hojas Sueltas de un Catecismo Españolista. By Eugenio Sellés Dasí. Toledo, 1905.

Appendix Four

The Soldier's Moral Duties

Duty	Virtues	Summary
Duty to the *patria*	Love for the *patria*	Patriotism
	Loyalty to the *bandera*	
	Subordination	
	Obedience	
Duty to his superiors	Respect	Subordination
	Submission	
	Deference	
Duty in his relations to the civil population	Civil duty	
	Accuracy and punctuality	
	Vigilance	
	Courtesy	
	Health	
	Steadfastness	
	Abnegation	
	Loyalty-adhesion	
Personal virtues and duties of the soldier	Sacrifice	Abnegation
	Patience-suffering	
	Selflessness	
	Valor	
	Love of glory	Valor
	Humanity	
	Military honor	
	Loyalty	
	Rectitude	
	Corps spirit	Honor
	Branch spirit	
Duties in his relations with other soldiers	Military spirit	
	Confidence	
	Solidarity	

Source: Enrique Ruiz-Fornells, *La educación moral del soldado*, prologue by Pedro Berenguer, 8th ed. (Toledo, 1918), 127.

Notes

INTRODUCTION

1. I use the term *modernist* to describe the outlook of fin-de-siècle intellectuals who rejected the dominant cultural values of nineteenth-century Europe—which rested largely on the Enlightenment legacies of rationalism and liberalism—in favor of radically new moralities and ways of looking at the world, such as those espoused by Nietzsche.

2. Even long after Spain's transition to democracy, for example, the magazines *Ejército* (Madrid) and *La Legión* (Torrejón de Ardoz, Madrid) still include articles and illustrations strikingly consistent with the conservative, religious imagery seen in the mural described earlier.

3. Recent works treating Spanish nationalism include José Álvarez Junco's articles "The Nation-Building Process in Nineteenth-Century Spain," in *Nationalism and the Nation in the Iberian Peninsula: Competing and Conflicting Identities*, ed. Clare Mar-Molinero and Angel Smith (Oxford, 1996), 89–106, and "El nacionalismo español como mito movilizador: Cuatro guerras," in *Cultura y movilización en la España contemporánea*, ed. Rafael Cruz and Manuel Pérez Ledesma (Madrid, 1997), 35–67; Andrés de Blas Guerrero, *Tradición republicana y nacionalismo español* (Madrid, 1991), and *Sobre el nacionalismo español* (Madrid, 1989); Carolyn P. Boyd, *Historia Patria: Politics, History, and National Identity in Spain, 1875–1975* (Princeton, 1997); Inman Fox, *La invención de España* (Madrid, 1997); Juan Pablo Fusi, *España: La evolución de la identidad nacional* (Madrid, 2000); J. M. Jover, "Cáracteres del nacionalismo español (1854–1874)," *Zona Abierta* 31 (June 1984): 1–22; M. Moreno Alonso, "El sentimiento nacionalista en la historiografía española del siglo XIX," *Nation et nationalités en Espagne, XIXe–XXe siècles* (Paris, 1984); and Luis Moreno, *La federalización de España; Poder político y territorio* (Madrid, 1997). On the recent historiography of Spanish nationalism see also José Álvarez Junco's two-part essay "L'eclosió d'estudis sobre el nacionalisme," *L'Avenç* 215 (June 1997): 66–69, and 216 (July–Aug. 1997): 60–65.

4. E. J. Hobsbawm, *Nations and Nationalism since 1780: Programme, Myth, Reality*, 2nd ed. (Cambridge, U.K., 1992). John Breuilly, *Nationalism and the State*, 2nd ed. (Chicago, 1994). Linda Colley has recognized the importance of military culture in the making of British national identity, noting that military attitudes "desperately need separate and detailed attention" (*Britons: Forging the Nation, 1707–1837* [New Haven, 1992], 7). But the case of modern Spain, where the military's influence on civil society was undoubtedly greater, has remained largely unexplored by scholars. As some scholars have noted, the similarities between Spanish and British (and also English) national-

ism do not end there. For just as the latter has attracted little attention in comparison to the peripheral nationalist (or "subnationalist") Welsh and Scottish movements, the Basque and Catalan cases have shown more dynamism and generated far more scholarship than Spanish nationalism itself.

5. The classic study is Pedro Lain Entralgo, *La generación del noventayocho* (Madrid, 1945). The term *Generation of '98* was invented, as Robert Wohl notes in *The Generation of 1914* (Cambridge, Mass., 1979), 125–26, simply to describe the group of writers who shared the regeneration of Spain as their common goal, and it "implied a unity of concern and action that no one at the time doubted, even if literary critics have since found the concept difficult to apply." Sebastian Balfour's recent book *The End of the Spanish Empire, 1898–1923* (Oxford, 1997) surveys the period of the "Disaster" of 1898, regenerationism, and subsequent developments in Restoration Spain.

6. Most historians define Spanish traditionalism in such terms. See, for example, Martin Blinkhorn's "Conservatism, Traditionalism, and Fascism in Spain, 1898–1937," in *Fascists and Conservatives: The Radical Right and the Establishment in Twentieth-Century Europe,* ed. Martin Blinkhorn (London, 1990), 118–37. Begoña Urigüen endeavors to define and analyze the origins, development, and politics of nineteenth-century Spanish traditionalism and other related movements in *Origenes y evolución de la derecha española: El neo-catolicismo* (Madrid, 1986).

7. Thilo Jens Wittenberg draws attention to and examines some aspects of the general philosophical shift within the officer corps that took place during the Restoration, but his work focuses primarily on the period before 1898. See his "Mut und Ehre: Die professionelle, ideologische und politische Entwicklung des spanischen Offizierkorps im 19. Jahrhundert (1808–1908)" (Ph.D. dissertation, Albert-Ludwigs-Universität zu Freiburg i. Br., 1995). Other studies covering the political and social developments of the Spanish military during the Restoration include Manuel Ballbé, *Orden público y militarismo en la España constitucional (1812–1983)* (Madrid, 1983); Miguel Alonso Baquer, *El Ejército en la sociedad española* (Madrid, 1971); Carolyn P. Boyd, *La política pretoriana en el reinado de Alfonso XIII* (Madrid, 1990), which is a revised and expanded version of her *Praetorian Politics in Liberal Spain* (Chapel Hill, 1979); Julio Busquets, *El militar de carrera en España,* 2nd, rev. ed. (Barcelona, 1971); Gabriel Cardona, *El poder militar en la España hasta la guerra civil* (Madrid, 1983); Daniel R. Headrick, *Ejército y política en España (1866–1898)* (Madrid, 1981); Rafael Núñez Florencio, *Militarismo y antimilitarismo en España (1888–1906)* (Madrid, 1990); Carlos Seco Serrano, *Militarismo y civilismo en la España contemporánea* (Madrid, 1984); and Stanley G. Payne's classic *Politics and the Military in Modern Spain* (Stanford, 1967). The Restoration military is also treated in Sebastian Balfour and Pablo La Porte's recent article "Spanish Military Cultures and the Moroccan Wars, 1909–36," *European History Quarterly* 30, no. 3 (July 2000), 307–32.

8. By *ideology* I simply mean a system of ideas used to interpret the world and as a basis for action. As Keith Michael Baker notes, the terms *ideological* and *intellectual* have largely the same meaning if the concept of "ideology" is understood in what he considers its "original sense": "concerned with the study of the process by which the world of phenomena is given order and meaning through the activity of signification"

(*Inventing the French Revolution: Essays on French Political Culture in the Eighteenth Century* [Cambridge, U.K., 1990], 16).

9. Jeffrey Herf, *Reactionary Modernism: Technology, Culture, and Politics in Weimar and the Third Reich* (Cambridge, U.K., 1984).

10. Adrian Shubert, *A Social History of Modern Spain* (London, 1990), 1–7. Shubert refers to David Blackbourn and Geoff Eley, *The Peculiarities of German History* (Oxford, 1984).

11. See Stanley G. Payne, *The Franco Regime, 1936–1975* (Madison and London, 1987), 3–18, for a succinct analysis of the political development of modern Spain from a broad historical perspective.

12. Bergson proposed his vitalistic evolutionary theory in *L'evolution créatice*, 4th ed. (Paris, 1908).

13. Zeev Sternhell strongly emphasizes the contributions of "leftist" thinkers to French and Italian "fascism," a term he tends to apply rather liberally, in *Neither Right nor Left: Fascist Ideology in France*, trans. David Maisel (Berkeley and Los Angeles, 1986) and *The Birth of Fascist Ideology: From Cultural Rebellion to Political Revolution*, with Mario Sznajder and Maia Asheri, trans. David Maisel (Princeton, 1994).

14. Sternhell, *Birth*, 32.

15. Paul Preston, *Franco: A Biography* (New York, 1994), 8–13. Antoni Jutglar also acknowledged the importance of Spanish military education in his *Ideologías y clases en la España contemporánea* (Madrid, 1968), 48–50.

16. For a provocative analysis of military education in Spain during a later period see Carlos Blanco Escolá, *La Academia General Militar de Zaragoza (1928–1931)* (Barcelona, 1989). Roberto Sánchez Abal's *La enseñanza militar en el reinado de Alfonso XII* (Madrid, 1991), the published version of the author's 1989 dissertation for Spain's Universidad Nacional de Educación a Distancia, offers useful information, but little analysis or interpretation. The same holds true for José Luis Isabel Sánchez, *La Academia de Infantería*, 2 vols. (Toledo, 1991).

17. Richard Herr, *An Historical Essay on Modern Spain* (Berkeley, Los Angeles, and London, 1971), 35.

18. See Boyd, *Historia*, and Fox, *Invención*.

19. As late as the 1970s children playing hopscotch in Madrid recited verses referring to the tragedies and hardships brought on by military service in Morocco (André Bachoud, *Los españoles ante las campañas de Marruecos* [Madrid, 1988], 392).

20. Daniel Pick, *War Machine: The Rationalisation of Slaughter in the Modern Age* (New Haven and London, 1993), esp. 75–87.

21. Keith Michael Baker discusses recent reinterpretations of the French Revolution by historians who stress its linguistic and semiotic aspects in the introduction to his *Inventing*, 1–11.

22. Hobsbawm, *Nations*, 102; Andrés de Blas Guerrero, *Nacionalismos y naciones en Europa* (Madrid, 1995), 17.

23. Breuilly, *Nationalism*.

24. The idea of "imagined political communities" comes from Benedict Anderson, *Imagined Communities*, rev. ed. (London, 1991).

25. See José Álvarez Junco, "La invención de la Guerra de la Independencia," *Studia Histórica-Historia Contemporánea* 12 (1994), 75–99.

26. On nineteenth-century Spanish nationalism, Álvarez Junco, "Nation-Building." On the endeavors of intellectual elites to use history to achieve this end see also Boyd, *Historia,* and Fox, *Invención.*

27. Stanley G. Payne, *Historia del Carlismo* (Madrid, 1995), 24.

28. This is in a sense understandable, since Spanish nationalism was notably weak during this period. On the reasons for this weakness see Álvarez Junco, "Nation-Building," and Payne, *Franco Regime,* 3–31. As Wittenberg demonstrates, notions of "the nation" and national identity played roles in the dominant intellectual movements within the officer corps during this period. See his "Mut."

29. Sebastian Balfour, "'The Lion and the Pig': Nationalism and National Identity in *fin-de-siècle* Spain," in *Nationalism,* ed. Mar-Molinero and Smith, 115. He expands on the analysis of Spanish military nationalism in his *End of the Spanish Empire,* 164–87.

30. Anderson, *Imagined,* 80.

31. See Wittenberg, "Mut." Krausismo, a movement in Spain based on the writings of Karl Friedrich Krause, had a great impact on nineteenth-century Spanish intellectual life. Krausists advocated a kind of secular pursuit of knowledge that assumed that science served a divine plan. Spanish Krausists, many of whom held university chairs, "found in Krausism an idealist philosophy of law and history with which to critique neo-Thomist orthodoxy and upon which to build an intellectual foundation for a more humane, productive, and industrial society" (Boyd, *Historia,* 31).

32. Deutsch makes this argument, which anticipates aspects of Anderson's subsequent approach, in his *Nationalism and Social Communication: An Inquiry into the Foundations of Nationality,* 2nd ed. (Cambridge, Mass., 1966). On the military clubs see Chapter 1 of this book.

33. They were, in fact, far more significant than most historians have acknowledged. See Wittenberg, "Mut."

34. Bernard Semmel, *Imperialism and Social Reform: English Social-Imperial Thought (1895–1914)* (London, 1960).

35. Anderson, *Imagined,* 71.

36. Breuilly, *Nationalism,* 49.

37. I use the term *historicist* simply to refer to the idea, often associated with the German writer Herder, that each society, or "nation," is unique—with a unique historical character and destiny that cannot be understood through the rationalist methods of the social sciences. On this definition of *historicism* and its use in nationalist ideologies see ibid., 56–64.

38. Ibid., 57.

39. See Boyd, *Historia,* and Fox, *Invención.*

40. Tom Nairn also writes of this dual nature of nationalism, which he calls "the modern Janus," noting the distinction between its manifestation as "a morally and politically positive force in modern history," such as in the struggles of societies against stronger outside oppressors, and its employment in such "negative" movements as Italian fascism. In addition, he stresses "the complex of refractory, unassimilable phenom-

ena linked to nationalism and its many derivatives (racism, anti-semitism, etc.) which time and time again appeared to undermine and thoroughly discredit Western rationality." Nairn argues that because nationalists often had to rely on populism, "a romantic culture quite remote from Enlightenment rationalism always went hand-in-hand with the spread of nationalism. The new middle-class intelligentsia of nationalism had to invite the masses into history; and the invitation-card had to be written in a language they understood" (*The Break-Up of Britain: Crisis and Neo-Nationalism* [London, 1977], 331, 337, 340). In the Spanish case the intimate ties between republican liberalism and ideas of the Spanish nation are indisputable. One author devotes an entire book to "el significado fundamental que el nacionalismo democrático español habrá de tener en nuestra tradición republicana hasta la llegada misma del régimen de 1931" (Andrés de Blas Guerrero, *Tradición republicana y nacionalismo español* [Madrid, 1991], 138).

41. Breuilly, *Nationalism,* 13. Hobsbawm notes that "intellectual vagueness" characterized nineteenth-century liberal discourse on the matters of nations and nationality. Liberal economists, for example, "could only recognize the economic significance of nations in practice, but not in theory" (*Nations,* 25–26).

42. Similarly, the nineteenth-century Polish intellectuals known as the "Positivists," whom Brian A. Porter argues did in fact embrace nationalism, helped set the stage for fin-de-siècle rightist nationalists, albeit in a more indirect fashion. As Porter argues, the rightists would appropriate such English liberals as Herbert Spencer, with whom the Positivists had been infatuated, but reconfigure his ideas. Spencer's writings were particularly susceptible to this kind of alterations, since he employed what was essentially militarist rhetoric and imagery even when making pacifist arguments. See Brian A. Porter, "The Social Nation and Its Futures: English Liberalism and Polish Nationalism in Late Nineteenth-Century Warsaw," *American Historical Review* 101, no. 5 (Dec. 1996), 1476. As is discussed later, Burguete also found much to like in Spencer.

43. Enrique Ruiz-Fornells, *La educación moral del soldado,* prologue by Pedro A. Berenguer, 8th ed. (1894; reprint, Toledo, 1918).

44. Miguel Alonso Baquer, "La selección de la elite militar española," in *Las Fuerzas Armadas Españolas. Historia Institucional y Social,* ed. Mario Hernández Sánchez-Barba and Miguel Alonso Baquer, vol. 5 (Madrid, 1986), 33–34.

CHAPTER ONE. LIBERALISM, TRADITION, AND WAR

1. John Lawrence Tone, *The Fatal Knot: The Guerrilla War in Navarre and the Defeat of Napoleon in Spain* (Chapel Hill and London, 1994), 49–53; Gabriel H. Lovett, *Napoleon and the Birth of Modern Spain,* vol. 1 (New York, 1965), 140–68; Charles J. Esdaile, *The Spanish Army in the Peninsular War* (Manchester, 1988), 76–77.

2. See José Álvarez Junco, "La invención de la Guerra de la Independencia," *Studia Histórica-Historia Contemporánea* 12 (1994), 75–99.

3. Tone, *Fatal Knot,* 53–54.

4. Esdaile, *Spanish Army,* 75–114.

5. Antonio Alcalá Galiano, "De nuestras costumbres políticas," in his *Obras escogidas: Biblioteca de Autores Españoles,* ed. Jorge Campos, vol. 84 (Madrid, 1955), 319, cited in Thilo Jens Wittenberg, "Mut und Ehre: Die professionelle, ideologische und politische Entwicklung des spanischen Offizerskorps im 19. Jahrhundert (1808–1908)" (Ph.D. dissertation, Albert-Ludwigs-Universität zu Freiburg i.Br., 1995), 13.

6. Tone, *Fatal Knot,* 55–56.

7. For example, Carlos Seco Serrano, *Militarismo y civilismo en la España contemporánea* (Madrid, 1984), 25–27.

8. Helen Nader, *Liberty in Absolutist Spain* (Baltimore, 1990).

9. Esdaile, *Spanish Army,* 102–3.

10. See Álvarez Junco, "La invención."

11. For example, Wellington's letter to Lord Castlereagh, Merida, August 23, 1809, excerpted in Julian Rathbone, *Wellington's War: His Peninsular Dispatches* (London, 1984), 74–77. See also Esdaile, *Spanish Army,* 115–27, which dates the letter to Castlereagh from August 25, 1809, and David Gates, *The Spanish Ulcer: A History of the Peninsular War* (London, 1986), 192. In the early twentieth century an astute, reform-minded Spanish officer would begin his highly critical report on the state of the Spanish army with another damning description attributed to Wellington (El Capitán Equis, *El problema militar en España: Apuntes para un estudio sincero y al alcance de todos,* vol. 1 [Burgos, 1916], v).

12. Stanley G. Payne, *Politics and the Military in Modern Spain* (Stanford, 1967), 1.

13. Esdaile, *Spanish Army,* 168–74; Fernando María Puell de la Villa, "Origen, vida y reclutamiento del infante español (1700–1912)" (Ph.D. dissertation, Universidad Nacional de Educación a Distancia, Madrid, 1995), 242, subsequently published as *El soldado desconocido: De la leva a la "mili"* (Madrid, 1996).

14. For a discussion of the motives of the guerrillas in Navarre, a stronghold of resistance to the French, see Tone, *Fatal Knot,* 146–71.

15. Richard Herr, *An Historical Essay on Modern Spain* (Berkeley, 1974), 73.

16. On the impact of the War of Independence on the Spanish military, see Esdaile, *Spanish Army,* which also includes a good account of the Spanish army in the eighteenth century.

17. Rafael Altamira, *Psicología del Pueblo Español,* 2nd ed. (Barcelona, [1917]), 152.

18. Puell, "Origen," 185–91, 119–37, 251.

19. Wittenberg, "Mut;" 27–29.

20. Payne, *Politics,* 16–18.

21. See Wittenberg, "Mut," for a much more comprehensive discussion than is possible here of what Wittenberg labels the "guerrilla syndrome" and of military thought in general in nineteenth-century Spain. He argues that the War of Independence fostered the creation of a peculiar "myth of Spanish aptitude [Mythos des 'spanischen Talents']" for individual initiative and action, which was perceived to have the potential to thrive in *all* Spaniards and thus came to carry more value than traditional measures of noble blood. The myth served as the "first crystallization point of a national identity" and also facilitated the rise of a middle-class *Aristocracia del talento.* This new aristoc-

racy combined with its older counterpart to create the oligarchy that would establish hegemony over the country (11).

22. Puell, "Origen," 197.

23. Payne, *Politics*, 14. On the Spanish *pronunciamiento* in general see ibid., 14–16, and Miguel Alonso Baquer, *El modelo español de Pronunciamiento* (Madrid, 1983).

24. Puell, "Origen," 269–73.

25. The only major study to explore the intellectual and philosophical world of the nineteenth-century Spanish officer corps in depth is Wittenberg, "Mut."

26. On the revolution in general and the military's role in it, see C. A. M. Hennessey, *The Federal Republic in Spain: Pi y Margall and the Federal Republican Movement, 1868–74* (Oxford, 1962).

27. Esdaile, *Spanish Army*, 168–73; Puell, "Origen," 292–94.

28. Núria Sales de Bohigas, *Sobre esclavos, reclutas y mercaderes de quintos* (Barcelona, 1974); Daniel R. Headrick, *Ejército y política en España (1866–1898)* (Madrid, 1981), 101–4, 143, 153–54; Puell, "Origin," 292–94.

29. Miguel Gistau Ferrando, *Monografía y Catálogo de la Biblioteca del Centro del Ejército y de la Armada* (Madrid, 1917), xi–xiv; Wittenberg, "Mut," 92–93.

30. *Correo Militar*, March 26, 1871, cited in Gistau Ferrando, *Monografía*, xii.

31. Wittenberg, "Mut," 103–29. By the early twentieth century the different types of military periodicals clearly revealed this distinction between officer elites, who played direct roles in shaping military policies, doctrine, education, and even—under Primo de Rivera and Franco—most areas of civilian government policy, and the "masses" of the officer corps and noncommissioned officers. The historian Rafael Núñez Florencio acknowledges these differences, but he refuses to concede that the more intellectually oriented officer elites represented anything but "isolated reformist intellectuals" far removed from what he sees as the true "military mentality" and "military thought [*el pensamiento militar*]" in Spain (*Utopistas y autoritarios en 1900* [Madrid, 1994], 130). For this reason his belief that "the military mentality" in Spain as a single entity represents a useful analytical category cannot hold true in a more nuanced study of Spanish military culture. But his reading of the mass-circulation military dailies in *Utopistas* and in his previous book, *Militarismo y antimilitarismo en España (1888–1906)* (Madrid, 1990), sheds some light on the politics of these dailies' readers. In his view, regardless of the diversity within the corps, which he admits existed to some degree, the officers were all united in their opposition to "a common enemy" (149).

32. Gistau Ferrando, *Monografía*, xiv.

33. On the Centro, originally known as the Círculo de Instrucción y Recreo del Ejército y de la Armada and then as the Centro Militar del Ejército y de la Armada, see ibid., xv–lli. For a critical analysis of its political and philosophical tendencies during its early period, see Wittenberg, "Mut," 156–86.

34. On the extraordinary history of the Centro's gambling activities, see Wittenberg, "Mut," 266–68.

35. Gistau Ferrando, *Monografía*.

36. Manuel Antolín Becerro, *Centro del Ejército y de la Armada Biblioteca: Memo-*

ria correspondiente al año 1918 y suplemento al catálogo general de 1917 (Madrid, 1919), iii–v.

37. Julio Busquets, *El militar de carrera en España,* 2nd ed. (Barcelona, 1984), 78–80.

38. See the following chapters of this book.

39. On discussions of nationalism in the Academia General Militar, see Wittenberg, "Mut," 189–212.

40. Miguel Alonso Baquer, *El ejército en la sociedad española* (Madrid, 1971), 170–204; Esdaile, *Spanish Army,* 22–23; Wittenberg, "Mut," 189–212.

41. Carolyn P. Boyd, *Historia Patria: Politics, History, and National Identity in Spain, 1875–1975* (Princeton, 1997), 70.

42. Ibid., 67–72.

43. Stanley G. Payne, *Historia del Carlismo* (Madrid, 1995), 24. On Carlist ideology, its royalist origins, and its later influence on Spanish politics, see also Martin Blinkhorn, *Carlism and Crisis in Spain* (Cambridge, U.K., 1975); José Luis Rodríguez Jiménez, *La extrema derecha española en el siglo XX;* and Alexandra Wilhelmsen, *La formación del pensamiento político del Carlismo (1810–1875)* (Madrid, 1995).

44. On non-Carlist Spanish traditionalism—including what some historians call "neo-Catholicism," see Begoña Urigüen, *Orígenes y evolución de la derecha española: El neo-catolicismo* (Madrid, 1986), and Stanley G. Payne, *Spanish Catholicism: An Historical Overview* (Madison, 1984), esp. 69–103.

45. José Álvarez Junco, "El nacionalismo español como mito movilizador: Cuatro guerras," in *Cultura y movilización en la España contemporánea,* ed. Rafael Cruz and Manuel Pérez Ledesma (Madrid, 1997), 35–67.

46. Francisco Villamartín, *Nociones del arte militar* (Madrid, 1862), excerpted in Francisco Barado, *Literatura Militar Española* (1890; reprint, Madrid, 1996), 423–29.

47. José Gómez de Arteche, *Guerra de independencia: Historia militar de España de 1808 a 1814,* 14 vols. (Madrid, 1868–1903), excerpted in Barado, *Literatura,* 409.

48. Miguel A. Espina, *La civilización y la espada: Estudios histórico-filosóficos* (Manila, 1886), 24–25.

49. Espina, *Civilización,* 29–69.

CHAPTER TWO. THE NIETZSCHEAN WARRIOR

1. Except where otherwise noted, all information on Burguete's military career has been gleaned from his personal service record: Archivo General Militar, Segovia, Expedientes Personales (AGM), sect. 1, legajo B-3995.

2. For an example of the quasi-hagiographical portrayals of Burguete that appeared in the Spanish press see Rogelio P. Olivares, "Un Paseo por la Moncloa: Impresiones particulares de una conversación con el General Burguete," *Mundial Revista Gráfica* 1, no. 9 (Sept. 9, 1922). Burguete's status as a public figure is also demonstrated by his inclusion in articles surveying prominent Spanish personalities about contemporary issues. For Burguete's remarks recorded beside those of the likes of Antonio Maura, Azorín, Unamuno, Alejandro Lerroux, Melquiades Álvarez, and Ramiro de Maeztu see

"¿Qué desea V. y qué espera para nuestra Patria en el año 1917?" undated article from *Heraldo de Aragón,* a private archive of Manuel Burguete Herrero, and "De todos los libros que ha leído en su vida, ¿cuál le ha impresionado más?" *Estampa,* March 7, 1931.

Commentary on Burguete's literary endeavors includes Ramiro de Maeztu, "El arma y el hombre," *Nuevo Mundo,* Oct. 27, 1916, and Maeztu's comments cited in R. Gómez de la Serna, *Azorín* (Madrid, 1930), 131. The fascist thinker Ernesto Giménez Caballero later copied Maeztu's passage, which included Burguete's response to the crisis of 1898 along with the comments of Costa, Azorín, Benavente, Baroja, and Unamuno, in his *Genio de España,* 7th ed. (Madrid, 1971), 44. The original exchange, which took place at a 1902 banquet in honor of Baroja where Burguete shared a table with the likes of Maeztu, Azorín, Galdós, Ortega Munilla, and Valle-Inclán, is briefly recounted in José Luis Calvo Carilla, *La cara oculta del 98: Místicos e intelectuales en la España del fin de siglo (1895–1902)* (Madrid, 1998), 359–60. Calvo Carilla bases his description on a subsequent account by Baroja. See also the comments on Burguete in Baroja's *Desde la ultima vuelta del camino: Memorias: Final del siglo XIX y principios del XX* (Madrid, 1945), 231–32, and in Miguel de Unamuno, "Almas de Jovenes," *Obras completas,* vol. 1, *Paisajes y ensayos* (Madrid, 1966), 252–62. The latter was first published in *Nuestro Tiempo,* May 1904.

3. Matei Calinescu, *Five Faces of Modernity* (Durham, 1987), 42.

4. As discussed in the Introduction, the term comes from Jeffrey Herf's *Reactionary Modernism: Technology, Culture, and Politics in Weimar and the Third Reich* (Cambridge, U.K., 1984). "Reactionary modernism" in a Spanish context has received little attention, although Enric Ucelay Da Cal uses the term in his study of the influence of Catalan intellectuals on the Spanish fascist thinker Ernesto Giménez Caballero. See his "Vanguardia, fascismo y la interacción entre nacionalismo español y catalán: El proyecto catalán de Ernesto Giménez Caballero y algunas ideas corrientes en círculos intelectuales de Barcelona, 1927–1933," in *Los nacionalismos en la España de la II. República,* ed. Justo G. Benmendi and Ramón Maíz (Madrid, 1991), 39–95.

5. Pierre Drieu La Rochelle, *Socialisme fasciste* (Paris, 1934).

6. Allen Douglas, *From Fascism to Libertarian Communism: Georges Valois Against the Third Republic* (Berkeley, 1992).

7. See Thilo Jens Wittenberg, "Mut und Ehre: Die professionelle, ideologische und politische Entwicklung des spanischen Offizerskorps im 19. Jahrhundert (1808–1908)" (Ph.D. dissertation, Albert-Ludwigs-Universität zu Freiburg I.Br., 1995), 268–72.

8. Carolyn P. Boyd, *La política pretoriana en el reinado de Alfonso XIII,* trans. Mauro Hernández Benítez (Madrid, 1990), 228–29, 261. An earlier edition appeared as *Praetorian Politics in Liberal Spain* (Chapel Hill, 1979).

9. *Yo acuso: Carta del General Burguete a Queipo de Llano* (Valencia, n.d.), 4. On Burguete after 1923 see also the epilogue to this book.

10. There are, however, brief discussions of Burguete in Boyd, *Praetorian Politics,* Appendix B, 286; Andrée Bachoud, *Los españoles ante las campañas de Marruecos* (Madrid, 1988), 133–34, 139; Wittenberg, "Mut," 268–75; and José Luis Calvo Carilla's recent book *La cara oculta del '98: Místicos e intelectuales en la España del fin de siglo (1895–1902),* 354–60.

11. Joaquín Fanjul, *Misión social del Ejército* (Madrid, 1907).

12. For example, José Luis Gómez-Navarro, *El régimen de Primo de Rivera* (Madrid, 1991); Carlos Navajas Zubeldía, *Ejército, Estado y Sociedad en España* (Logroño, 1991); Manuel Espadas Burgos, "La Institución Libre de Enseñanza y la formación del militar español durante la Restauración," *Temas de Historia Militar,* Colección ADALID, no. 2 (Madrid, 1983), 495–514; and Espadas Burgos, "Orden social en la mentalidad militar española a comienzos del siglo XX," in *España, 1898–1936: Estructuras y cambio* (Madrid, 1984), 345–59.

13. *Enciclopedia Universal Ilustrada, Europeo-Americana,* vol. 9 (Barcelona, n.d.), 1482–83, and the *Appendice,* vol. 2 (Bilbao, Madrid, and Barcelona, 1931), 716. The supplement for the period of the Civil War, published during the Franco regime's most repressive phase, has an entry for Fanjul: *Suplemento 1936–1939,* part 1 (Bilbao, Madrid, and Barcelona, 1944), 367.

14. Baroja, *Desde la ultima vuelta,* 231–32; Calvo Carilla, *Cara oculta,* 354, 359; Augusto Vivero, *Los sucesos de agosto ante el Parlamento: Discursos íntegros de los señores Largo Caballero, Anguiano, Saborit . . . etc. Biografía de los mencionados oradores, por Torralva Becci. Interesantísimas notas explitivos. Copiosa colección de documentos . . . Prólogo del doctor Simarro* (Madrid, 1918), 172, cited in Wittenberg, "Mut," 263 n.

15. See, for example, the very positive portrayal of Fanjul in Maximiano García Venero, *El General Fanjul: Madrid en el Alzamiento Nacional* (Madrid, 1967).

16. El Comandante *** [Ricardo Burguete], *Así hablaba Zorrapastro* (Valencia, n.d.) (hereafter *Zorrapastro*). Gonzalo Sobejano categorizes Burguete with Maeztu and Azorín in *Nietzsche en España* (Madrid, 1967), 144. In *Cara oculta,* 354–60, Calvo Carilla includes a brief discussion of Burguete in the context of Maeztu, Baroja, and Azorín. Although the analyses of Burguete by Calvo Carilla and Sobejano are relatively brief, they are the only works to analyze the military writer satisfactorily in the context of more famous Spanish literary figures. Udo Rukser, in *Nietzsche in der Hispania* (Bern and Munich, 1962), 182, and Paul Ilie, in "Nietzsche in Spain, 1890–1910," *PMLA* 79, no. 1 (March 1964), include cursory discussions of Burguete's writings, although the former fails to identify "El Comandante ***," wrongly characterizes his book as a "thoroughly cynical" satire, and misunderstands the work's key concept of the "*hombre hábil.*"

17. In *Nietzsche,* 127, 440–41, Sobejano reasons that the book was probably published in late 1899 or early 1900, because on Feb. 21, 1900, the satirical magazine *Gedeón* included an article with what was probably an allusion to *Así hablaba Zorrapastro.*

18. Ricardo Burguete, *Mi rebeldía* (Madrid, 1904); Unamuno, "Almas," 1157.

19. *Zorrapastro,* 5–6, 98–100. Subsequent page references are cited in the text.

20. *¡La guerra! Cuba (diario de un testigo)* (Barcelona, 1902), 41–43.

21. See E. Inman Fox's introduction to his edition of Ángel Ganivet, *Idearium Español con El Porvenir de España* (Madrid, 1990), 9–10.

22. See Chapter 4 of this book.

23. See, for example, Sorel's letter to Daniel Halevy, reprinted in Georges Sorel, *Reflections on Violence,* trans. T. E. Hulme (New York, 1941), 1–42.

24. See Julio Caro Baroja, *El mito del carácter nacional: Meditaciones a contrapelo* (Madrid, 1970).

25. See Raúl Morodo, *Los orígenes ideológicos del franquismo: "Acción Española"* (Madrid, 1985), 139–48, on how *Acción Española* writers condemned "encyclopedism, liberalism and democracy" (147). A more recent study is Pedro Carlos González Cuevas, *"Acción Española": Teología política y nacionalismo autoritario en España (1913–1936)* (Madrid, 1998).

26. "El más perverso y amotinado contra Dios que hay" (quoted in José Luis Abellán, "Limites en la historiografía de Menéndez Pelayo," in *Menéndez Pelayo: Hacía una nueva imagen,* ed. Manuel Revuelta Sañudo [Santander, 1983], 42). On Menéndez y Pelayo and his subsequent influence on Spanish academia see also Carolyn P. Boyd, *Historia Patria: Politics, History, and National Identity in Spain, 1875–1975* (Princeton, 1997), esp. 101–4 and 237–38.

27. In 1938 a book by the Francoist Instituto de España called Menéndez y Pelayo the "Spanish Fichte," and the Falangist Onésimo Redondo labeled him the founder of "Revolutionary Nationalism" (Boyd, *Historia,* 238).

28. Eugen Weber, *"Action Française": Royalism and Reaction in Twentieth-Century France* (Stanford, 1962), 9.

29. Many Spaniards explicitly compared their "Disaster" of 1898 with France's defeat by Prussian troops at Sedan in 1870. Examples from within the military establishment include "Efeele," *El desastre nacional y los vicios de nuestras instituciones militares* (Madrid, 1901), which had appeared in somewhat different form as "La preparación del desastre nacional" in *Estudios Militares* (*EM*) 18 (1899); Florencio León Gutiérrez, "España sin sus colonias," and Servando Marenco, "Ante el abismo," both in *EM* 18 (1899). Vicente Caho Viu compares the effect of 1870 on French intellectuals with the effect of 1898 on Spanish civilian thinkers in *Repensar el noventa y ocho* (Madrid, 1997), 77–115.

30. On Maurras and *Action Française* during this period see Robert Soucy, *French Fascism: The First Wave, 1924–1933* (New Haven and London, 1986), 1–26, and Weber, *"Action Française,"* 3–43. On their influence outside of France and in Spain in particular see González Cuevas, *"Acción Española,"* 83–88; Morodo, *Los origenes;* Juan Olabarría Agra, "Las Fuentes Francesas de *"Acción Española," Historia Contemporánea* 3 (1990), 219–35; and Weber, *"Action Française,"* 479–500.

31. Boyd, *Praetorian Politics,* 13–14.

32. Joaquín Romero-Maura, "The Spanish Army and Catalonia: The '¡Cu-Cut! Incident' and the Law of Jurisdictions, 1906," *Sage Research Papers in the Social Sciences,* Contemporary European Studies Series, no. 90-033, vol. 5 (Beverly Hills, 1976), 22–23; E. Inman Fox, *Ideología y política en las letras de fin de siglo (1898)* (Madrid, 1988), 237–43.

33. Joaquín Costa, *Colectivismo agrario en España: Doctrinas y hechos* (Madrid, 1898). Some historians have since argued that the communal tradition in rural Spain helps explain the popularity of anarchism among Spanish peasants. See, for example, Gerald Brenan, *The Spanish Labyrinth: An Account of the Social and Political Background of the Spanish Civil War* (1943; Cambridge, U.K., 1990), 87–169.

34. See Espadas Burgos, "Orden social," 358.

35. Racial thought and notions of racial identity surfaced in much Spanish social and

cultural thought, although varieties of racial discourse and their influence varied widely throughout the nineteenth and twentieth centuries. See Joshua Seth Goode, "The Racial Alloy: The Science, Politics, and Culture of Race in Spain, 1875–1923" (Ph.D. dissertation, University of California, Los Angeles, 1999).

36. On Maeztu's early views on capitalism see Fox, *Ideología,* 259–311.

37. Ramiro de Maeztu, "Bilbao. Una excursión a las minas," *El Imparcial,* Aug. 20, 1901, reproduced in Ramiro de Maeztu, *Artículos desconocidos, 1897–1904,* ed. E. Inman Fox (Madrid, 1977), 160–64.

38. Gabriel Cardona, *El poder militar en la España contemporánea hasta la guerra civil* (Madrid, 1983), 39–40. On Burguete's actions in 1917 see also Maximiano García Venero, *Melquiades Alvarez: Historia de un liberal,* 2nd ed., prologue by Azorín (Madrid, 1974), 362–66.

39. Stanley G. Payne, *Politics and the Military in Modern Spain* (Stanford, 1967), 137. Interview with Manuel Burguete, July 8, 1997, Madrid. Like the English military theorist J. F. C. Fuller, Burguete was clearly familiar with works by Carlyle, whom he cited on occasion.

40. On the political developments of working-class Gijon see Pamela Beth Radcliff, *From Mobilization to Civil War: The Politics of Polarization in the Spanish City of Gijon, 1900–1937* (Cambridge, U.K., 1996).

41. Interview with Manuel Burguete, July 8, 1997, Madrid. García Venero, *Melquiades Alvarez,* 337–38.

42. García Venero, *Melquiades Alvarez,* 351.

43. Francisco J. Romero Savadó makes this argument in "Spain and the First World War: The Structural Crisis of the Liberal Monarchy," *European History Quarterly* 25 (1995): 343–45. See also his recent book *Spain, 1914–1918: Between War and Revolution* (London, 1999).

44. See the many documents pertaining to the incident in Public Records Office, FO 371/3034. In his *A Diplomatist in Europe* (London, 1927) Arthur H. Hardinge noted that Lema had been educated in England and described him as "friendly to British interests" and "a sincere Anglophile" (253).

45. On traditionalist social thought in Spain see Martin Blinkhorn, *Carlism and Crisis in Spain, 1931–1939* (Cambridge, U.K., 1975). See also Chapter 4 of this book.

46. See the brief analysis in Rafael Núñez Florencio, *Militarismo y antimilitarismo en España (1888–1906)* (Madrid, 1990), 183–89, on the "distant but respectful comprehension" by the military press of the late-nineteenth-century workers' movement, although the author's assertion that military opinion was far more negative toward the anarchists than toward the socialists (185) clearly does not hold for Burguete. See also Espadas Burgos, "Orden social."

47. Francisco Barado, *Revista Técnica de Infantería y Caballería (RTIC)* 17 (1899): 1–2.

48. Francisco Barado, *Discurso leído en el solemne acto de la apertura del curso de 1904 á 1905 en la Escuela de Estudios Militares* (Madrid, 1904), 21.

49. Justo Pérez Hernández, *La Sociologia del Soldado. Un curso de conferencias sociales en los cuarteles* (Badajoz, 1921).

50. Raymond Carr, *Spain, 1808–1975*, 2nd ed. (Oxford, 1982), 356.

51. See, for example, the strong praise for Wilhelm II's military orientation in "Rey, Soldado y Estadista," *RTIC* 11 (1900), and the advice directed at Alfonso XIII in "La obra del nuevo reinado," *RTIC*, 2nd ser., 2 (1902), and also José Muñiz y Terrones, *Concepto del mando y deber de la obediencia Cartas a Alfonso XIII* (1895), cited in C. Rey Joly, "Educación popular militar," *RTIC* 11 (1900): 383. José Ibañez Marín praises Wilhelm II's support for the buildup of the German navy in "El poder militar y maritimo," *RTIC* 11 (1900).

52. On the intellectual history of Spanish anarchism see José Álvarez Junco, *La ideología política del anarquismo español, 1868–1910* (Madrid, 1991). Temma Kapalan makes a case for the rational nature of practical anarchism in *Anarchists of Andalusia, 1868–1903* (Princeton, 1977).

53. On the widening in late-nineteenth-century France of the gap between the anarchism of the working classes and that of artists and intellectuals, who would display relatively little interest in the more practical anarcho-syndicalism of the early twentieth century, see Richard D. Sonn, *Anarchism and Cultural Politics in Fin de Siècle France* (Lincoln, Neb., 1989), 19–30.

54. Sobejano, *Nietzsche*, 483.

55. Quoted in Stanley G. Payne, *Falange: A History of Spanish Fascism* (Stanford, 1961), 8.

56. Sonn, *Anarchism*, 38–39. On Barrès see also Robert Soucy, *Fascism in France: The Case of Maurice Barrès* (Berkeley, 1972), and Zeev Sternhell, *Maurice Barrès et le nationalisme française* (Paris, 1972).

57. Zeev Sternhell, *La droite révolutionnare, 1885–1914: Les origines françaises du fascisme* (Paris, 1978), and *Neither Right nor Left: Fascist Ideology in France*, trans. David Maisel (Berkeley, 1986). For a different view see Soucy, *Fascism*, and his *French Fascism: The First Wave, 1924–1933* (New Haven, 1986). On the controversy engendered by Sternhell's works see Robert Wohl, "French Fascism, Both Right and Left: Reflections on the Sternhell Controversy," *Journal of Modern History* 63 (March 1991), 91–98, and António Costa Pinto, "Fascist Ideology Revisited: Zeev Sternhell and His Critics," *European History Quarterly* 16 (1986): 465–83.

58. For example, William D. Irvine, *The Boulanger Affair Reconsidered: Royalism, Boulangism, and the Origins of the Radical Right in France* (New York and Oxford, 1989).

59. Sonn, *Anarchism*, 36–48.

60. George Richard Esenwein, *Anarchist Ideology and the Working-Class Movement in Spain, 1868–1898* (Berkeley, Los Angeles, and Oxford, 1989), 190–204; Rafael Pérez de la Dehesa, *Política y sociedad en el Primer Unamuno, 1894–1904* (Madrid, 1966), 67–73; Fox, *Ideología*, 25–63. See also Álvarez Junco, *Ideología*.

61. Sebastian Balfour, *The End of the Spanish Empire, 1898–1923* (Oxford, 1997), 138.

62. See Goode, "Racial Alloy."

63. Cardona, *El poder militar*, 24.

64. Burguete criticized tariffs in *El problema militar: 200 mil soldados; más de cincuenta millones de economia: España ante los grandes imperios del porvenir* (Palma,

1905), 64, and *Dinamismo espiritualista: Cuestiones previas. La vida en sus tres dimensiones. Proceso histórico de ética española* (Madrid, 1905), 111–12. See also Chapter 4 of this book.

65. Clemente Libertino [Francisco Manuel de Melo], *Historia de los movimientos, separación y guerra de Cataluña en tiempo de Felipe IV* (n.p., 1645).

66. José Álvarez Junco, *El Emperador del Paralelo: Lerroux y la demagogia populista* (Madrid, 1990), 133–76; Fox, *Ideología*, 13–23; Esenwein, *Anarchist Ideology*, 191–97.

67. Berenguer is a prominent name in Catalan history, going back to a line of counts who ruled the city in the Middle Ages.

68. This is the book Unamuno praised.

69. Burguete, *Mi rebeldía*, 326.

70. Ibid., 139.

71. José Andrés-Gallego, *Un '98 distinto: Restauración, desastre, regeneracionismo* (Madrid, 1998), 262.

72. Calvo Carilla, *Cara oculta*, 354–56.

CHAPTER THREE. SPIRITUAL COMBAT AND THE AESTHETICS OF WAR

1. Ricardo Burguete, *La guerra y el hombre: Psicología de las tropas. Melilla, 1909–1910* (Madrid, 1911), 237–38.

2. On Fuller see Azar Gat, *Fascist and Liberal Visions of War: Fuller, Liddell Hart, Douhet, and Other Modernists* (Oxford, 1998), 13–42; Brian Holden Reid, *J. F. C. Fuller, Military Thinker* (London, 1987); and A. J. Trythall, *"Boney" Fuller: The Intellectual General* (London, 1977).

3. Gat, *Fascist and Liberal Visions*, 40.

4. Unless otherwise noted, biographical information on Burguete has been gleaned from his (incomplete) personal service record and the accompanying reports, telegrams, and other correspondence I found in the Archivo General Militar, Segovia, Expedientes Personales (AGM), sect. 1, legajo B-3995. There is also a brief professional biography of Burguete in "Infantes ilustres: General de división D. Ricardo Burguete," *Memorial de Infantería* (Madrid) 9 (June 1920), 429–30. After returning from overseas duty Burguete served briefly in Paris as military tutor to the sons of Infanta Eulalia de Borbón and Prince Antonio de Orleans. See Pilar García Louapre, *Eulalia de Borbón Infanta de España: Lo que no dijo en sus Memorias* (Madrid, 1995), 329–41.

5. Ricardo Burguete, *¡La guerra! Cuba (diario de un testigo)* (Barcelona, 1902) and *¡La guerra! Filipinas (Memorias de un herido)* (Barcelona, 1902).

6. "Hablando con Burguete," *La Correspondencia Militar*, July 27, 1909. Burguete said that he requested the transfer himself after learning of the death in combat of Colonel José Ibáñiz Marín, another prolific military writer who shared many of his interests and beliefs. See also Burguete, *Guerra y el hombre*, 281, which includes the text of a speech he delivered in Tenerife in November 1910 describing his recent experiences in northern Africa. In 1914 Burguete attracted much publicity again when he—possibly at the behest of General Francisco Jordana y Villalba—publicly criticized Madrid's Moroc-

can policies and Gabriel Maura in particular. On this affair and its immediate consequences for Burguete and the government see María Jesús González, *El universo conservador de Antonio Maura: Biografía y proyecto de Estado* (Madrid, 1997), 300–301.

7. Ricardo Burguete, *La ciencia militar ante la guerra europea: Su evolución y transformación hasta el presente y el porvenir* (Barcelona, [1918]).

8. On Burguete's views and actions regarding Morocco see the following chapter of this book.

9. The military press was filled with such arguments for obligatory military service. See, for example, Francisco Barado, "Las clases de tropa," *Revista Técnica de Infantería y Caballería (RTIC)* 10 (1899), and Florencio León Gutiérrez, "España sin sus colonias," *Estudios Militares* 18 (1899). For an analysis of the problem and military responses to it see Núria Sales de Bohigas, *Sobre esclavos, reclutas y mercaderes de quintos* (Barcelona, 1974), 216, 241–44, and Manuel Espadas Burgos, "Orden social en la mentalidad militar española a comienzos del siglo XX," in *España, 1898–1936: Estructuras y cambio* (Madrid, 1984), 345–59.

10. Walter Kaufmann interprets Nietzsche's thoughts in "On War and Warriors" as an argument that "those still seeking knowledge must fight, must wage war, for their thoughts"—not a literal praise of soldiers and war. See his edition of Nietzsche's *Thus Spoke Zarathustra: A Book for None and All* (New York, 1978), 6–7.

11. El Comandante *** [Ricardo Burguete], *Así hablaba Zorrapastro* (Valencia, n.d.), 48–49.

12. See John Gooch, *Armies in Europe* (London, Boston, and Henley, 1980), 109–44, on how between 1871 and 1914 all the major European powers adopted policies of general military conscription.

13. Burguete, *Zorrapastro*, 47–49.

14. Other Spaniards held similarly romantic views of the cavalry's offensive capabilities. For example, see Ricardo Caruncho, "La Caballería," *RTIC* 10 (1899).

15. Burguete, *Zorrapastro*, 50–53.

16. Ricardo Burguete, *Mi rebeldía* (Madrid, 1904).

17. Mariano Prestamero, "El Ejército y la Patria," *RTIC* 10 (1900), 83–90.

18. Burguete's entry was reproduced in his *El Problema militar: 200 mil soldados; más de cincuenta millones de economía. España ante los grandes imperios del porvenir* (Palma, 1905), 21–42. The winning entry, by Eduardo Gallego Ramos, was published as *Proyecto de reorganización y mejora del ejército de tierra* (Guadalajara, 1905). Although Gallego's views on universal military service resembled those of Burguete, in many ways he represented the rationalist and scientifically minded segment of the Spanish military that Burguete most opposed. A captain in the corps of engineers who had won several science contests, Gallego strongly praised the general staff and believed that this institution would take the leading role in the army's regeneration.

19. Under Primo de Rivera a system linking the fees of recruits to the incomes of their parents was in fact established. See Carolyn P. Boyd, *La política pretoriana en el reinado de Alfonso XIII* (Madrid, 1990), 343. Burguete later presented another detailed plan for military reform in *Ciencia militar*, 525–39.

20. Burguete, *Zorrapastro,* 57.

21. Burguete wrote most extensively on Clausewitz and the idea of friction in war in his *Ciencia del valor: Psicología de la guerra. Aplicación al desarrollo episódico de la batalla de Mukden* (Madrid, 1907), 73–108. Here he also cited observations by John Ruskin on war and morale.

22. Quoted in Michael Howard, *Clausewitz* (Oxford and New York, 1983), 26. See the essays by Howard, Peter Paret, and Bernard Brodie in Carl von Clausewitz, *On War,* ed. and trans. Michael Howard and Peter Paret (Princeton, 1976).

23. For example, G. Gil Juste, "La ofensiva táctica," *RTIC* 11 (1900). Jan Bloch presented his views in *La guerre future,* 6 vols. (Paris, 1899–1900), which appeared in abbreviated form as *Is War Impossible?* in 1900. For a brief analysis of Bloch's thinking see James J. Schneider, *The Structure of Strategic Revolution: Total War and the Roots of the Soviet Warfare State* (Novato, Calif., 1994), 86–92. On Bloch's ideas and the general historical context of the Hague Conferences see also Barbara Tuchman, *The Proud Tower* (New York, 1966); Geoffrey Best, *Humanity in Warfare* (New York, 1980); and Peter van den Dungan, *The Making of Peace: Jean de Bloch and the First Hague Conference* (Los Angeles, 1983).

24. Burguete conveniently ignored a remark by Moltke, noted by a more tactically cautious Spanish officer, that despite the "moral superiority" of the offensive it was still better to wait for the enemy's attack. S., "Las ideas del Mariscal Moltke sobre la ofensiva y la defensiva," *RTIC,* 2nd ser., 1 (1901): 385–90. Most Spanish officers, however, interpreted the Russo-Japanese War along the lines of Burguete, as articles in all the Spanish military journals of the day illustrate. On European reactions to the war and their contributions to the cult of the offensive see Jack Snyder, *The Ideology of the Offensive: Military Decision Making and the Disasters of 1914* (Ithaca, N.Y., 1984); Michael Howard, "Men Against Fire: The Doctrine of the Offensive in 1914," in *Makers of Modern Strategy,* ed. Peter Paret (Princeton, 1986); and Gary P. Cox, "Of Aphorisms, Lessons, and Paradigms: Comparing the British and German Official Histories of the Russo-Japanese War," *Journal of Military History* 56 (July 1992): 389–401.

25. Luigi Barzini, *Guerra russo-japonesa: La battaglia de Mukden,* 3rd ed. (Milan, 1907).

26. Charles T. Payne, "The Russo-Japanese War [*sic*] Impact on Western Military Thought Prior to 1914" (M.A. thesis, University of Georgia, 1990), 13, cited in Cox, "Of Aphorisms," 393 n.

27. Ricardo Burguete, *Teoría y práctica de la guerra: Evolución en el arte* (Madrid, 1913), 242. Mendigorría's report on Burguete's plan for tactical reform, which was later published as Luis Fernández de Córdova, "Táctica del Comandante Burguete," *RTIC,* 2nd ser., 2 (1902): 11–20, 63–71, and 109–16, is cited in various documents archived with Burguete's personal service record (AGM, sect. 1, legajo B-3995).

28. Burguete, *Ciencia del valor,* 5–6. For an earlier expression of his views on individual and collective national valor see Burguete, *Mi rebeldía.*

29. Burguete, *Ciencía del valor,* 6–7.

30. Ibid., 221–24.

31. Ibid., 235.

32. Ricardo Burguete, *Preparación de las tropas para la guerra (Nuevo Vegecio): Estudios de ética militar* (Madrid, 1905), 128.

33. See Chapter 7 of this book.

34. Andrée Bachoud, *Los españoles ante las campañas de Marruecos* (Madrid, 1988), 118–19.

35. Boyd, *Política pretoriana*, 55.

36. On the differences between various kinds of Spanish military periodicals see Rafael Núñez Florencio, *Militarismo y antimilitarismo en España (1886–1906)* (Madrid, 1990), 6–8.

37. Modesto Navarro, *Cuestiones tácticas: Observaciones sobre la táctica de Burguete* (Madrid, 1904), 5.

38. For example, D. Miguel Primo de Rivera, *Conferencía pronunciada el sábado 8 de marzo de 1919* [at the Centro del Ejército y de la Armada] (Madrid, 1919), and José Millán-Astray, "La Legión extranjera en Argelia y el Tercio de extranjeros español," *Memorial de Infantería* 18 (1920). See also Chapter 6 of this book on the endeavors of Enrique Ruiz-Fornells as an editor.

39. See Boyd, *Política pretoriana.*

40. Miguel de Unamuno, "Almas de jovenes," *Obras Completas,* vol. 1, *Paisajes y Ensayos* (Madrid 1966), 1157, and Ramiro de Maeztu, "El arma y el hombre," *Nuevo Mundo,* Oct. 27, 1916. The former originally appeared in *Nuestro Tiempo* 4 (May 1904): 252–62.

41. For example, Antonio Martín Ballesteros, "Preponderancia militar y económica," *RTIC* 11 (1900). For a discussion of the Spanish military's strong interest in its German counterpart see Miguel Alonso Baquer, *El Ejército en la sociedad española* (Madrid, 1971), 170, 199–290.

42. For example, C. Rey Joly, "Educación popular militar," *RTIC* 11 (1900), 381. Costa's comment is cited in Alonso Baquer, *Ejército,* 199.

43. Burguete, *Zorrapastro,* 57, and *Ciencia del valor,* 55.

44. Burguete, *Zorrapastro,* 59–60.

45. Ibid., 61.

46. Ricardo Burguete, *Dinamismo espiritualista: Cuestiones previas. La vida en sus tres dimensiones. Proceso histórico de ética española* (Madrid, 1905), 102.

47. Conversely, conservatives used similar rhetoric and accused the secular schools *(institutos)* of failing to provide a true "education" to pupils. Although the Institución Libre prohibited textbooks, the liberal textbooks used in standard schools resembled their conservative counterparts in their reliance on rote memorization (Carolyn P. Boyd, *Historia Patria: Politics, History, and National Identity in Spain, 1875–1975* [Princeton, 1997], 105, 118, 179).

48. Joaquín Fanjul, *Misión social del ejército* (Madrid, 1907).

49. On the interest of military officers in the Institución and Krausism see Manuel Espadas Burgos, "La Institución Libre de Enseñanza y la formación del militar español durante la Restauración," *Temas de Historia Militar* (*Colección ADALID,* n. 2) (Madrid, 1983), 495–514, and Alonso Baquer, *Ejército,* 199–209. On Spanish views on pedagogy in general see Boyd, *Historia.*

50. "Casi pudiera deciros, ¡oh madres! que cuando disciplinéis el útero tendréis soldados" (Burguete, *Zorrapastro*, 62).

51. Gat, *Fascist and Liberal Visions*, 20.

52. Burguete, *Dinamismo*, 104.

53. Burguete, *Ciencia del valor*, 55–56 (italics in original).

54. Burguete equated the academies' emphasis on "nemo-tecnia," or mnemonics, to "memo-tecnia" (*memo* means "silly" or "stupid" in Spanish) (ibid., 56).

55. Ibid., 57.

56. Every officer's personal service record that I have examined attests to the role of publishing in attaining promotions. On the professional interests of civilian textbook authors see Boyd, *Historia*, 55, 78.

57. El Capitán Equis, *El problema militar en España: Apuntes para un estudio sincero y al alcance de todos*, vol. 2 (Burgos, 1917), 41–103. In *Ejército*, 299, Miguel Alonso Baquer identifies Captain X as Nazario Cebreiros, who later wrote *Las reformas militares* (Santander, 1931), a perceptive analysis of Azaña's restructuring of the Spanish military.

58. El Capitán Equis, *Problema militar*, 62–63.

59. Burguete, *Ciencia del valor*, 59–61.

60. Years earlier he had written that "the strategic plan of 1870 entailed the right moral temperature" (Burguete, *Mi rebeldía*, 321).

61. Burguete, *Teoría*, 393. See also the following chapter of this book. Nevertheless, after the war in 1914 failed to unfold as most military thinkers had expected, Burguete himself devoted extensive analysis to Clausewitz's thought and the wars of German unification as part of his efforts to better understand World War I. See his *Ciencia militar*.

62. Burguete, *Teoría*, 328–29.

63. Ángel Ganivet, *Idearium Español con El porvenir de España*, ed. E. Inman Fox (Madrid, 1990), 77–87. On the influence of Ganivet on Burguete's thought see also the following chapter of this book.

64. Burguete, *Ciencia del valor*, 227.

65. See, for example, the pamphlet reproduction of José Ibáñez Marín's 1905 speech at the Centro del Ejército y de la Armada: *La unidad de doctrina en el ejército* (Madrid, 1904). For a discussion of the Prussian general staff as a model for Spanish officers see Alonso Baquer, *Ejército*.

66. Burguete reiterated the link he perceived between democracy and the organizational ills of modern armies in *Ciencia militar*, 228.

67. Burguete, *Zorrapastro*, 69–73.

68. Thomas F. Glick, *Einstein in Spain: Relativity and the Recovery of Science* (Princeton, 1988), 13–14. A similar literary characterization of a more progressive engineer is Pepe Rey in Galdos's *Doña Perfecta*, 10th ed. (Madrid, 1902). Although not a military officer, he is an ally of the army in its struggle against the reactionary Carlists.

69. See F. García Sarría's prologue to his reprint of Genaro Alas, *El Darwinismo: Conferencias pronunciadas en el Casino de Oviedo en los dias 25 de febrero, 4 y 11 de marzo de 1887*, Exeter Hispanic Texts, vol. 21 (Exeter, 1978). A newspaper column by

Alas on the Boer War provoked a response by Maeztu, as E. Inman Fox notes in his edition of Ramiro de Maeztu, *Articulos desconocidos, 1897–1904* (Madrid, 1977), 149 n. On Darwin's reception in Spain see Thomas F. Glick, *Darwin en España* (Barcelona, 1982), and the articles in *Anthropos*, nn. 16–17, special issue 2 (October 1982).

70. Glick, *Einstein*, 315.

71. Genaro Alas, *El cerebro militar de los estados: Conferencia pronunciada en el Centro del Ejército y de la Armada* [. . .] *el día 14 de marzo de 1903* (Madrid, 1903), 28–29, 11.

72. Alonso Baquer, *Ejército*, 170–71.

73. Glick, *Einstein*, 139.

74. Burguete dedicated *Ciencia militar* to his "dear *compañeros* from the unforgettable Academia General Militar."

75. Boyd, *Política pretoriana*, 57–59.

76. Ganivet, *Idearium*, 83–85.

77. Ricardo Burguete, *Nuevos métodos de combate: Proyecto de reglamento de ejercicios y maniobras para infantería*, 3rd ed. (Madrid, 1907). According to the foreword the first two editions were longer and appeared in 1900 and 1903. Copies of the 1903 and the 1907 editions at the Biblioteca Nacional in Madrid have, respectively, 236 and 116 pages.

78. Navarro, *Cuestiones*, 12. Navarro's work was first published several years earlier in *Estudios Militares*.

79. AGM, sect. 1, legajo N-142. For a positive review of Navarro's work see S., "Bibliografía," *RTIC*, 2nd ser., 4 (1904): 379–84.

80. AGM, sect. 1, legajo B-3995. Mendigorría's report had been published as Luis Fernández de Córdova, "Táctica del comandante Burguete," *RTIC*, 2nd ser., 2 (1902): 11–20, 63–71, 109–16.

81. AGM, sect. 1, legajo B-3995. See also Hilario Hernández Rivera's criticism of Navarro and praise for Burguete in his "Sobre el espirítu que debe informar un reglamento táctico," *RTIC*, 2nd ser., 2 (1902), and Juan Serrano Altamira, "La táctica y el proyecto de Burguete," in the same issue.

82. Zeev Sternhell, *Neither Right nor Left: Fascist Ideology in France*, trans. David Maisel (Berkeley, Los Angeles, and London, 1986), 34. First published as *Ni droite ni gauche: L'Idéologie fasciste en France* (1983).

83. Burguete, *Guerra y el hombre*, 32–36. Burguete also cited Le Bon extensively in *Ciencia militar*, 137–39.

84. León Fernández Fernández, *Utilidad de la ciencia de las muchedumbres* (Toledo, 1903). Fernández later wrote the book *Psicología militar*, which won him official decoration by Royal Order of August 11, 1916 (AGM, sect. 1, legajo F-908). By this time writings by military officers devoted to psychology were more common. For another example see Rogelio Gorgojo, "Notas para un estudio de psicología militar," *Memorial de Infantería* (Madrid) 16, no. 91 (Aug. 1919): 118–25, which cited Burguete's *Morbo nacional: Vida defensiva* (Madrid, 1906).

85. José Álvarez Junco, *El emperador del paralelo: Lerroux y la demagogia populista* (Madrid, 1990), 154.

86. Burguete, *Guerra y el hombre*, 32–33, 57, 67–71.

87. Álvarez Junco, *Emperador*, 232.

88. Burguete, *Ciencia del valor*, 98–99. In this work Burguete quoted extensively from the section of Clausewitz's *On War* devoted to "military genius" (book 1, chap. 3).

89. Daniel Pick, *War Machine: The Rationalisation of Slaughter in the Modern Age* (New Haven and London, 1993), 114.

90. Burguete, *Zorrapastro*, 149–51.

91. General Don Ricardo Burguete, prologue to Carmela Eulate Sanjurjo, *La mujer en la historia*, 2nd ed. (Seville, 1915), 13.

92. Burguete, *Preparación*, 134, 132.

93. Unamuno as quoted in Christopher Cobb's prologue to his edition of Miguel de Unamuno, *Artículos olvidados sobre España y la Primera Guerra Mundial* (London, 1976), xx. José Ortega y Gasset's *España invertebrada* was first published in 1921.

94. H. Ramdsen, *The 1898 Movement in Spain* (Manchester, U.K., 1974), 52. The author analyzes the impact of Taine on Spanish thinkers and the similarities between his ideas and those of Unamuno and Ganivet (41–95). For a brief overview of Taine's thought see Edward T. Gargan's introduction to his edition of Hippolyte Adolphe Taine, *The Origins of Contemporary France* (Chicago and London, 1974), xi–xlv.

95. Cited in Ramsden, *1898*, 50.

96. For example, Burguete, *Mi rebeldía*, 221–30, and *Teoría*, 273.

97. Burguete, *Teoría*, 273.

98. Burguete, *Zorrapastro*, 64.

99. Matei Calinescu, *Five Faces of Modernity* (Durham, 1987), 68–78.

100. Maeztu objected to the impreciseness of the term *modernist* in his essay "Todos modernistas," which appeared in *Diario Universal* on March 15, 1903. Cited by E. Inman Fox in his introduction to Ramiro de Maeztu, *Artículos desconocidos, 1897–1904* (Madrid, 1977), 45–46.

101. Recounted by Baroja, quoted in Sebastian Juan Arbo, *Pío Baroja y su tiempo* (Barcelona, 1963), 309.

102. Burguete, *Zorrapastro*, 64–65.

103. Burguete, *¡La guerra! Filipinas*, 210–20, 133.

104. Burguete, *Guerra y el hombre*, 80.

105. See Chapter 7 of this book.

106. Burguete, *Guerra y el hombre*, 81. Burguete described how he was wounded and his subsequent stay in a hospital in *¡La guerra! Filipinas*, 154–207.

107. See the epilogue of this book.

108. Burguete, *Teoría*, 361–62.

109. See Pick, *War*.

CHAPTER FOUR. HISTORY, DESTINY, AND NATIONAL REGENERATION

1. For example, León Fernández Fernández, "Reflexiones sobre el modo de escribir la historia," *Memorial de Infantería* 8, no. 93 (Oct. 1919): 241–54.

2. See the partial list in José María Gárate Córdoba, "La Cultura Militar en el Siglo XIX," in *Las Fuerzas Armadas Españolas: Historia Institucional y Social,* ed. Marío Hernández Sánchez-Barba and M. Alonso Baquer, vol. 4 (Madrid, 1986), 264–66. General José Gómez de Arteche, author of *Guerra de Independencia: Historia militar de España de 1808 a 1814,* 14 vols. (Madrid, 1868–1903), drew attention in a speech at the academy to the growing interest in military science and history both within and outside the institution's doors and to the increase in publications of all kinds by officers ("Lusitania y su primer Coronel," *Revista Técnica de Infantería y Caballería* [*RTIC*], 2nd ser., 3 [1903]).

3. On civilian attempts to identify the Spanish nation and the national culture, on efforts to foster nationalism and a Castile-centered national identity, and on the political agendas that often underlay these attempts see Carolyn P. Boyd, *Historia Patria: Politics, History, and National Identity in Spain, 1875–1975* (Princeton, 1997), and Inman Fox, *La invención de España* (Madrid, 1997).

4. On the meaning of Ganivet's *Idearium español* to Spanish national Catholics see Boyd, *Historia,* 180–82.

5. Ricardo Burguete, *Dinamismo espiritualista: Cuestiones previas. La vida en sus tres dimensiones. Proceso histórico de ética española* (Madrid, 1905), 7–22.

6. Salvador de Madariaga, *Englishmen, Frenchmen, Spaniards* (Oxford, 1931).

7. Edouard Schuré, *The Great Initiates: A Study of the Secret History of Religions,* trans. Gloria Rasberry, intro. Paul M. Allen (San Francisco, 1961). First published as *Les Grands Initiés* (Paris, 1889). The first part of Burguete's description of the Pythagorean categories (in *Dinamismo,* 7–8) was copied directly from Schuré, *Initiates,* 351–52. These categories, which correspond to the stages of Pythagorean initiation, are echoed in Freemasonic doctrine. Burguete's frequent copying of text from other authors was typical of civilian academic authors in Spain as well. As Boyd writes in *Historia,* they "tended to paraphrase or even plagiarize (usually without attribution, although sometimes with quotation marks) the work of earlier historians when constructing their own narratives. Identical phrases and interpretations thus echoed through the pages of the most diverse texts" (78).

8. Captain J. F. C. Fuller, *The Star in the West: A Critical Essay upon the Works of Aleister Crowley* (London and New York, 1907), 70 n.

9. Burguete, *Dinamismo,* 14.

10. Ibid., 10. Burguete used the term *positivism* here and elsewhere in the same manner as many contemporary writers: as a broad and imprecise term for the overly rationalist, "materialist," and "scientific" mind-set that served as "the reigning philosophy of the upper middle class—the self-satisfied cult of material progress" (H. Stuart Hughes, *Consciousness and Society: The Reorientation of European Social Thought, 1890–1930,* rev. ed. [New York, 1977], 41).

11. Fred Leeman, "Redon's Spiritualism and the Rise of Mysticism," in *Odilon Redon: Prince of Dreams, 1840–1916,* ed. Douglas W. Druick (Chicago, 1994), 215–36. This is a catalogue of an exhibition held at the Art Institute of Chicago, the Van Gogh Museum (Amsterdam), and the Royal Academy of Arts (London).

12. Burguete discussed telepathy as a manifestation of "spiritualist dynamism" in *Dinamismo,* 106–9.

13. Ibid., 115.

14. Ibid., 120–21. Most of Burguete's colleagues unreservedly praised Cervantes and Quixote. See, for example, the text of José Ibañez Marín's 1905 speech at the Ateneo of Madrid: "Don Quixote y las armas," *El Ateneo de Madrid en el III Centenario de la publicación de El Ingenioso Hidalgo Don Quixote de la Mancha* (Madrid, 1905), which also appeared in *RTIC*, 2nd ser., 5 (1905), and Teniente Coronel García Pérez's pamphlet *Cervantes, Soldado de la Española Infantería* [*sic*] (n.p., n.d.). For a discussion of the broader context of the debate on the meaning of Quixote at this time see José Carlos Mainer, "De historiografía literaria española: El fundamento liberal," *Estudios de Historia Social* (Madrid) 2 (1981): 439–72, and Boyd, *Historia*, 182–83.

15. E. Inman Fox, *Ideología y política en las letras de fin de siglo (1898)* (Madrid, 1988), 304–7.

16. Pedro Laín Entralgo, *La generación del noventa y ocho* (Madrid, 1945), as quoted in Douglas W. Foard, *The Revolt of the Aesthetes: Ernesto Giménez Caballero and the Origins of Spanish Fascism* (New York, 1989), 12.

17. Burguete, *Dinamismo*, 117.

18. Ibid., 117, 134–35.

19. Antonio Cánovas del Castillo, *Historia de la decadencia de España desde el advenimiento de Felipe III al trono hasta la muerte de Carlos II* (1854; rev. eds. 1868 and 1888), discussed in Fox, *Invención*, 41–42.

20. Burguete, *Dinamismo*, 117.

21. See, for example, Ángel Ganivet, *Idearium Español con El porvenir de España*, ed. E. Inman Fox (Madrid, 1990), 75.

22. Ricardo Burguete, *La ciencia del valor: Psicología de la guerra. Aplicación al desarrollo episódico de la batalla de Mukden* (Madrid, 1907), 34.

23. Burguete, *Dinamismo*, 40–41.

24. Burguete, *¡La guerra! Filipinas (memorias de un herido)* (Barcelona, 1902), 49.

25. Burguete, *Dinamismo*, 40–41.

26. Ibid., 194. On the interest of writers of Burguete's day in anarchist ideas see Chapter 2 of this book.

27. Ricardo Burguete, *El problema militar: 200 mil soldados; más de cincuenta millones de economia. España ante los grandes imperios del porvenir* (Palma, 1905), 64, 45–46, 74.

28. Burguete, *Ciencia del valor*, 1.

29. Burguete, *Problema militar*, 46, 54–56.

30. On Maeztu's early economic views see Fox, *Ideología*, 259–311.

31. Burguete, *Problema militar*, 14–17.

32. Burguete, *Dinamismo*, 111–12. The Catalan manufacturing classes, toward which Burguete had already expressed considerable disdain in *Zorrapastro*, had in fact worked through the Fomento del Trabajo Nacional to promote the 1891 tariff. Moreover, just as Burguete was voicing his criticism of such protectionism, representatives of Catalan industry were forming an alliance with their counterparts from Basque metallurgical companies to promote their common interest in maintaining and strengthening protective trade policies. The product of their endeavors was the Spanish tariff that went into

effect on July 1, 1906 (R. J. Harrison, "Catalan Business and the Loss of Cuba, 1898–1914," *Economic History Review*, 2nd ser., 27, no. 3 [Aug. 1974]: 431–41).

33. Azar Gat, *Fascist and Liberal Visions of War: Fuller, Liddell Hart, Douhet, and Other Modernists* (Oxford, 1998), 35.

34. Ricardo Burguete, *Teoría y práctica de la guerra: Evolución en el arte* (Madrid, 1913), 377, 379.

35. H. W. Koch, "Social Darwinism as a Factor in the 'New Imperialism,'" in *Origins of the First World War: Great Power Rivalry and German War Aims* (Basingstoke, 1984), 319–42; Bernard Semmel, *Imperialism and Social Reform: English Social-Imperial Thought (1895–1914)* (London, 1960).

36. Shannon E. Fleming, *Primo de Rivera and Abd-el-Krim* (New York and London, 1991), 11–15.

37. Burguete, *Problema militar*, 57. Burguete shared such thinking with many of his colleagues. See, for example, E. Venegas, "Espana: Potencia militar y maritima," *RTIC*, 2nd ser., 2 (1902): 277–84.

38. Burguete, *Problema militar*, 71–75.

39. Ganivet, *Idearium*, 75.

40. Burguete, *Teoría*, 357–61.

41. Ibid., 431–36.

42. Ibid., 372–73.

43. C. R. Pennell, *A Country with a Government and a Flag: The Rif War in Morocco, 1921–1926* (Cambridgeshire, U.K., 1986), 36.

44. Ibid., 40–61.

45. "Para escarmentarlas es preciso ocuparlas para aniquilarlas con *razzias*" (Burguete, *Teoría*, 391). Hubert Lyautey, an advocate of "peaceful penetration" whom Burguete greatly admired, had already employed the *razzia* as an instrument of terror while directing the French forces in Morocco (Douglas Porch, *The Conquest of Morocco* [London, 1986], 122–46).

46. Burguete, *Teoría*, 392.

47. Ibid., 383–87.

48. Ibid., 362–63.

49. Melchor Fernández Almagro, *Historia política de la España contemporánea*, vol. 1, 3rd ed. (Madrid, 1972), 424–25; Fleming, *Primo*, 19–22.

50. Burguete, *Teoría*, 363, 375.

51. Ibid., 363.

52. Ibid., 374–75. Actually, Unamuno expressed considerably more skepticism about Arabic influence in Spain than Burguete, whose emphasis on the impact of the Arabs appears to have been more like that of Ganivet. H. Ramsden compares the views of Unamuno and Ganivet on Spain's "European" and "African" qualities in *The 1898 Movement in Spain: Towards a Reinterpretation with Special Reference to 'En torno al casticismo' and 'Idearium español'* (Manchester, 1974), 33–39.

53. Edward W. Said, *Orientalism* (London, 1978), 115.

54. Carolyn P. Boyd, *La política pretoriana en el reinado de Alfonso XIII*, trans. Mauro Hernández Benítez (Madrid, 1990), 242–43.

55. On the conflict between the junteros and the africanistas see ibid.

56. Also one of the army's most important figures, Berenguer himself would rule Spain briefly after the fall of Primo de Rivera's regime in early 1930.

57. Boyd, *Política pretoriana,* 228; Stanley G. Payne, *Politics and the Military in Modern Spain* (Stanford, 1967), 179–80.

58. José Riquelme to José Marina, Gobierno Militar de Melilla y Plazas Menores de Africa. E. M. [Estado Mayor], Sección Asuntos Indígenas [July 1908], Archivo General Militar, Segovia, Expedientes Personales (AGM), sect. 2, div. 8, legajo 84. Vincent Sheean, an American writer who visited Morocco during the early 1920s, called Riquelme "the one Spanish leader who really knows the Arab and can manage Arab populations," writing that the the Rifian rebel Mhammed ben Abd-el-Krim had shown "genuine respect" for Riquelme (*An American Among the Riffi* [New York, 1926], 240). This Rifian rebel was the head of the Moroccan insurgents' military forces and the brother of the overall leader of the rebellion, Muhammed ben Abd-el-Krim. (Note: Because this book focuses on Spanish ideas and actions, Arabic names have been transliterated and employed according to Spanish custom.)

59. Report of Major Reginald B. Cocroft (United States Military Attaché in Spain), Madrid, July 24, 1922 (correspondence of the Military Intelligence Division Relating to General, Political, Economic, and Military Conditions in Spain, 1918–1941, National Archives and Records Administration, Washington, D.C. [hereafter "NARA Military Intelligence"], 2041/151).

60. Ibid., July 27, 1922.

61. Ibid., July 24, 1922.

62. Boyd, *Política pretoriana,* 265; Fleming, *Primo,* 76–77; Payne, *Politics,* 180–81; Pennell, *Country,* 109–10; David A. Woolman, *Rebels in the Rif: Abd-el-Krim and the Rif Rebellion* (Stanford, 1968), 106.

63. Report of Cocroft, August 26, 1922 (NARA Military Intelligence, 2041/151).

64. On the events and political dealings between the major players in the Rif during this period see Pennell, *Country,* 110–16.

65. Boyd, *Política pretoriana,* 282–83.

66. Woolman, *Rebels,* 214.

67. General [Ricardo] Burguete, *Rectificaciones históricas: De Guadalete a Covadonga y primer siglo de la Reconquista de Asturias. Ensayo de un nuevo método de investigación é instrumento de comprobaciones para el estudio de la historia* (Madrid, 1915), 305, 315–17. The issue of the contrast between evaluations of the "mixed race" of Spaniards and northern European arguments for "racial purity" is explored in Joshua Seth Goode, "The Racial Alloy: The Science, Politics, and Culture of Race in Spain, 1875–1923" (Ph.D. dissertation, University of California, Los Angeles, 1999).

68. The encyclopedia was called *Enciclopedia Universal Ilustrada Europeo-Americana,* vol. 43 (Bilbao, Madrid, and Barcelona, 1921), 22–25; Gárate Córdoba, "Cultura militar," 227–28. Burguete was a "corresponding" member of the academy. "Numerary" memberships were much harder to attain and were held by far fewer people.

69. Burguete, *Rectificaciones,* 3.

70. Ibid., 310.

71. Ibid., 75.

72. Rafael Altamira, *Psicología del pueblo español,* 2nd ed. (Barcelona, [1917]), especially 218 ff. The first edition appeared in 1902. For an analysis of Altamira's views on history and their regenerationist context see Boyd, *Historia,* 122–64.

73. Burguete, *Rectificaciones,* 301.

74. Burguete directs his criticism at the contributions of Aureliano Fernández-Guerra and Eduardo de Hinojosa to the *Historia General de España, escrita por individuos de número de la Real Academia de la Historia, bajo la dirección del excmo. Sr. D. Antonio Cánovas del Castillo,* vol. 3, *Los pueblos Germánicos hasta la ruina de la Monarquía Visigoda* (Madrid, 1891–93).

75. Burguete, *Rectificaciones,* 27.

76. Cited in Boyd, *Historia,* 127. As Boyd writes, for Ortega "myths embodied the creative spirit of the pueblo" (163). On Dozy and reactions to his debunking of popular conceptions of medieval Spain see ibid., 89, 148–49.

77. Burguete, *Rectificaciones,* 28.

78. On Menéndez Pidal see Boyd, *Historia,* 148–49.

79. Miguel de Unamuno, *En torno al casticismo,* 11th ed. (Madrid, 1991), 50. On the views of Unamuno and others on "*intrahistoria,*" "internal history," and historicism see Boyd, *Historia,* especially 80–98, 128–64.

80. Altamira explained his notion of *historia interna* in the prologue to his *Historia de España y de la civilización española,* 4 vols. (Madrid, 1899–1911). On Altamira see Boyd, *Historia,* 134–64.

81. *Enciclopedia,* 186–89.

82. E. Inman Fox, "Spain as Castile: The Invention of a National Culture," working paper 4 of the Spanish Studies Round Table at the University of Illinois at Chicago, presented Jan. 29, 1993, 5.

CHAPTER FIVE. FIGHTING FOR GOD AND KING

1. Stanley G. Payne, *Spanish Catholicism: An Historical Overview* (Madison, 1984), 75; Guy Hermet, *Les Catholiques dans l'Espagne Franquiste,* vol. 1 (Paris, 1980), 88. Studies of Carlism include Martin Blinkhorn, *Carlism and Crisis in Spain* (Cambridge, U.K., 1975), and Alexandra Wilhelmsen, *La formación del pensamiento político del Carlismo (1810–1875)* (Madrid, 1995).

2. See Appendix 3 for a bibliography of his works.

3. Archivo General Militar, Segovia, Expedientes Personales (AGM), sect. 1, legajo G-610; Antonio García Pérez, *Militarismo y socialismo: Conferencía pronunciada en la noche del sábado 27 de enero de 1906* (Madrid, 1906), 7–8.

4. Antonio García Pérez, *La Marina en la Cruzada* (Canarias, n.d.), 2.

5. The bibliography and self-serving biographical description of García Pérez at the book's beginning, however, draw attention to his past honors and status as a former victim of the Republic (ibid., 2).

6. Paul Preston, *Franco: A Biography* (New York, 1994), 9–12.

7. Ibid.

8. Antonio García Pérez, *Consejos á los caballeros alumnos de la Academia de Infantería* (Toledo, [1910]), 10–11.

9. El Capitán Equis, *El problema militar en España: Apuntes para un estudio sincero y al alcance de todos*, vol. 2 (Burgos, 1917), 58–64.

10. AGM, sect. 1, legajo N-142.

11. Andrée Bachoud, *Los españoles ante las campañas de Marruecos* (Madrid, 1988), 128.

12. For example, his *Un programa para la enseñanza primaria en España* (Madrid, 1905), won the first prize for its category in the writing contest of Seville's "Juegos Florales" of May 1904. This work was also published in *Nuestro Tiempo* in January and February 1905.

13. AGM, sect. 1, legajo G-610.

14. El Capitán Equis, *Problema militar*, 62–64.

15. Antonio García Pérez, "Estudio político-social de la España del siglo XVI," *Nuestro Tiempo* 7, no. 99 (May 1907): 177–219, and *Destellos de grandeza* (Madrid, n.d.), 11–71.

16. Capitán García Pérez, *Posesiones españolas en Africa* (Toledo, 1909). Some of his works, such as the fifty-eight-page *La casa solariega de la Infantería Española* (Toledo, n.d.), 57–58, reveal their intended readership by including pages with blanks in which cadets were to fill in data regarding their entry to and progress in the academy.

17. Examples of such works by García Pérez include *Compendio de moral* (n.p., n.d.), *Ejemplos de moral militar* (n.p., n.d.), *Máximas de mando y obediencia* (Toledo, n.d.), *Patria y bandera* (Toledo, n.d.), and *Marina*. Examples of similar works by other officers include Juan García Caminero, *Ideas y maximas* (Valladolid, 1933), and Modesto Navarro y García, *Cartilla para el soldado: Máximas de moral militar* (Madrid, [1920]).

18. Antonio García Pérez, *Heroicas infantes en Marruecos* (n.p., n.d.). This edition of this pamphlet, found in the Biblioteca Nacional of Madrid in the Biblioteca García Figueras, Colección de Varios, vol. 54, saw publication as an "Obsequio de la 'Stokes Gun Company á la Oficialidad de la española infantería,'" and it includes descriptions of the company's line of weapons (3).

19. For example, García Pérez's *Compendio histórico del Regimiento de Córdova* (Malaga, 1917).

20. At the urging of Granada's city authorities, who were impressed with his essays on Juan Vázquez Afán de Ribera, a local hero from the War of Independence, García Pérez was awarded by royal order on February 25, 1909, the *recompensa* of the Encomienda de Carlos III.

21. José Ibáñez Marín, *Violación supuesta: Defensa de un capitán acusado de tal delito, leída ante el Consejo de Guerra de Oficiales Generales*, 2nd ed. (Madrid, 1900).

22. Comandante A. García Pérez, *Siete años de mi vida (1905–12)* (Madrid, n.d.), 51. This work was originally published in *Estudios Militares* (1912).

23. Antonio García Pérez, *Un Programa para la Enseñanza Primaria en España* (Madrid, 1905), 22–23.

24. Ibid., 14–17.

25. "Conferencias y enseñanza agraria en el Ejército," *Revista Técnica de Infantería y Caballería* (*RTIC*), 2nd ser., 4 (1904): 557–60.

26. "de la Historia poética que ensalza las luchas del progreso; de la Historia del mártir del trabajo caído en el áspero sendero de la gloria" (García Pérez, *Programa,* 45).

27. He became a corresponding member of the Royal Academy of History in 1909, of the Real Academia Sevillana de Buenas Letras in 1910, and of the Academia de Ciencias, Bellas Letras y Nobles Artes de Córdoba in 1916. In 1907 he had become a "socio" of the Real Sociedad Geográfica de Madrid (AGM, sect. 1, legajo G-610; Antonio García Pérez, *Zona española del norte de Marruecos* [Toledo, n.d.], 96).

28. Antonio García Pérez, *Estudio político-militar de la campaña de Méjico, 1861–1867* (Madrid, 1900). Another edition appeared in 1901.

29. Antonio García Pérez, "Necesidad de estudiar la geografía y la historia de América," *RTIC,* 2nd ser., 1 (1901): 209–15. His other works about the American continent include *Organización militar de América. República del Ecuador* (Madrid, 1902) and *Organización militar de México* (Madrid, 1902).

30. García Pérez, *Destellos,* 86.

31. Ibid., 21–29. For his account of the military reforms under Ferdinand and Isabel, García Pérez drew heavily upon the historical writings of Francisco Martín Arrúe.

32. Ibid., 43–44.

33. Ibid., 39.

34. On Menéndez Pelayo's profound influence on *Acción Española* writers see Raul Morodo, *Los orígines ideológicos del franquismo: "Acción Española"* (Madrid, 1985), 52–57, 141–48.

35. Comandante [Antonio] García Pérez, *Juan Soldado y Juan Obrero* (Madrid, 1916). Originally published in *Nuestro Tiempo* (Dec. 1915).

36. García Pérez, *Militarismo,* 27.

37. Ibid., 14–15.

38. See Chapter 7 of this book.

39. García Pérez, *Militarismo,* 17–27.

40. Martin Blinkhorn, *Carlism and Crisis in Spain, 1931–1939* (Cambridge, U.K., 1975), 2.

41. Stanley G. Payne, *Spanish Catholicism: A Historical Overview,* 161–63; Blinkhorn, *Carlism,* 20–27.

42. He reiterated his view of the Catholic Church as guarantor of true "freedom" and "progress" in his *Catolicismo y libertad* (Badajoz, 1909).

43. Blinkhorn, *Carlism,* 21–27; R. Martin Blinkhorn, "Ideology and Schism in Spanish Traditionalism, 1876–1931," *Iberian Studies* 1, no. 1 (spring 1972): 21–22.

44. Blinkhorn, "Ideology," 18.

45. Antonio García Pérez, *La religión y la guerra* (Madrid, 1912), 23. During the early twentieth century articles discussing the religious qualities of warfare also appeared occasionally in military periodicals.For example, see S., "El sentimiento religioso en la guerra," *RTIC,* 2nd ser., 1 (1901): 309–12.

46. See Chapter 6 of this book.

47. *Ejército,* supp. ("dedicado al Primer Centenario de la Proclamación de la Purisima e Inmaculada Concepcion como Patrona de la Infantería Española"), Nov. 1992. On the history of the infantry's patron saints see José Luis Isabel Sánchez, "Los orígenes del centenario de la Inmaculada," ibid., 48–54. For an example of García Pérez's praise for the Virgin Mary and the holy alliance between "the cross and the sword" see his *Glorias de María Inmaculada en los hechos de armas más salientes del ejército español,* prologue by José Ibáñez Marín (Madrid, 1905).

CHAPTER SIX. ENLIGHTENING THE SOLDIERS

1. Modesto Navarro García, prologue to Enrique Ruiz-Fornells, *Fuegos de la infantería: Conferencias pronunciadas en la Escuela de Estudios Militares del Centro del Ejército y de la Armada,* 2nd ed. (Toledo, 1908), viii.

2. [Enrique Ruiz-Fornells,] "Memorias del Excmo. D. Enrique Ruiz-Fornells Regueiro General Subsecretario del Ministerio de la Guerra" (unpublished memoirs dated Feb. 8, 1935), 2–4. These memoirs were typed and made available to me by the author's grandson José Enrique Ruiz-Fornells Bonet, Madrid. Unless otherwise indicated, the following biographical information has been gleaned from this source and from Enrique Ruiz-Fornells' personal service record at the Archivo General Militar in Segovia, Expedientes Personales (AGM), sect. 1, legajo R-3459.

3. Ruiz-Fornells, "Memorias," 4–5. On Cassola's reforms see Daniel R. Headrick, *Ejército y política en España (1866–1898)* (Madrid, 1981), 236–39; Fernando Puell de la Villa, "Las reformas del General Cassola," *Revista de Historia Militar* 23, no. 46 (1979): 143–74; and Miguel Alonso Baquer, *El ejército en la sociedad española* (Madrid, 1971), 181–89.

4. Enrique Ruiz-Fornells and Alfredo Melgar Mata, *Organización militar de España y algunas potencias extranjeras,* 19th ed. (Toledo, 1917) (first published in 1893); Enrique Ruiz Fornells, *La educación moral del soldado,* prologue by Pedro A. Berenguer, 8th ed. (Toledo, 1918) (first published in 1894).

5. Ruiz-Fornells, "Memorias," 11, 13, 15.

6. For example, he blamed the king for blocking his appointment to the directorship of the Infantry Academy in 1924 and for preventing his promotion to major general before he reached the mandatory age for entrance into the reserves (Ruiz-Fornells, "Memorias," 39, 48). Military men figured prominently in the young king's education: naval officer Patricio Guirre held the position of director of the king's studies, and the young king's governors were Lieutenant Colonel Juan Loriga and Colonel Miguel Gonzales de Castejon of the general staff. One biography, *Don Alfonso XIII: A Study of Monarchy* (London, 1931), by Princess Pilar of Bavaria and Major Desmond Chapman-Huston, makes the extraordinary and probably false claim that the military instruction directed by Ruiz-Fornells "was exactly the same as that of any other recruit in the Spanish army" (57).

7. For example, Ruiz-Fornells, *Educación moral,* 133–34, 144. In the 1900 edition he used the same block of text on pp. 125–26, in the 1894 edition on pp. 119–20.

8. Ruiz-Fornells, "Memorias," 23 n.

9. On Azaña's habitually disrespectful treatment of military officers in general, including those who supported his republican politics, see Albert A. Nofi, "General Officer Loyalties in the Spanish Civil War" (Ph.D. Dissertation, City University of New York, 1991), 153–67, and Stanley G. Payne, *Spain's First Democracy* (Madison, 1993), 95.

10. On his opposition to Burguete's tactical project see his "Memorias," 15–16 n.

11. Ibid., 13–16.

12. Ibid., 26–27.

13. Ibid., 28. For a good, brief analysis of the Anual debacle and its immediate politicomilitary fallout see Carolyn P. Boyd, *Praetorian Politics in Liberal Spain* (Chapel Hill, 1979), 175–82.

14. Ruiz-Fornells, "Memorias," 28.

15. Works by León Fernández Fernández include *A los cien años del dos de mayo* (Madrid, 1908), *De la enseñanza militar* (Madrid, 1907), *La educación é instrucción del elemento armado* (Madrid, 1911), *Ideas acerca de la educación de la sensibilidad y felicidad del pensamiento* (Toledo, 1902), *Reflexiones filosóficas acerca de la guerra y los militares* (Madrid, 1909), and *Utilidad de la ciencia de las muchedumbres* (Toledo, 1903).

16. Ruiz-Fornells, "Memorias," 31.

17. Ibid., 47.

18. Ibid., 47–48. On the artillery crisis see Stanley G. Payne, *Politics and the Military in Modern Spain* (Stanford, 1967), 237–40; José Luis Gómez-Navarro, *El régimen de Primo de Rivera* (Madrid, 1991), 371–86; and Carolyn P. Boyd, *La política pretoriana en el reinado de Alfonso XIII*, trans. Mauro Hernández Benítez (Madrid, 1990), 345–48.

19. Ruiz-Fornells, "Memorias," 48.

20. Ibid., 55.

21. See the epilogue to this book for more on his activities after 1923.

22. Ruiz-Fornells, *Educación moral*, 96–97.

23. Enrique Ruiz-Fornells, *La instrucción en el ejército* (Toledo, 1902), 6–8.

24. Ibid., 7–8.

25. Ibid., 7.

26. Ibid., 9–10, 27–28.

27. Ibid., 10.

28. Ibid., 11.

29. Ibid., 12–13.

30. Ibid., 14.

31. Ibid., 14–15.

32. Ibid., 15–16.

33. Ruiz-Fornells, "Memorias," 28.

34. Ruiz-Fornells, *Instrucción*, 19.

35. On Guibert's military thought see Azar Gat, *The Origins of Military Thought from the Enlightenment to Clausewitz* (Oxford, 1989), 43–53; Geoffrey Best, *War and Society in Revolutionary Europe, 1770–1870* (New York and Oxford, 1982), 56–58; and Michael Howard, *War in European History* (Oxford and New York, 1976), 74, 79.

36. Ruiz-Fornells, *Instrucción*, 20–21.

37. Ibid., 22–25.

38. Francisco Martín Arrúe, *Curso de Historia Militar (Obra de texto en las Academias Militares, premiada en concurso que se verificó en la General Militar en 1887, y con Medalla de Primera Clase en la Exposición Universal de Barcelona en 1888)*, 6th ed. (Toledo, 1912), 232–48.

39. On Lyautey's "Du Rôle social de l'officier" see Douglas Porch, *The Conquest of Morocco* (London, 1986; copyright by author 1982), 81–84.

40. Carlo Corsi, *Della Educazione Morale del Soldato*, 2nd ed. (Florence, 1874); Paul Simon, *L'instruction des officiers, l'éducation des troupes et la puissance nationale; étude sociologique*, 2nd ed. (Paris, 1907).

41. Except where otherwise noted, the following discussion and references draw on the 1918 edition of *Educación moral*, which represented the most elaborate and refined exposition of the same basic arguments Ruiz-Fornells had introduced in earlier editions of the book.

42. Ruiz-Fornells, *Educación moral*, 57.

43. José Millán-Astray, prologue to Inazo Nitobe, *El Bushido (El alma de Japón)*, trans. Gen. Millán-Astray (Madrid, 1941), 9–10. See also the following chapter of this book.

44. Pedro A. Berenguer, prologue to Ruiz-Fornells, *Educación moral*, iv. Berenguer's prologue appeared in all editions of the book, from 1894 through 1918.

45. Ruiz-Fornells' prologue to ibid., vii. This prologue, dated May 1918, did not appear in earlier editions of this book.

46. Ruiz-Fornells, *Instrucción*, 45.

47. Best, *War*, esp. 52–121; Howard, *War*, 75–93; Eugen Weber, *Peasants into Frenchmen: The Modernization of Rural France, 1870–1914* (Stanford, 1976), 292–302.

48. On early-nineteenth-century liberal ideas of citizen-armies in Spain and the molding of civic virtue through conscription see Charles J. Esdaile, *The Spanish Army in the Peninsular War* (Manchester, 1988), 168–73.

49. Ruiz-Fornells, *Educación moral*, 121.

50. Ibid., 201–9.

51. Jean Jaurès, *L'Armée nouvelle* (Paris, 1915); Michael Alpert, *La reforma militar de Azaña (1931–1933)* (Madrid, 1982), 22–24, 54–57.

52. Ruiz-Fornells, *Educación moral*, 141.

53. Ibid., 142.

54. Emilio Mola Vidal, *El pasado, Azaña y el porvenir: Las tragedias de nuestras instituciones militares* (Madrid, 1934), 25.

55. Ruiz-Fornells, *Educación moral*, 145. The appendix to this edition of his book includes an excerpt from infantry captain A. Benzo's pamphlet *Lecturas para el soldado* on socialism, which Ruiz-Fornells presented as exemplary of the type of speeches officers should deliver to their men (209–11).

56. Ibid., 145.

57. Ibid., 147.

58. Ibid., x–xi.

59. Ruiz-Fornells, "Memorias," 6.

60. Ruiz-Fornells, *Instrucción*, 42.

61. In early editions of his textbook he included some analysis, albeit somewhat different and in a briefer and less developed form, of the roles ostensibly played by these forces in human behavior (*Educación moral*, 1894 ed., 33–53; 1900 ed., 41–62).

62. Ibid., 17.

63. For example, ibid., 33 n.

64. Ibid., 11.

65. Ibid., 14.

66. Ibid., 43–44.

67. Ibid., 48.

68. Ibid., 46. For his earlier attempts to define moral education and instruction see the 1894 and 1900 versions of his textbook, pp. 9–21 and 17–29, respectively.

69. J. F. C. Fuller, *Educación del soldado para la guerra*, trans. Emilio Castellano Gállego, prologue by Enrique Ruiz-Fornells (Madrid, 1925). This book first appeared as J. F. C. Fuller, *Training Soldiers for War* (London, 1914).

70. Ruiz-Fornells, *Educación moral*, 55–58, 94–101.

71. Ibid., 76–77.

72. Ibid., 74.

73. Ibid., 86.

74. Ángel Ganivet, *Idearium Español con El porvenir de España*, ed. E. Inman Fox (Madrid, 1990), 46.

75. Ruiz-Fornells, *Educación moral*, 87.

76. Ibid., 88.

77. Ibid., 89.

78. Ibid., 90. In the earlier versions of his textbook he presented these words in the form of a quotation from Mariscal's *Geografía militar de España* (1894 ed., 49; 1900 ed., 58–59).

79. Ruiz-Fornells, *Fuegos*.

80. Ruiz-Fornells, *Instrucción*, 6; *Educación moral*, 5.

81. Ruiz-Fornells, *Instrucción*, 46.

82. Enrique Ruiz-Fornells, "Consequencias tácticas de la Guerra Europea," *Curso de Conferencias de la Guarnición de Valladolid: Organizado por el General de la 7.a División Orgánica Excmo. Sr. D. Juan García Gómez-Caminero* (Valladolid, 1933), 9–28.

83. Ruiz-Fornells, *Educación moral*, 1894 ed., 116; 1900 ed., 122–23.

84. Ibid., 1918 ed., 128 (italics in original). The same phrase appeared at various places in all previous editions as well.

85. Ibid., 100.

CHAPTER SEVEN. "LONG LIVE DEATH!"

1. See, for example, Joaquin de Entrambasaguas's pamphlet "La posible clave de un incidente ya histórico: Unamuno y Millán-Astray," in *Punta Europa* 11, no. 108 (1966).

Entrambasaguas forwards the elaborate but unconvincing argument that Unamuno did not use the words *convencer* and *vencer.* He does not deny, however, that Millán-Astray shouted, "Mueran los intellectuales!" although he dismisses the outburst as insignificant. For more plausible reconstructions of the incident see Carlos Rojas, *¡Muera la inteligencia! ¡Viva la muerte! Salamanca 1936* (Barcelona, 1995), 130–47, and Paul Preston, *¡Comrades! Portraits from the Spanish Civil War* (London, 1999), 29–31.

2. Arturo Barea, *Unamuno,* trans. Emir Rodríguez Monegal (Buenos Aires, 1959), 78.

3. Carlos de Silva, *General Millán-Astray (El Legionario)* (Barcelona, 1956), 182–83, 187–89.

4. As late as 1991 it was still possible at the *Corte Inglés* department stores in Madrid to buy keychains and other objects explicitly glorifying Millán-Astray and his feats. A letter to the editor published in *El País* on July 3, 1992, discussed American vice president Dan Quayle and his inability to spell *potato* with reference to Millán-Astray and his cry "¡Muera la inteligencia!" Most extraordinarily, the Museum of Dar-Rifien, located between the north African cities of Ceuta and Tetuán, has a bottle on display containing what is claimed to be the remains of Millán-Astray's extracted eye.

5. Literature professor Carlos Rojas's recent book *¡Muera la inteligencia!* makes up for much of this scholarly inattention, as does the first chapter of Preston, *¡Comrades!* On the composition, organization, and military operations of the Spanish Foreign Legion during the 1920s see José E. Álvarez, *The Betrothed of Death: The Spanish Foreign Legion during the Rif Rebellion, 1920–1927* (Westport, Conn., 2001). John H. Galey's "Bridegrooms of Death: A Profile Study of the Spanish Foreign Legion," in *Journal of Contemporary History* 4, no. 2 (1969), is based largely on an uncritical reading of Millán-Astray's *La Legión.* Although Galey presents an interesting picture of the Legion and its founder's self-proclaimed role therein, he does not grasp the full ramifications of Millán-Astray's ideology for Franco's Spain. *General Millán-Astray,* by Millán's colleague General Carlos de Silva, is much too partial to be reliable. For strong criticism of Silva's portrayal of Millán-Astray see Carlos Blanco Escolá, *La Academia General Militar de Zaragoza (1928–1931)* (Barcelona, 1989), 85–93. Despite the problems in Silva's account, most histories of the Tercio have relied heavily on it. See, for example, the official history Subinspección de la Legión, *La Legión Española (Cincuenta años de historia),* 2 vols. (Madrid, 1970), discussed later. A more recent but essentially hagiographical portrayal of Millán-Astray can be found in Carlos de Arce, *Historia de la Legion Española* (Barcelona, 1984).

6. José Millán-Astray, *Memorias,* vol. 1 (Madrid, [1918]), 10–11.

7. Rojas, *¡Muera!* 72–80.

8. Álvarez, *Betrothed,* 245–46; Carolyn P. Boyd, *Praetorian Politics in Liberal Spain* (Chapel Hill, 1979), 39, 289–90; Silva, *General,* 39–82.

9. José Millán-Astray, *La Legión Extranjera en Argelia y el Tercio de Extranjeros Español: Conferencia pronunciada el día 14 de mayo de 1920 en el Centro del Ejército y de la Armada* (Madrid, 1920), 25–26. His report also appeared in *Memorial de Infantería* (Madrid) 18 (1920): 264–73, 372–89.

10. Blanco Escolá, *Academia,* 79–87; Boyd, *Praetorian,* 172; Gabriel Cardona, *El poder*

militar en la España contemporanea hasta la Guerra Civil (Madrid, 1983), 8. Blanco argues that the idea of the Spanish Foreign Legion did not originate with Millán-Astray, despite the legionnaire's subsequent assertions.

11. "La Legión Extranjera," *El Ejército Español* (Madrid), Aug. 28, 1920.

12. See Álvarez, *Betrothed.*

13. Except where otherwise noted, the discussion of the conflict between the *africanistas* and the *junteros,* Millán-Astray's reaction to it, and its consequences is drawn from Boyd, *Praetorian Politics,* 209–29, 290. The letter to Sánchez Guerra is quoted as it appeared in *Ejército Español,* November 11, 1920.

14. "Millán-Astray pide su separación del Ejército," *Heraldo de Madrid,* November 10, 1922; "La figura de Millán-Astray," *Heraldo de Madrid,* November 11, 1922.

15. *Ejército Español,* November 10–15, 1922; *Heraldo de Madrid,* November 10–16, 1922.

16. José Millán-Astray, *La Legión,* 2nd ed. (Madrid, 1980).

17. Ibid., 32, 63, 104, 55. Accounts by other Spanish soldiers in Africa during this period confirm that Millán-Astray promoted an exalted vision of death within the Tercio. See Arturo Barea, *The Forging of a Rebel,* trans. Ilsa Barea (New York, 1972), 299–306; Manuel González Iglesias, *Los novios de la Muerte* (Madrid, 1968); Carlos Micó España, *Los caballeros de la Legión* (Madrid, 1922); and Julio de la Torre Galán, *!La Legión! . . . !Esa novia! . . .* (Madrid, 1969). The last book is a sort of updated version of Millán-Astray's *La Legión*; it also takes the form of a handbook for legionnaires, instructing readers on everything from the proper way to salute to how to "die well" (28).

18. Richard Sablotny, *Legionnaire in Morocco* (Los Angeles, 1940), 117. Such acts were not uncommon, as other accounts demonstrate (Preston, *¡Comrades!* 16–18).

19. Paul Preston, *Franco* (New York, 1994), 29–30.

20. Cardona, *Poder,* 33.

21. Boyd, *Praetorian,* 172; Francisco Franco, *Marruecos: Diario de una Bandera* (1922; Seville, 1939).

22. Cardona, *Poder,* 32–33; Blanco Escolá, *Academia,* 86.

23. Cardona, *Poder,* 33; Millán-Astray, *La Legión,* 29, 115.

24. Millán-Astray, *La Legión,* 29, 115.

25. Francisco Franco Bahamonde, *Papeles de la guerra de Marruecos* (Madrid, 1986), 84–86. This section of *Papeles* is a reprint of Franco's *Marruecos: Diario de una Bandera.*

26. Millán-Astray, *La Legión,* 29, 115.

27. Millán-Astray, prologue to R. P. Ascunce, *Iñigo de Loyola: Capitán español y el Castillo de Pamplona* (Madrid, [1941–42]), 10.

28. Millán-Astray, *La Legión,* 16, 21–22. Gabriel Cardona speculates that the Catalans joined the Tercio in desperation after the government's repression of the Barcelona syndicalist movement. See Cardona, *Poder,* 37.

29. Sablotny, *Legionnaire,* 26–27.

30. "Paraphrase of Cablegram Received," from U.S. Consulate General, Madrid, dated Nov. 20, 1921; received Nov. 21, 1921 (NARA Military Intelligence, 2041/151).

31. Major R. B. Cocroft, U.S. Military Attaché in Madrid, to Major M. Churchill, Chief, Military Intelligence Division, Washington, D.C., Jan. 25, 1922 (NARA Military Intelligence, 2041/151).

32. Millán-Astray, *La Legión,* 21–22, 111–26; Manuel González Iglesias, *Los novios de la muerte* (Madrid, 1968) and Galey, "Bridegrooms," 61 n.

33. Millán-Astray, *La Legión,* 126, 106.

34. José Millán-Astray, prologue to Inazo Nitobe, *El Bushido (El alma de Japón),* trans. Gen. Millán-Astray (Madrid, 1941), 9–10. Another edition supposedly translated by Millán-Astray appeared in 1943.

35. Julio Busquets, *El militar de carrera en España,* 2nd, rev. ed. (Barcelona, 1971), 228.

36. Millán-Astray, prologue to Nitobe, *Bushido,* 12, 8, 10–11. The text of the prologue has been reproduced in Blanco Escolá, *Academia,* 238–39.

37. Inazo Nitobe, *Bushido: El alma de Japón,* trans. Gonzalo Jiménez de la Espada (Madrid, 1909), 15. In the introduction to the 1941 edition Millán-Astray claimed that he had translated his edition of the book from French into Castilian (9). The title page and the back cover of this edition include notes prohibiting the book's sale and requesting that the book be widely distributed among school youth.

38. Juan Carlos Losada Malvárez, *Ideología del ejército franquista, 1939–1959* (Madrid, 1990), 58. See also the epilogue to this book.

39. Ángel Ganivet, *Idearium Español y El Porvenir de España,* 5th ed. (Madrid, 1957), 97.

40. Millán-Astray, quoted in "Ceuta ha elevado un monumento a González Tablas," *Africa* (Ceuta) 11 (Aug. 1935): 158. Franco echoed such sentiments in his attempts to propagate "*Hispanidad*" after the war, often drawing on references to such "Spanishness" from the writings of 1898. See Stanley G. Payne, *The Franco Regime, 1936–1975* (Madison and London: 1987), 360–62; and Paul Preston, *The Politics of Revenge: Fascism and the Military in Modern Spain* (London: 1990), 30–33.

41. Ganivet, *Idearium,* 96–97. For a brief summary of the critical disagreement regarding Ganivet's positions on Africa and other matters see H. Ramsden, *Ángel Ganivet's "Idearium español"* (Manchester, 1967), 29–32.

42. Barea, *Forging,* 295.

43. Millán-Astray, prologue to Fidel Fernández, *Aben Humeya* (Barcelona, 1935), 16.

44. Craig Cameron gives an overview of this idea of the influence of myth and imagination on U.S. actions in World War II in his *American Samurai: Myth, Imagination, and the Conduct of Battle in the First Marine Division, 1941–1951* (Cambridge, 1994), 1–20.

45. On the operational history of the Legion in the 1920s see Álvarez, *Betrothed.*

EPILOGUE

1. Carolyn P. Boyd, *La política pretoriana en el reinado de Alfonso XIII,* trans. Mauro Hernández Benítez (Madrid, 1990).

2. For a very sympathetic account of his arrest and sentence see the front-page articles in *La Tierra* and *La Voz,* March 28, 1931. After his release much of the republican

press would treat him as a hero. The text of the speech he delivered to reporters is reproduced in Rafael Sánchez Guerra, *España republicana: Lecciones de sus hombres* (n.p., 1931), 43–49, and Emilo Mola Vidal, *Obras completas* (Valladolid, 1940), 804–8. On the trial and its impact see also Mariano Aguilar Olivencia, *El ejército español durante la Segunda República (claves de su actuación posterior)* (Madrid, 1986), 27–28; Manuel Ballbé, *Orden público y militarismo en la España constitucional (1812–1983)* (Madrid, 1983), 315–16; Boyd, *Política pretoriana*, 374–75; Gabriel Cardona, *El poder militar en la España contemporánea hasta la guerra civil* (Madrid, 1983), 114; and Stanley G. Payne, *Politics and the Military in Modern Spain* (Stanford, 1967), 363–64.

3. Mola, *Obras*, 744–50, 803–4; Cardona, *Poder*, 40 n, 114.

4. "El teniente general Ricardo Burguete explica su ingreso en el Partido Socialista," *El Socialista*, n.d., private archive of Manuel Burguete Herrero, Madrid; Maximiano García Venero, *Melquiades Álvarez: Historia de un liberal*, prologue by Azorín, 2nd ed. (Madrid, 1974), 362 n.

5. On the Deutsche Friedensgesellschaft see the introductions in Helmut Donat and Lothar Wieland, eds., *Das Andere Deutschland: Unabhängige Zeitung für entschiedene republikanische Politik. Eine Auswahl (1925–1933)* (Königstein/Ts., 1980).

6. "Friedensfundgebung mit Krach," *Hamburger Fremdenblatt*, Oct. 3, 1931; "Die öffentlichen Versammlungen," *Das Andere Deutschland*, Sept. 28, 1931. Characteristically, in his diary Azaña had ridiculed Burguete after learning of his intention to attend the peace conference in Germany (Manuel Azaña, *Memorias políticas, 1931–1933* [Madrid, 1978], 169).

7. Lehmann-Russbüldt was active in the Deutsche Friedensgesellschaft and a contributor to the pacifist newspaper *Das Andere Deutschland*. His book that Burguete drew upon was *Die blutige Internatione der Rüstingsindustrie* (Hamburg-Bergedorf: Fackelreiter Verlag, 1929). The book also appeared as *War for Profits*, trans. and intro. Pierre Loving (New York: A. H. King, 1930).

8. "Por última vez," *La Voz*, Aug. 3, 1931; "Guerra o revolución," *La Voz*, July 27, 1931; "La conferencia . . . ," *Ahora*, Nov. 30, 1933, 33–35.

9. The *Heraldo de Madrid* subsequently published Burguete's letter (private archive of Manuel Burguete Herrero, Madrid).

10. Letter from the secretary-general of the Spanish Red Cross awarding Margarita Reparaz de Burguete the Medal of First Class, Feb. 25, 1925; letter from Ricardo Burguete to the vice president of the Spanish Red Cross, July 2, 1936. Both documents from ibid.

11. Major R. B. Cocroft (U. S. military attaché), "Plans of the Present High Commissioner in Morocco," Aug. 26, 1922 (NARA Military Intelligence, 2041/151).

12. In his diary Azaña portrays Burguete as a ridiculous, vain, and bothersome figure (*Memorias*, 14, 169–70, 405).

13. The following is gleaned from Ricardo Burguete, *Yo acuso: Carta del General Burguete a Queipo de Llano* (Valencia, n.d.); interview with Manuel Burguete Herrero, July 8, 1997, Madrid; and Cardona, *Poder*, 40 n.

14. The still-surviving brother, Manuel, believed at the time that Luis—possibly still alive—was thrown from a plane into the Mediterranean en route to a prison in Ceuta.

But Manuel's son, Manuel Burguete Herrero, says a witness told him years later that Luis was shot by Falangists while imprisoned (interview with Manuel Burguete Herrero, July 8, 1997, Madrid).

15. Burguete did not mention the charge made earlier by some officers that his ruling against Queipo had represented an attempt to punish Queipo for his public criticism of dictator Primo de Rivera in 1924 (report of Major Campbell B. Hadges [U. S. military attaché in Madrid], Sept. 27, 1924 [NARA Military Intelligence, 2041/232]).

16. Burguete, *Yo acuso*, 3–5.

17. Ibid., 4, 6.

18. Letter from Margarita Reparaz to Araquistain, April 4, 1937, Paris (Archivo Histórico Nacional, Diversos Araquistain, legajo 37, R 33). After the war she would submit several requests to military authorities for her pension as a military widow (Archivo General Militar, Segovia, Expedientes Personales [AGM], sect. 1, legajo B-3995).

19. Quoted in Jorge Aspizua Turrión, Ramon Bernabeu Urbina, and Julio Molina Benayas, "La Colección Bibliográfica Militar (1928–1936)," *Revista de Estudios Políticos* 64 (April–June 1989): 305.

20. Fuller wrote a special prologue for the Spanish translation expressing doubts over the utility for the Spanish army of the mechanized equipment he described (ibid., 308).

21. Vicente Rojo, instruction to *Colección Bibliográfica Militar* (Toledo) 16 (December 1929): 6.

22. Aspizua, Bernabeu, and Molina, "La Colección," 307.

23. Coronel García Caminero [sic], *De la guerra* (Cadiz, [1925]). The text concludes with the dateline June 24, 1923, Madrid; a note on the last page states that the printing of the book was completed on November 23, 1925.

24. He also cited Kant, Goethe, Darwin, Spinoza, Mahan, Gobineau, and Quevedo, among others.

25. García Caminero, *De la guerra*, 59–60. He reiterated his criticism of positivist, empirical science in 1933, presenting the thesis "that the sense of imagination is far superior to scientific observation, and that the former is responsible for all progress in science and arts" (Juan García Gómez-Caminero, "Rumbos sobre pedagogía militar," in *Curso de Conferencias de la Guarnición de Valladolid: Organizado por el General de la 7.a División Orgánica Excmo. Sr. D. Juan García Gómez-Caminero* [Valladolid, 1933], 338).

26. García Caminero, *De la guerra*, 27.

27. Ibid., esp. 121–36. Ironically, perhaps the most famous civilian supporter of the Second Republic, Manuel Azaña, had a radically different view of *Idearium español* than did Burguete and Gómez-Caminero. See E. Inman Fox's introduction to Ángel Ganivet, *Idearium español con El porvenir de España*, 12th ed. (Madrid, 1990), 31–34.

28. AGM, sect. 1, legajo G-1353.

29. Albert A. Nofi, "General Officer Loyalties in the Spanish Civil War" (Ph.D. dissertation, City University of New York, 1991), 337–38, 398 n, 401, 423 n, 439–40.

30. AGM, sect. 1, legajo G-610. Antonio García Pérez, *La marina en la Cruzada* (Carias, n.d.), 2. See appendix 3 for a bibliography of his works.

31. On the Azaña reforms see Michael Alpert, *La reforma militar de Azaña (1931–1933)* (Madrid, 1982); Carolyn P. Boyd, "Las reformas militares," in *Historia General de España y América*, ed. L. Suárez Fernández, vol. 17 (Madrid, 1986), 141–73; Aguilar, *Ejército*; and Cardona, *Poder*, 116–37.

32. [Enrique Ruiz-Fornells], "Memorias del Excmo. D. Enrique Ruiz-Fornells Regueiro General Subsecretario del Ministerio de la Guerra" (unpublished memoirs dated Feb. 8, 1935), 2–4. These memoirs were typed and made available to me by the author's grandson José Enrique Ruiz-Fornells Bonet, Madrid.

33. Ibid., 18, 25, 31, 59.

34. Letter from Ruiz-Fornells' grandson José Enrique Ruiz-Fornells Bonet, Madrid, Nov. 8, 1994.

35. Subinspección de la Legión, *La Legión Española (Cincuenta años de historia)*, 2 vols. (Madrid, 1970), 1–2.

36. Carlos Rojas, *¡Muera la inteligencia! ¡Viva la muerte! Salamanca 1936* (Barcelona, 1995), 36.

37. Casa de España en Roma, *Conferencia pronunciada por el Coronel D. José Millán-Astray ante la Colonia Española de Roma con motivo de la entrega de un rame de laurel del Monte Palatino y de un Album de firmas de los españoles residentes en Italia, como homenaje de gratitud y cariño para el glorioso Legionario español mutilado* (Rome, 1926), 3, 7–12. Millán-Astray would return to Mussolini's Rome during the Civil War to participate in a commemoration of solidarity between Francoist Spain and Italy (Javier Tusell, *Franco en la guerra civil: Una biografía política* [Barcelona, 1992], 202).

38. Stanley G. Payne, *The Franco Regime, 1936–1975* (Madison, 1987), 199.

39. Paul Preston, *¡Comrades! Portraits from the Spanish Civil War* (London, 1999), 26–27.

40. Paul Preston, *Franco* (New York, 1994), 208.

41. Stanley G. Payne, *Falange: A History of Spanish Fascism* (Stanford, 1961), 121.

42. On the rise of the term *crusade* as a key element of Nationalist propaganda see José Andrés-Gallego, "El nombre de 'Cruzada' y la Guerra de España," *Aportes: Revista de Historia Contemporánea* 8 (June 1988): 65–71.

43. Gen. Millán-Astray, *El caudillo Franco y nuestro glorioso estado mayor: Conferencia a los cadetes de la Academia de Estado Mayor en Valladolid* (n.p., n.d.), 2, 5 (on pp. 2–3 he speaks of "this third triumphal year"); Millán-Astray, prologue to Adro Xavier [Alejandro Rey Stolle], *Caballero legionario* (Madrid, n.d.), 11–12.

44. Bernardo de Ramay, *Romanceros de la Nueva España*, prologue by Millán-Astray, illus. A. Ituarte and D. Olivares (Buenos Aires, 1937).

45. Paul Preston, *The Politics of Revenge: Fascism and the Military in Modern Spain* (London, 1990), 32, 40.

46. José Millán-Astray, *Academica del Cuerpo Jurídico Militar: Curso 1940–1941. Conferencias culturales* (Madrid, 1940–41), 25–26.

47. José Millán-Astray, prologue to R. P. Enrique Ascunce, *Iñigo de Loyola: Capitán español y el Castillo de Pamplona* (Madrid, [1941–42]), 10.

48. Ibid., 10–12.

49. José-Mario Armero, *España fue noticia: Corresponsales extranjeros en la guerra civil española* (Madrid, 1976), 69; Augustín García Laforga, *Mutilados de la guerra por la patria (soldados, viejos y estropeados): Siglos XVI al XX* (Saragossa, 1971). See General Millán-Astray, *Franco el Caudillo* (Salamanca, 1939), for the texts of the speeches he delivered during the war. For a colorful account of his ever dramatic, often bizarre behavior during and after the Civil War see Preston, *¡Comrades!* 24–42.

50. John H. Galey, "Bridegrooms of Death: A Profile Study of the Spanish Foreign Legion," *Journal of Contemporary History* 4, no. 2 (1969): 62.

51. Adolfo Maíllo, *Patria* (Zaragoza, [1940?]), 46–47, quoted in Gregorio Cámara Vilar, *Nacional-Catolicismo y escuela: La socialización política del Franquismo (1936–1951)* (Jaen, 1983), 311. For a detailed examination of national-Catholic themes stressed in the school textbooks of Franco Spain see pp. 293–385.

52. Raymond Carr, *Spain, 1808–1975*, 2nd ed. (Oxford, 1982), 701.

53. Lorenzo Delgado Gómez-Escalonilla, *Imperio de papel: Acción cultural y política exterior durante el primer franquísmo* (Madrid, 1992), 249 n, 256 n, 274 n.

54. Payne, *Franco Regime*, 204.

55. Alfonso Botti, *Cielo y dinero: El nacionalcatolicismo en España (1881–1975)* (Madrid, 1992), 104–7.

APPENDIX THREE. PARTIAL BIBLIOGRAPHY OF WORKS BY ANTONIO GARCÍA PÉREZ

1. Archivo General Militar, Segovia, Expedientes Personales, sect. 1, legajo G-610.

2. Although García Pérez's personal service records as made available to me by the staff of the Archivo General Militar list no promotion after that of December 1918 to lieutenant colonel, the title page of *¡Arriba España!* (Larache, [1943]) identifies him as a "retired colonel" (*coronel retirado*).

Bibliography

MAJOR PRIMARY SOURCE COLLECTIONS (WITH ABBREVIATIONS USED IN NOTES)

Archivo General Militar (AGM). Segovia.
Archivo Histórico Nacional. Madrid. Diversos Araquistaín.
Biblioteca Nacional. Madrid. Colección García Figueras.
Hemeroteca Municipal. Madrid.
National Archives and Records Administration (NARA Military Intelligence). Washington, D.C. Correspondence of the Military Intelligence Division Relating to General, Political, Economic, and Military Conditions in Spain, 1918–1941.
Personal Papers of Ricardo Burguete. Madrid.
Public Records Office. London.
Servicio Histórico Militar. Madrid.

CONTEMPORARY NEWSPAPERS AND PERIODICALS (WITH ABBREVIATIONS USED IN NOTES)

Africa. Ceuta.
Ahora. Madrid.
Das Andere Deutschland. Hannover.
La Correspondencia Militar. Madrid.
Ejército. Madrid.
Ejército y Armada. Madrid.
El Ejército Español. Madrid.
Estudios Militares. Toledo, Madrid.
Hamburger Fremdenblatt.
El Heraldo de Madrid.
El Imparcial. Madrid.
La Legión. Torrejón de Ardoz, Madrid.
Memorial de Infantería. Madrid.
Nuestro Tiempo. Madrid.
Revista Técnica de Infantería y Caballería (*RTIC*). Madrid.
El Socialista. Madrid.
La Tierra. Madrid.
La Voz. Madrid.

CONTEMPORARY BOOKS AND PAMPHLETS

Alas, Genaro. *El cerebro militar de los estados: Conferencia pronunciada en el Centro del Ejército y de la Armada.* Madrid, 1903.

———. *El Darwinisimo: Conferencias pronunciadas en el Casino de Oviedo en los días 25 de febrero, 4 y 11 de marzo de 1887.* Reprinted in *Exeter Hispanic Texts.* Vol. 21. Prologue by F. García Serría. Exeter, 1978.

Altamira, Rafael. *Enseñanza de la historia.* 2nd ed., revised and expanded. Madrid, 1895.

———. *Historia de España y de la civilización española.* 4 vols. Madrid, 1899–1911.

———. *Psicología del pueblo español.* 2nd ed. Barcelona, [1917].

Azaña, Manuel. *Memorias políticas, 1931–1933.* Madrid, 1978.

Barado, Francisco. *Discurso leído en el solemne acto de la apertura del curso de 1904 á 1905 en la Escuela de Estudios Militares.* Madrid, 1904.

Barea, Arturo. *The Forging of a Rebel.* Trans. Ilsa Barea. New York, 1972.

Baroja, Pío. *Desda la última vuelta del camino: Memorias. Final del siglo XIX y principios del XX.* Madrid, 1945.

Barzini, Luigi. *Guerra russo-japonesa: La battaglia de Mukden.* 3rd ed. Milan, 1907.

Bergson, Henri. *Creative Evolution.* Trans. Arthur Mitchell. New York, 1911.

Bloch, Jan. *La guerra future.* 6 vols. N.p., 1899.

Burguete, Ricardo. [El Comandante ***, pseud.]. *Así hablaba Zorrapastro.* Valencia, n.d.

———. *La ciencia del valor: Psicología de la guerra. Aplicación al desarrollo episódico de la batalla de Mukden.* Madrid, 1907.

———. *La ciencia militar ante la guerra europea: Su evolución y transformación hasta el presente y el porvenir.* Barcelona, [1918].

———. *Corsarios y piratas: La leyenda del mediterráneo.* Barceolona, [1902].

———. *Dinamismo espiritualista: Cuestiones previas. La vida en sus tres dimensiones. Proceso histórico de ética española.* Madrid, 1905.

———. *¡La guerra! Cuba (diario de un testigo).* Barcelona, 1902.

———. *¡La guerra! Filipinas (memorias de un herido).* Barcelona, 1902.

———. *La guerra y el hombre: Psicología de las tropas. Melilla, 1909–1910.* Madrid, 1911.

———. *Habla un soldado: El problema de Marruecos. Un cuarto á espadas.* Madrid, 1914.

———. *Mi rebeldía.* Madrid, 1904.

———. *Morbo nacional: Vida defensiva.* Madrid, 1906.

———. *Nuevos métodos de combate: Proyecto de reglamento de ejercicios y maniobras para infantería.* 3rd ed. Madrid, 1907.

———. *Preparación de las tropas para la guerra (Nuevo Vegecio): Estudios de ética militar.* Madrid, 1905.

———. *El problema militar: 200 mil soldados; más de cincuenta millones de economía. España ante los grandes imperios del porvenir.* Palma, 1905.

———. Prologue to *La mujer en la historia,* by Carmela Eulate Sanjurjo. 2nd ed. Seville, 1915.

———. *Rectificaciones históricas: De Guadalete á Covadonga y Primer Siglo de la Reconquista de Asturias. Ensayo de un nuevo método de investigación é instrumento de comprobaciones para el estudio de la historia.* Madrid, 1915.

———. *Teoría y práctica de la guerra: Evolución en el arte.* Madrid, 1913.

———. *Yo acuso: Carta del General Burguete a Queipo de Llano.* Valencia, n.d.

Cánovas del Castillo, Antonio. *Historia de la decadencia de España desde el advenimiento de Felipe III al trono hasta la muerte de Carlos II.* 1854. Rev. eds., 1868 and 1888.

Cebreiros, Nazario [El Capitán Equis, pseud.]. *El problema militar en España: Apuntes para un estudio sincero y al alcance de todos.* 2 vols. Burgos, 1916–17.

Clausewitz, Carl von. *On War.* Ed. and trans. Michael Howard and Peter Paret. Princeton, 1976.

Corsi, Carlo. *Della educazione morale del soldato.* 2nd ed. Florence, 1874.

Costa, Joaquín. *Colectivismo agrario en España. Doctrinas y hechos.* Madrid, 1898.

"Efeele." *El desastre nacional y los vicios de nuestras instituciones militares.* Madrid, 1901.

Fanjul, Joaquín. *Misión social del ejército.* Madrid, 1907.

Fernández Fernández, León. *A los cien años del Dos de Mayo.* Madrid, 1908.

———. *La educación é instructión del elemento armado.* Madrid, 1911.

———. *De la enseñanza militar.* Madrid, 1907.

———. *Ideas acerca de la educación de la sensibilidad y felicidad del pensamiento.* Toledo, 1902.

———. *Reflexiones filosóficas acerca de la guerra y los militares.* Madrid, 1909.

———. *Utilidad de la ciencia de la muchedumbres.* Toledo, 1903.

Franco, Francisco. *Marruecos: Diario de una bandera.* Seville, 1939.

Gallego Ramos, Eduardo. *Proyecto de reorganización y mejora del Ejército de Tierra.* Guadalajara, 1905.

Ganivet, Ángel. *Idearium Español con El Porvenir de España.* Ed. E. Inman Fox. Madrid, 1990.

García [Gómez-]Caminero, Juan. *De la guerra.* Cadiz, [1925].

———. *Ideas y maximas.* Valladolid, 1933.

García Gómez-Caminero, Juan. "Rumbos sobre pedagogía militar." In *Curso de conferencias de la Guarnición de Valladolid: Organizado por el General de la 7.ª División Orgánica Excmo. Sr. D. Juan García Gómez-Caminero.* Valladolid, 1933.

García Pérez, Antonio. *La casa solariega de la infantería española.* Toledo, n.d.

———. *Catolicismo y libertad.* Badajoz, 1909.

———. *Cervantes, Soldado de la Española Infantería.* N.p., [1921].

———. *Compendio de moral.* N.p., [1927].

———. *Compendio histórico del Regimiento de Córdova.* Malaga, 1917.

———. *Consejos á los caballeros alumnos de la Academia de Infantería.* Toledo, [1910].

———. *Destellos de grandeza.* Madrid, n.d.

———. *Ejemplos de moral militar.* N.p., [1928].

———. *Estudio político-militar de la campaña de Méjico, 1861–1867.* Madrid, 1900.

———. *Glorias de María Inmaculada en los hechos de armas más salientes del ejército español.* Prologue by José Ibáñez Marín. Madrid, 1905.
———. *Heroicas infantes en Marruecos.* N.p., n.d.
———. *La Marina en la Cruzada.* Canarias, n.d.
———. *Máximas de mando y obediencia.* Toledo, n.d.
———. *Militarismo y socialismo: Conferencia pronunciada en la noche del sábado 27 de enero de 1906.* Madrid, 1906.
———. *Patria y bandera.* Toledo, n.d.
———. *Posesiones españolas en Africa.* Toledo, 1909.
———. *Un programa para la enseñanza primaria en España.* Madrid, 1988.
———. *La religión y la guerra.* Madrid, 1912.
———. *Siete años de mi vida (1905–12).* Madrid, [1912].
———. *Zona española del norte de Marruecos.* Toledo, n.d.
Giménez Caballero, Ernesto. *Genio de España.* 7th ed. Madrid, 1971.
Gómez de la Serna, R. *Azorín.* Madrid, 1930.
Historia general de España, escrita por individuos de número de la Real Academia de la Historia, bajo la direccion del excmo. Sr. D. Antonio Cánovas del Castillo. 3 vols. Madrid, 1891–1893.
Ibáñez Marín, José. "Don Quixote y las armas." In *El Ateneo de Madrid en el III. Centenario de la publicación de El Ingenioso Hidalgo Don Quixote de la Mancha.* Madrid, 1905.
———. *La unidad de doctrina en el ejército.* Madrid, 1904.
———. *Violación supuesta: Defensa de un capitán acusado de tal delito, leída ante el Consejo de Guerra de Oficiales Generales.* 2nd ed. Madrid, 1900.
Jaurès, Jean. *L'Armée nouvelle.* Paris, 1915.
Maeztu, Ramiro de. *Artículos desconocidos, 1897–1904.* Ed. E. Inman Fox. Madrid, 1977.
Maíllo, Adolfo. *Patria.* Zaragoza, [1940?].
Martín Arrúe, Francisco. *Curso de historia militar (Obra de texto en las academias militares, premiada en concurso que se veificó en la General Militar en 1887, y con Medalla de Primera Clase en la Exposición Universal de Barcelona en 1888.* 6th ed. Toledo, 1912.
Micó España, Carlos. *Los caballeros de la Legión.* Madrid, 1922.
Millán-Astray, José. *Academia del Cuerpo Jurídico Militar: Curso, 1940–1941. Conferencias culturales.* Madrid, 1940–41.
———. *Casa de España en Roma: Conferencia pronunciada por el Coronel D. José Millán-Astray ante la Colonia Española de Roma con motive de la entrega de un rame de laurel del Monte Palatino y de un Album de firmas de los españoles residentes en Italia, como homenaje de gratitud y cariño para el glorioso Legionario español mutilado.* Rome, 1926.
———. *El Caudillo Franco y nuestro glorioso Estado Mayor: Conferencia a los Cadetes de la Academia de Estado Mayor en Valladolid.* N.p., n.d.
———. *Franco el Caudillo.* Salamanca, 1939.
———. *La Legión.* 2nd ed. Madrid, 1980.

———. *La Legión Extranjera en Argelia y el Tercio de Extranjeros español: Conferencia pronunciada el día 14 de mayo de 1920 en el Centro del Ejército y de la Armada.* Madrid, 1920.

———. Prologue to *Aben Humeya,* by Fidel Fernández. Barcelona, 1935.

———. Prologue to *El Bushido (El alma de Japón),* by Inazo Nitobe. Trans. José Millán-Astray. Madrid, 1941.

———. Prologue to *Caballero legionario,* by Alejandro Rey Stolle [Adro Xavier, pseud.]. Madrid, n.d.

———. Prologue to *Iñigo de Loyola: Capitán español y el Castillo de Pamplona,* by R. P. Enrique Ascunce. Madrid, [1941–42].

———. Prologue to *Romanceros de la nueva España,* by Bernardo de Ramay. Illus. A. Ituarte and D. Olivares. Buenos Aires, 1937.

Millán-Astray, José [father of the officer]. *Memorias.* Madrid, [1918].

Mola Vidal, Emilio. *El pasado, Azaña y el porvenir: Las tragedias de nuestras instituciones militares.* Madrid, 1934.

Navarro y García, Modesto. *Cartilla para el soldado: Maximas de moral militar.* Madrid, [1920].

———. *Cuestiones tácticas: Observaciones sobre la táctica de Burguete.* Madrid, 1904.

Nietzsche, Friedrich Wilhelm. *Thus Spoke Zarathustra: A Book for None and All.* Trans. Walter Kaufmann. New York, 1978.

Nitobe, Inazo. *Bushido: El Alma de Japón.* Trans. Gonzalo Jiménez de la Espada. Madrid, 1909.

Ortega y Gasset, José. *España invertebrada: Bosquejo de algunos pensamientos históricos.* 2nd ed., revised and expanded. Madrid, 1921.

Pérez Hernández, Justo. *La sociología del soldado: Un curso de conferencias sociales en los cuarteles.* Badajoz, 1921.

Ruiz-Fornells, Enrique. "Consequencias tácticas de la guerra europea." In *Curso de conferencias de la Guarnición de Valladolid: Organizado por el General de la 7.a División Orgánica Excmo. Sr. D. Juan García Gómez-Caminero.* Valladolid, 1933.

———. *La educación moral del soldado.* Prologue by Pedro A. Berenguer. 8th ed. Toledo, 1918.

———. *Fuegos de la infantería: Conferencias pronunciadas en la Escuela de Estudios Militares del Centro del Ejército y de la Armada.* 2nd ed. Prologue by Modesto Navarro y García. Toledo, 1908.

———. "Memorias del Excmo. D. Enrique Ruiz-Fornells Regueiro General Subsecretario del Ministerio de la Guerra." Unpublished memoirs dated Feb. 8, 1935. Madrid.

———. Prologue to *Educación del soldado para la guerra,* by J. F. C. Fuller. Trans. Emilio Castellano Gallego. Madrid, 1925.

Ruiz-Fornells, Enrique, and Alfredo Melgar Mata. *Organización militar de España y algunas potencias extranjeras.* 19th ed. Toledo, 1917.

Sablotny, Richard. *Legionnaire in Morocco.* Los Angeles, 1940.

Sánchez Guerra, Rafael. *España republicana: Lecciones de sus hombres.* N.p., 1931.

Schuré, Edouard. *Les Grandes Initiés.* Paris, 1889. English edition: *The Great Initiates.* Trans. Gloria Rasberry. Intro. Paul M. Allen. San Francisco, 1961.

Simon, Paul. *L'instruction des officiers, l'éducation des troupes et la puissance nationale: Étude sociologique.* 2nd ed. Paris, 1907.

Sorel, Georges. *Reflections on Violence.* Trans. T. E. Hulme. New York, 1941.

Taine, Hippolyte. *De l'idéal dans l'art.* Paris, 1867.

Unamuno, Miguel de. "Almas de jovenes." In *Obras completas.* Vol. 1, *Paisajes y ensayos.* Madrid, 1966.

———. *Artículos olvidados sobre España y la Primera Guerra Mundial.* Prologue by Christopher Cobb. London, 1976.

———. *En torno al casticismo.* Madrid, 1902.

SECONDARY BOOKS, ARTICLES, AND UNPUBLISHED DISSERTATIONS

Abellán, José Luis. "Limites en la historiografía de Menéndez Pelayo." In *Menéndez Pelayo: Hacía una nueva imagen,* ed. Manuel Revuelta Sañudo. Santander, 1983.

Aguilar Olivencia, Mariano. *El ejército español durante the Segunda República (claves de su actuación posterior).* Madrid, 1986.

Alonso Baquer, Miguel. *El ejército en la sociedad española.* Madrid, 1971.

———. "La selección de la élite militar española." In *Las fuerzas armadas españolas. Historia institucional y social,* ed. Mario Hernández Sánchez-Barba and Miguel Alonso Baquer. Vol. 5. Madrid, 1986.

Alpert, Michael. *La reforma militar de Azaña (1931–1933).* Madrid, 1982.

Álvarez, José E. *The Betrothed of Death: The Spanish Foreign Legion During the Rif Rebellion, 1920–1927.* Westport, Conn., 2001.

Álvarez Bolado, Alfonso. *El experimento del nacional catolicismo.* Madrid, 1976.

Álvarez Junco, José. *El emperador del paralelo: Lerroux y la demagogia populista.* Madrid, 1990.

———. *La ideología política del anarquismo español.* Madrid, 1976.

———. "La invención de la Guerra de la Independencia." *Studia Histórica-Historia Contemporánea* 5, no. 12 (1994): 75–99.

———. "El nacionalismo español como mito movilizador: Cuatro guerras." In *Cultura y movilización en la España contemporánea,* ed. Rafael Cruz and Manuel Pérez Ledesma, 35–67. Madrid, 1997.

———. "The Nation-Building Process in Nineteenth-Century Spain." In *Nationalism and the Nation in the Iberian Peninsula: Competing and Conflicting Identities,* ed. Care Mar-Molinero and Angel Smith, 89–106. Oxford, 1996.

Anderson, Benedict. *Imagined Communities.* Rev. ed. London, 1991.

Andrés-Gallego, José. *Un 98 distinto: Restauración, desastre, regeneracionismo.* Madrid, 1998.

———. "El nombre de 'Cruzada' y la Guerra de España." In *Aportes: Revista de Historia Contemporánea* no. 8 (June 1988): 65–71.

Arbo, Sebastian Juan. *Pío Baroja y su tiempo.* Barcelona, 1963.

Arce, Carlos de. *Historia de la Legión Española.* Barcelona, 1984.

Aspizua Turrión, Jorge, Ramón Bernabeu Urbina, and Julio Molina Benayas. "La Colección Bibliográfica Militar (1928–1936)." In *Revista de Estudios Políticos* 64 (April–June 1989): 299–319.

Bachoud, André. *Los españoles ante las campañas de Marruecos.* Madrid, 1988.

Baker, Keith Michael. *Inventing the French Revolution: Essays on French Political Culture in the Eighteenth Century.* Cambridge, 1990.

Balfour, Sebastian. *The End of Spanish Empire, 1898–1923.* Oxford, 1997.

———. "'The Lion and the Pig': Nationalism and National Identity in Fin-de-Siécle Spain." In *Nationalism and the Nation in the Iberian Peninsula,* ed. Clare Mar-Molinero and Angel Smith. Oxford, 1996.

Balfour, Sebastian, and Pablo La Porte, "Spanish Military Cultures and the Moroccan Wars, 1909–36." In *European History Quarterly* 30, no. 3 (July 2000), 307–32.

Ballbé, Manuel. *Orden público y militarismo en la España constitucional (1812–1983).* Madrid, 1983.

Barea, Arturo. *Unamuno.* Trans. Emir Rodríguez Monegal. Buenos Aires, 1959.

Best, Geoffrey. *Humanity in Warfare.* New York, 1980.

———. *War and Society in Revolutionary Europe, 1770–1870.* Oxford and New York, 1982.

Blackbourn, David, and Geoff Eley. *The Peculiarities of German History.* Oxford, 1984.

Blanco Escolá, Carlos. *La Academia General Militar de Zaragoza (1928–1931).* Barcelona, 1989.

Blas Guerrero, Andrés de. *Nacionalismos y naciones en Europa.* Madrid, 1995.

———. *Sobre el nacionalismo español.* Madrid, 1989.

———. *Tradición republicana y nacionalismo español.* Madrid, 1991.

Blinkhorn, Martin. *Carlism and Crisis in Spain.* Cambridge, 1975.

———. "Ideology and Schism in Spanish Traditionalism, 1876–1931." *Iberian Studies* 1, no. 1 (spring 1972).

———, ed. *Fascists and Conservatives: The Radical Right and the Establishment in Twentieth-Century Europe.* London, 1990.

Botti, Alfonso. *Cielo y dinero: El nacionalcatolicismo en España (1881–1975).* Madrid, 1992.

Boyd, Carolyn P. *Historia Patria: Politics, History, and National Identity in Spain, 1875–1975.* Princeton, 1997.

———. "History in the Schools and the Problem of Spanish Identity." In *Iberian Identity: Essays on the Nature of Identity in Portugal and Spain,* ed. Richard Herr and John H. R. Polt. Berkeley, 1989.

———. *La política pretoriana en el reinado de Alfonso XIII.* Trans. Mauro Hernández Benítez. Madrid, 1990.

———. *Praetorian Politics in Liberal Spain.* Chapel Hill, 1979.

———. "Las reformas militares." In *Historia general de España y América,* ed. Luis Suárez Fernández et al., 17: 141–73. N.p., n.d.

Brenan, Gerald. *The Spanish Labyrinth: An Account of the Social and Political Background of the Spanish Civil War.* 1943; Cambridge, U.K., 1990.

Breuilly, John. *Nationalism and the State.* 2nd ed. Chicago, 1994.

Busquets, Julio. *El militar de carrera en España.* 2nd, rev. ed. Barcelona, 1971.

Cachinero, Jorge. "Intervencionismo y reformas militares en España a comienzos del siglo XX." *Zona Abierta* 39–40 (Apr.–Sept. 1986): 115–49.

Cacho Viu, Vicente. *Repensar el noventa y ocho.* Madrid, 1997.

Calinescu, Matei. *Five Faces of Modernity.* Durham, 1987.

Calvo Carilla, José Luis. *La cara oculta del 98: Místicos e intelectuales en la España del fin de siglo (1895–1902).* Madrid, 1998.

Cámara Vilar, Gregorio. *Nacional-Catolicismo y escuela: La socialización política del Franquismo (1936–1951).* Jaén, 1983.

Cameron, Craig. *American Samurai: Myth, Imagination, and the Conduct of Battle in the First Marine Division, 1941–1951.* Cambridge, U.K., 1994.

Cardona, Gabriel. *El poder militar en la España hasta la guerra civil.* Madrid, 1983.

Carr, Raymond. *Spain, 1808–1975.* 2nd ed. Oxford, 1982.

Coffey, Mary Louise. "The *Episodios Nacionales*: A Sociological Study of the Historical Novels of Benito Pérez Galdós." Ph.D. dissertation, Northwestern University, 1996.

Colley, Linda. *Britons: Forging the Nation, 1707–1837.* New Haven, 1992.

Cox, Gary P. "Of Aphorisms, Lessons, and Paradigms: Comparing the British and German Official Histories of the Russo-Japanese War." *Journal of Military History* 56 (July 1992): 389–401.

Delgado Gómez-Escalonilla, Lorenzo. *Imperio de papel: Acción cultural y política exterior durante el primer franquismo.* Madrid, 1992.

Deutsch, Karl W. *Nationalism and Social Communication: An Inquiry into the Foundations of Nationality.* 2nd ed. Cambridge, Mass., 1966.

Donat, Helmut, and Lothar Wieland, eds. *Das Andere Deutschland: Unabhängige Zeitung für entschiedene republikanische Politik. Eine Auswahl (1925–1933).* Königstein/Ts., 1980.

Dungan, Peter van den. *The Making of Peace: Jean de Bloch and the First Hague Conference.* Los Angeles, 1983.

Echevarria, Antulio J. "On the Brink of the Abyss: The Warrior Identity and German Military Thought Before the Great War." *War and Society* 13, no. 2 (1995).

Enciclopedia Universal Ilustrada Europeo-Americana. 70 vols. Barcelona, [1907–30].

Entrambasaguas, Joaquín de. "La posible clave de un incidente ya histórico: Unamuno y Millán-Astray." *Punta Europa* 11, no. 108 (1966).

Esdaile, Charles J. *The Spanish Army in the Peninsular War.* Manchester, U.K., 1988.

Esenwein, George Richard. *Anarchist Ideology and the Working-Class Movement in Spain, 1868–1898.* Berkeley, 1989.

Espadas Burgos, Manuel. "La Institución Libre de Enseñanza y la formación del militar español durante la Restauración." In *Temas de Historia Militar.* Colección ADALID, no. 2, 495–514. Madrid, 1983.

———. "Orden social en la mentalidad militar española a comienzos del siglo XX." In *España, 1898–1936: Estructuras y cambio,* 345–59. Madrid, 1984.

Fernández Almagro, Melchor. *Historia política de la España contemporánea.* 3rd ed. Madrid, 1972.

Fleming, Shannon E. *Primo de Rivera and Abd-el-Krim: The Struggle for Spanish Morocco, 1923–1927*. New York and London, 1991.
Foard, Douglas W. *The Revolt of the Aesthetes: Ernesto Gimzénez Caballero and the Origins of Spanish Fascism*. New York, 1989.
Fox, E. Inman. *Ideología y política en las letras de fin de siglo (1898)*. Madrid, 1988.
———. *La invención de España*. Madrid, 1997.
———. "Spain as Castile: The Invention of a National Culture." Working paper no. 4 of the Spanish Studies Round Table at the University of Illinois at Chicago, presented January 29, 1993.
Fusi, Juan Pablo. *España: La evolución de la identidad nacional*. Madrid, 2000.
Galey, John H. "Bridegrooms of Death: A Profile Study of the Spanish Foreign Legion." *Journal of Contemporary History* 4, no. 1 (1969).
Gárate Córdoba, José María. "La cultura militar en el siglo XIX." In *Las fuerzas armadas españolas: Historia institucional y social*, ed. Marío Hernández Sánchez-Barba and M. Alonso Baquer. Vol 4. Madrid, 1986.
García Laforga, Augustín. *Mutilados de guerra por la patria (Soldados, viejos y estropeados): Siglos XVI al XX*. Zaragoza, 1971.
García Venero, Maximiano. *El General Fanjul: Madrid en el Alzamiento Nacional*. Madrid, 1967.
———. *Melquiades Álvarez: Historia de un liberal*. Prologue by Azorín. 2nd ed. Madrid, 1974.
Gat, Azar. *The Development of Military Thought: The Nineteenth Century*. Oxford, 1992.
———. *Fascist and Liberal Visions of War: Fuller, Liddell Hart, Douhet, and Other Modernists*. Oxford, 1998.
———. *The Origins of Military Thought from the Enlightenment to Clausewitz*. Oxford, 1989.
Gellner, Ernest. *Nations and Nationalism*. Oxford, 1983.
Glick, Thomas F. *Darwin en España*. Barcelona, 1982.
———. *Einstein in Spain: Relativity and the Recovery of Science*. Princeton, 1988.
Gómez-Navarro, José Luis. *El régimen de Primo de Rivera*. Madrid, 1991.
González, María Jesús. *El universo conservador de Antonio Maura: Biografía y poryect de Estado*. Madrid, 1997.
González Cuevas, Pedro Carlos. *"Acción Española": Teología política y nacionalismo autoritario en España (1913–1936)*. Madrid, 1998.
González Iglesias, Manuel. *Los novios de la muerte*. Madrid, 1968.
Gooch, John. *Armies in Europe*. London and Boston, 1980.
Goode, Joshua Seth. "The Racial Alloy: The Science, Politics, and Culture of Race in Spain, 1875–1923." Ph.D. dissertation, University of California, Los Angeles, 1999.
Harrison, R. J. "Catalan Business and the Loss of Cuba." *Economic History Review*, 2nd ser., 27, no. 3 (Aug. 1974): 431–41.
Headrick, Daniel R. *Ejército y política en España (1866–1898)*. Madrid, 1981.
Hennessy, C. A. M. *The Federal Republic in Spain: Pi y Margall and the Federal Republican Movement, 1868–74*. Oxford, 1962.

Herf, Jeffrey. *Reactionary Modernism: Technology, Culture, and Politics in Weimar and the Third Reich.* Cambridge, U.K., 1984.

Hermet, Guy. *Les Catoliques dans l'Espagne Franquiste.* Vol. 1. Paris, 1980.

Herr, Richard. *An Historical Essay on Modern Spain.* Berkeley, 1971.

Hobsbawm, E. J. *Nations and Nationalism Since 1780: Programme, Myth, Reality.* 2nd ed. Cambridge, U.K., 1992.

Howard, Michael. *Clausewitz.* Oxford and New York, 1983.

———. "Men Against Fire: The Doctrine of the Offensive in 1914." In *Makers of Modern Strategy,* ed. Peter Paret. Princeton, 1986.

———. *War in European History.* Oxford and New York, 1976.

Hughes, H. Stuart. *Consciousness and Society: The Reorientation of European Social Thought, 1890–1930.* Rev. ed. New York, 1977.

Ilie, Paul. "Nietzsche in Spain: 1890–1910." *PMLA* 79, no. 1 (March 1964).

Isabel Sánchez, José Luis. *La Academia de Infantería.* 2 vols. Toledo, 1991.

Jutglar, Antoni. *Ideologías y clases en la España contemporánea.* Madrid, 1968.

Koch, H. W. "Social Darwinism as a Factor in the 'New Imperialism.'" In *Origins of the First World War: Great Power Rivalry and German War Aims,* 319–42. Basingstoke, 1984.

Laín Entralgo, Pedro. *La generación del noventayocho.* Madrid, 1945.

Lannon, Frances, and Paul Preston, eds. *Elites and Power in Twentieth-Century Spain: Essays in Honour of Sir Raymond Carr.* Oxford, 1990.

Leeman, Fred. "Redon's Spiritualism and the Rise of Mysticism." In *Odilon Redon: Prince of Dreams, 1840–1916,* ed. Douglas W. Druick. Chicago, 1994.

Linz, Juan J. "Spain: An Authoritarian Regime." In *Politics and Society in Twentieth-Century Spain,* ed. Stanley G. Payne. New York, 1976.

Llobera, Josep R. *The God of Modernity: The Development of Nationalism in Western Europe.* Oxford, 1994.

Losada Malvárez, Juan Carlos. *Ideología del ejército franquista (1939–1959).* Madrid, 1990.

Mainer, José Carlos. "De historiografía literaria española: El fundamento liberal." *Estudios de Historia Social* (Madrid) 2 (1981): 439–72.

Moreno, Luis. *La federalización de España: Poder político y territorio.* Madrid, 1997.

Morodo, Raul. *Los orígenes ideológicos del franquismo: "Acción Española."* Madrid, 1985.

Nairn, Tom. *The Break-Up of Britain: Crisis and Neo-Nationalism.* London, 1977.

Navajas Zubeldía, Carlos. *Ejército, estado y sociedad en España.* Logroño, 1991.

Nofi, Albert A. "General Officer Loyalties in the Spanish Civil War." Ph.D. dissertation, City University of New York, 1991.

Núñez Florencio, Rafael. *Militarismo y antimilitarismo en España (1888–1906).* Madrid, 1990.

———. *Utopistas y autoritarios en 1900.* Madrid, 1994.

Olabarría Agra, Juan. "Las fuentes francesas de *Acción Española.*" *Historia Contemporánea* 3 (1990): 219–35.

Payne, Stanley G. *Falange: A History of Spanish Fascism.* Stanford, 1961.

———. *The Franco Regime, 1936–1975.* Madison and London, 1987.

———. *Politics and the Military in Modern Spain.* Stanford, 1967.

———. *Spain's First Democracy.* Madison, 1993.

———. *Spanish Catholicism: An Historical Overview.* Madison, 1984.

Pennell, C. R. *A Country with a Government and a Flag: The Rif War in Morocco, 1921–1926.* Cambridgeshire, U.K., 1986.

Pérez de la Dehesa, Rafael. *Política y sociedad en el Primer Unamuno, 1894–1904.* Madrid, 1966.

Pick, Daniel. *War Machine: The Rationalisation of Slaughter in the Modern Age.* New Haven and London, 1993.

Pinto, António Costa. "Fascist Ideology Revisited: Zeev Sternhell and His Critics." *European History Quarterly* 16, no. 4 (1986): 465–83.

Porch, Douglas. *The Conquest of Morocco.* London, 1986.

Porter, Brian A. "The Social Nation and Its Futures: English Liberalism and Polish Nationalism in Late-Nineteenth-Century Warsaw." *American Historical Review* 101, no. 5 (1996).

Preston, Paul. *¡Comrades! Portraits from the Spanish Civil War.* London, 1999.

———. *Franco: A Biography.* New York, 1994.

———. *The Politics of Revenge: Fascism and the Military in Modern Spain.* London, 1990.

Puell de la Villa, Fernando. "Origen, vida y reclutamiento del infante español (1700–1902)." Ph.D. dissertation, Universidad Nacional de Educación a Distancia, Madrid, 1995.

———. "Las reformas del General Cassola." *Revista de Historia Militar* 23, no. 46 (1979): 143–74.

———. *El sodado desconocido: De la leva a la "mili."* Madrid, 1996.

Ramsden, H. *Ángel Ganivet's "Idearium Español."* Manchester, U.K., 1967.

———. *The 1898 Movement in Spain: Towards a Reinterpretation with Special Reference to 'En torno al casticismo' and 'Idearium español.'* Manchester, U.K., 1974.

Reid, Brian Holden. *J. F. C. Fuller: Military Thinker.* New York, 1987.

Rodríguez Jiménez, José Luis. *La extrema derecha española en el siglo XX.* Madrid, 1997.

Rojas, Carlos. *¡Muera la inteligencia! ¡Viva la muerte! Salamanca 1936.* Barcelona, 1995.

Romero Maura, Joaquín. "The Spanish Army and Catalonia: The 'Cu-Cut! Incident' and the Law of Jurisdictions, 1906." In *Sage Research Papers in the Social Sciences.* Contemporary European Studies Series no. 90-033, vol. 5. Beverly Hills, 1976.

Romero Salvadó, Francisco J. "The Failure of the Liberal Project of the Spanish Nation-State, 1909–1923." In *Nationalism and the Nation in the Iberian Peninsula,* ed. Clare Mar-Molinero and Angel Smith. Oxford, 1996.

———. *Spain, 1914–1918: Between War and Revolution.* London, 1999.

———. "Spain and the First World War: The Structural Crisis of the Liberal Monarchy." *European History Quarterly* 25 (1995): 529–54.

Rusker, Udo. *Nietzsche in der Hispania.* Bern and Munich, 1962.

Said, Edward S. *Orientalism.* New York, 1979.

Sales de Bohigas, Núria. *Sobre esclavos, reclutas y mercaderes de quintos.* Barcelona, 1974.

Sánchez Abal, Roberto. *La enseñanza militar en el reinado de Alfonso XII.* Madrid, 1991.

Seco Serrano, Carlos. *Militarismo y civilismo en la España contemporánea.* Madrid, 1984.

Semmel, Bernard. *Imperialism and Social Reform: English Social-Imperial Thought (1895–1914).* London, 1960.

Shubert, Adrian. *A Social History of Modern Spain.* London, 1990.

Silva, Carlos de. *General Millán-Astray (El Legionario).* Barcelona, 1956.

Snyder, Jack. *The Ideology of the Offensive: Military Decision Making and the Disasters of 1914.* Ithaca, N.Y., 1984.

Sobejano, Gonzalo. *Nietzsche en España.* Madrid, 1967.

Soucy, Robert. *French Fascism: The First Wave, 1924–1933.* New Haven and London, 1986.

Sternhell, Zeev. *The Birth of Fascist Ideology: From Cultural Rebellion to Political Revolution.* With Mario Sznajder and Maia Asheri. Trans. David Maisel. Princeton, 1994.

———. *Neither Right nor Left: Fascist Ideology in France.* Trans. David Maisel. Berkeley and Los Angeles, 1986.

Subinspección de la Legión. *La Legión Española (Cincuenta años de historia).* 2 vols. Madrid, 1970.

Torre Galán, Julio de la. *¡La Legión! . . . ¡Esa novia! . . .* Madrid, 1969.

Tuchman, Barbara. *The Proud Tower.* New York, 1966.

Tusell, Javier. *Franco en la guerra civil: Una biografía política.* Barcelona, 1992.

Urigüen, Begoña. *Origenes y evolución de la derecha española: El neo-catolicismo.* Madrid, 1986.

Vanaclocha Bellver, Francisco J. *Prensa político-militar y sistema de partidos en España.* Madrid, 1981.

Weber, Eugen. *"Action Française": Royalism and Reaction in Twentieth-Century France.* Stanford, 1962.

———. *Peasants into Frenchmen: The Modernization of Rural France, 1870–1914.* Stanford, 1976.

Wittenberg, Thilo. "Mut und Ehre: Die professionelle, ideologische und politische Entwicklung des spanischen Offizierskorps im 19. Jahrhundert (1808–1908)." Ph.D. dissertation, Albert-Ludwigs-Universität, Freiburg i. Br., 1995.

Wohl, Robert. "French Fascism, Both Right and Left: Reflections on the Sternhell Controversy." *Journal of Modern History* 63 (March 1991): 91–98.

———. *The Generation of 1914.* Cambridge, Mass., 1979.

Woolman, David A. *Rebels in the Rif: Abd-el-Krim and the Rif Rebellion.* Stanford, 1968.

Index